# POWERFUL WORDS

## Discover Your Secret Language for Personal Success and Maximizing Impact Through Emotional Connections

Dr. Clark Gaither

LIFESTYLE
ENTREPRENEURS
PRESS

*To Frank ~*

*All my best!*

*C. Gaither, M.D.*

*5/12/16*

Publisher: Jesse Krieger

LIFESTYLE ENTREPRENEURS PRESS

If you are interested in being published through Lifestyle Entrepreneurs Press, please email: Jesse@JesseKrieger.com

I have heard it said that experience is not the best teacher, evaluated experience is. In this book, Dr. Clark Gaither has created a roadmap for personal transformation. Each of us reach seasons in our lives when we long for a meaning and transformation. Dr. Gaither carefully leads us through the transformation process by eliciting from us the powerful words that are hidden in our life's experiences and expertly guides us through the reflection required to turn our words into the lessons that lead to transformation.

If you are eager to stay the same and never have or become more, do not read this book. But, if you are looking to transform into the best of yourself and maximize your potential then do the work Dr. Gaither lays out and move into real transformation.

Deb Ingino - CEO Strength Leader Development
(www.StrengthLeader.com)

To my father,

# Dent Turner Gaither
(1920-2007)

# FOREWORD
/////////////////////////////////////////////

When I was just 13 years old my life was dramatically impacted by listening to a little recording called *The Strangest Secret*. Prior to that event the direction of my life seemed to be obvious. I would grow up and help my Dad on the farm. And yet the message of that little recording said, "We become what we think about." Those six little words would profoundly change my future and open doors of opportunity that exceeded my biggest dreams.

I learned the power of feeding my mind positive, courage-building words as opposed to allowing the challenges of a legalistic religion and a poor farm life to determine my attitude and future. And I learned that by taking responsibility for my thinking, and the words I said and believed, I could determine the direction of my life.

In this very hopeful book Dr. Gaither shares his own story of early heartache, tragedy and misfortune – and how those experiences could have left him trapped in anger, fear and depression. But his continued search for answers and solutions also led to his discovery that he was not trapped – he had a choice. He could move beyond those negative emotions to be more empathetic and joyous than ever before by choosing words that were life-giving rather than soul-diminishing. He also shares how he would use words with hidden meanings. While in a stage of recovery he would still answer when asked the common question – "How are you?" with "Fine" while identifying with the joke that **FINE** stands for Freaked out, Insecure, Neurotic and Emotionally unbalanced.

In Proverbs 18:21 we read: "Words kill, words give life; they're either poison or fruit – you chose." (MSG) Think about the subtle yet powerfully different responses evoked when we hear the words "love" or "hate." When approaching a new challenge we can walk into a new opportunity by hearing the word "courage" or block a chance for a richer life by listening to "fear."

We all dream of and wish for lives of happiness, meaning and fulfillment. And yet, it seems the words we speak and believe have the power to open or close doors daily. With one little letter we change "can" to "can't." A child is shaped and molded by hearing "smart" or "dumb." "Stop" can protect us - or block us from a new adventure. Proverbs 15:4 confirms our choices: "The soothing tongue is a tree of life, but a perverse tongue crushes the spirit." (NIV)

In the award winning movie, *The King's Speech*, the Duke of York was thrust into the role of King George IV. He was challenged to "have faith in his voice" while dealing with a debilitating stammer. That faith was about much more than just pushing words out of his mouth. He had to believe he had a message worth sharing to find his voice. In that gut-wrenching but thrilling process the Duke found his voice, thus becoming confident and able to galvanize his countrymen for uncommon greatness.

Dr. Gaither describes the process by which we can all make the choices for finding our unique voice – even when circumstances seem to make us stammer. *Powerful Words* gently guides us through the process of opening up after being wounded. Of trusting after trust has been violated. Of stretching in areas that culture and tradition have warned us against. Of acting in our passion even when others say that's unrealistic and impractical. This is a book to help us know, and do, better. Forgiveness, peace, hope and compassion are characteristics that can be learned through saying words that we believe. Those healthy, spiritual traits may not seem natural in light of real-life circumstances but they can be learned in spite of those circumstances by repeating the words that build our belief and confidence.

I challenge you to open your heart and discover how the unexplained and often unwelcomed events in our lives can move us toward the greatness intended for each of us – if we allow words of hope and faith to guide us. By choosing the words we speak and believe, we release the best in ourselves and encourage the same in those around us.

You are doing something special for others and yourself – by reading *Powerful Words*. *The investment of your time will come back multiplied with more confidence and enthusiasm – and you'll discover a powerful voice you already have that will inspire and encourage others along the way.*

**Dan Miller**
New York Times Best-Selling Author of
*48 Days to The Work You Love*

# TABLE OF CONTENTS

# ABOUT THIS BOOK

This book is about Powerful Words, words which hold great significance and personal power for you, me, everyone. Some Powerful Words we will share in common. Many of them will be different, but we all share one greatly important aspect of these words - the emotional impact they have had on us and how they have shaped and reshaped our lives.

The words which hold the most power for you are the ones which move you on an emotional level. If you and another person share the same Powerful Words, you will be connected to that person and they to you, even if they are a stranger.

This book is about finding **your** Powerful Words and using them in whatever you do as you set out to help others in whatever capacity you choose. It is about telling your story, your personal truth. This is where your greatest influence resides.

Throughout this book I will share my own stories with you, using Powerful Words (the gray shaded ones) which hold great significance for me. You will connect with me on an emotional level through some of my words and stories or perhaps none of them. My hope is they will serve to inspire you. They are presented merely as guide for you to use to help bring out your own stories, using your own Powerful Words.

I want you to develop a practice of using your own stories and Powerful Words, words which hold the greatest significance for you. You will find at the end of each chapter a series of thought provoking questions. Answer as many or as few as you like, but you will get the most from this book if you answer all the questions which resonate with you on an emotional level.

As you write down your own words, stories and experiences, make them personal. Be vulnerable. You will find Powerful Words rising to the top of each of your life's stories, words which you can use to benefit and impact the lives of others in very meaningful ways.

Everyone has the capacity to be someone else's hero. You will be the hero to some who hear what you have to share. People are waiting for you to create for them, serve them, lead them, heal them, inspire them. You will, using your own Powerful Words.

# THIS PATH I AM ON.....

The seeds for this book were planted while on a hiking trip on the island of La Gomera, Spain, in November of 2013. I felt the need to get away over the Thanksgiving holiday that year. Feeling a need to clear my head and to think, I went solo. It was an awesome trip! Although I didn't manage to clear my mind of all that was troubling me at the time, I did a lot of thinking and in the process learned some things about myself I did not know before.

La Gomera is the second smallest of the Canary Islands. The islands are actually off the coast of Morocco, but they are owned and governed by Spain. It is truly a volcanic island paradise.

People from England, Ireland, Scotland, Holland and Germany frequent this island quite a bit for the spectacular hiking that is available year round. Even the Rother Walking Guide series has a guide book devoted to this particular island.

My flight took me from Raleigh, North Carolina (NC), to Madrid then from Madrid to the largest of the Canary Islands, Tenerife. From there it was a short one hour ferry ride to La Gomera. The weather was warm, as were the people. Everywhere I stayed the accommodations were comfortable and immaculate.

I lodged at a different hotel each night. The next morning I would send my bags ahead of me by taxi to the next hotel where I would stay the evening. Hiking across the island would get me to my next destination. In this way, I was able to hop-scotch from village to village, place to place across the island's valleys and mountainous peaks.

I set my own pace and would stop or detour at my leisure, logging somewhere between 40 and 50miles for the week while gaining and losing around 18,000 feet in altitude. The scenery was nothing short of spectacular!

There was a lot of time to think on this excursion. No more so than on the very first day. My first hike would take me from Hermiqua on the eastern side of the island over the island's highest peak to Chipude on the western side of the island.

It was to be a 7-1/2 hour hike that would take me from 200 feet above sea level in Hermigua to the 4,878 foot peak of Garajonay then back down to 3,500 feet at Chipude. I had very nearly bitten off more than I could chew.

I got a late start. Being up nearly 24 hours straight the day before while in transit caused me to sleep in a little longer than planned the next morning. I had a quick breakfast at the hotel, checked out and summoned a taxi to take me from San Sebastian over to Hermigua. Once there I sent my bag with the taxi driver on to Hotel Sonia Plaza de Chipude, my refuge for later that evening.

The taxi drove off for the other side of the island with my bags containing nearly everything I had brought with me. At this point, I was pretty much committed to hike the entire trail. I carried only a small back pack with water, snacks, minimal survival gear and a poncho.

It was 9:30 when I got out of the taxi in Hermigua. I was not sure where the trailhead was located for my hike and neither did the taxi driver so he let me off at a roundabout in the center of town. I stopped and asked one of the locals for directions to the trailhead. He spoke only broken English and I "no hablo espanol". He indicated where he thought the trailhead was located on my map. I struck out.

I marched up the street full of energy, ignoring the gathering clouds and gusting winds. I felt good and expectantly exuberant about what adventures might lie ahead of me on the trail. I was only on the trail for about five minutes before I began to doubt my direction.

Steadily, the trail kept taking me in what seemed like the wrong direction. Or, at least not the right direction. A great doubt began to creep into my thoughts. I began to feel like I was wasting time and I had no time to waste. I checked my hiking guide and then the map. A quick check of my compass confirmed it. I was definitely headed in the wrong direction.

Begrudgingly, I backtracked and trudged back down to the streets of Chipude to reconnoiter and reassess my bearings. I walked up and down the streets several times looking for someone who could speak English and knew where the right trailhead might be located.

I wasn't having much luck until I spied the Ibo Alfaro Hotel up on the side of a mountain, where I had reservations to stay in two days time. It had a distinctive appearance and I remembered what it looked like from their website. I walked up to the hotel thinking that someone on the staff would be able to help me. It was a good decision.

One of the staff members in charge of guest services was very helpful. He gave me very clear directions to the location of the proper trailhead. It turns out that the first set of directions were correct, but I had turned off of the highway too soon and mistakenly took a different trailhead instead.

There was a sign posted. I had glanced at it, but didn't take the time to read it carefully being convinced I was on the right path. It was my mistake.

Hurrying back down to the center of town, I made my way up the street past the errant pathway I had first taken and walked on up ahead a short distance to find the proper trailhead. I was already sweaty and slightly puffed from haste, trying to make up for time lost.

.cked my watch. It was 10:30. There was an 8 mile hike ahead
. me and 4,600 feet in altitude to gain. It would start getting dark
at 5:30 and I wanted to make the next hotel before nightfall. That is
when I first felt it - fear, and the first few drops of rain...

My ascent began through the mountain valley of Hermigua, past
banana palm groves and terraces for vegetable farming. I was moving
at a brisk pace fearing I would not make the hotel by nightfall. The
last thing I wanted was to be in unfamiliar territory on a dark trail at
night. It was going to be close.

In the beginning I stopped briefly many times along the way to snap
pictures because the views were just so breathtaking. Up until the
mist began to roll in and a slow, steady drizzle began. I donned my
poncho and squared off my hat to channel the rain down my back
instead of my front side.

Ascending the mountain, the mist got thicker and thicker until I
could see only a short distance in any direction. The path at my feet
though, was interesting and varied. At times it was just a barren dirt
stripe through the vegetation which would often turn into a rock
strewn cobbled walkway.

At first, longish flat stretches would concede to uphill slogs that were
relentless and at times rutted by water flowing off of the mountain.
Water pipes coming down from a mountain dam would often parallel
the trail. I supposed this made them easier to access for any needed
repairs.

As the trail got steeper, bulkheads crisscrossed the trail and made
steps. Lush tropical palms would give way to patches of laurel and
bracken. Surprisingly, there were very few bugs to contend with
on this island. I never saw a single fly. About every 30-45 minutes
I would stop and rest a bit and take some water or have a snack. No
one else was on the trail and I was rather enjoying the solitude.

Even after two hours of hiking I would occasionally pass by a dwelling set against the hillside that looked occupied with no service roads in sight. Beyond wondering who lived there or how a house came to be built in such an isolated location, I thought, "How the hell do they get here?" This trail I am on?

Once or twice, when the path inexplicably forked without a sign, I would invariably take the path which led to a dead end but usually with something interesting at the end - a huge mountain water dam, an awesome rock formation, or an overlook with what I assume was a stunning view but all that could be seen was white. This meant having to double back to the fork and continuing on up the alternate pathway.

About 2 hours into the hike I came to a set of steps that literally looked as though they were carved into the rock face of a mountain. They zigzagged back and forth in one switchback after another as they climbed, for all intents and purposes, straight up. Which they did.

I was on this segment of the trail for one solid hour, climbing up step after step after step. It felt like climbing a staircase which had no end. My legs were burning and I had to take more frequent rest stops. On many occasions I have run for two straight hours without stopping, no problem. But, this endless climbing was turning out to be much more difficult.

Getting water or a snack was an ordeal of sorts. Remove hat, remove poncho, remove backpack, get what was needed from backpack, reverse the whole process and repeat again some time later.

At one point I came up to a sign on the trail pointing off to the left which read Salto de Agua which was supposed to be a rather imposing waterfall, falling more than 500 feet in steps down a shear rock wall. There was a page devoted to it in my guide book and it was on my list of things to see.

The path lead to an observation platform supported by some rather substantial upright bollards. I took the steps up to the platform and walked over to the railing. Well it sounded beautiful, but all I could see was white.

The mountain was deep into a cloud. The visibility was maybe 30 feet past the end of my nose. It was rather disappointing to have come all that way and not see the waterfall when it was so close and I could hear it raging from all of the rain that was steadily pelting the mountain.

Time was swiftly flowing by as well. I turned around and headed back to the main trail.

That day, after some time and difficulty on the trail, in the back of my mind questions began to pop up. Am I going to make it? What the hell possessed me to come here in the first place? Am I in good enough shape for a week of this?

I had been running 12 miles a week on average for years but hiking like this uses a whole different set of muscles and the hikes I had planned lasted hours, not just 25 minutes as in a 5K run or two hours as in a half-marathon.

It was just about then the sound of voices began to come up from the trail below me. I was realizing I hadn't seen anyone else on the trail since leaving Hermigua. Bounding up the side of the mountain came three shirtless guys running! Not hiking, but running up the mountain.

Only one of them was carrying water, a small bottle that was mostly full. Stopping to chat with me he uncapped the bottle and took a sip as the others ran on past us without speaking a word. I'm sure he saw the question on my face when he quipped, "Oh, I'll catch up with them."

The accent was definitely English. These lads were on holiday from England and came to the island to run the trails rather than hike them. Of course, they were young and in superb physical condition. As he bounded off on up the trail he waved his hand in the general direction of the top of the mountain and said there was a restaurant about 10 minutes on up ahead with a fire place and good food.

My first thought was, "Ten minutes! At his pace or mine?" My next thought was that of welcome relief. I was soaked, not by rain but by my sweating underneath the poncho. I thought to myself, you should have bought a nicer, breathable, tech-style poncho instead of the light blue trash bag looking poncho picked up at the last minute from Walmart the day before leaving the states. I won't make that mistake again. In fact, I went to REI and bought a much nicer poncho soon after returning home.

Because of the cloud cover, misty rain and altitude it had turned much cooler. The thought of a hot meal by a fire was intensely appealing so I hurried on up the mountain. My legs were just about to call it quits when the La Vista Restaurant came into view. It looked like a log cabin on the outside.

The inside was filled with picnic tables with bench seats sitting on a concrete floor. There was a large woodstove against one wall. Several hikers were seated here and there, hunched over plates and bowls of steaming food. The trail runners must have kept on running past the restaurant. They were nowhere to be seen.

I peeled off all of my hiking accouterments and plopped down on a bench next to the woodstove. The place smelled of burning wood and baking bread, heavenly! A waitress came over who spoke a little English. Not waiting to hear what she recommended I asked, "What's the special?" She said, "carne de cabra. Eees berry goood!" I thought what the heck, "I'll have that."

She served me a loaf of fresh baked bread with red and green pepper dipping sauce and a plate of barbequed bone-in meat with roasted potatoes. The meat was spicy and tender with a rich flavorful broth. It was delicious. I drained the bowl of its contents in short order.

For those of you who don't know what carne de cabra is, let me just say that neither did I. While paying for the meal I asked the waitress what it was I had just eaten. "Roast goat", was her accented reply.

Now, I can't say if I would have ever ordered the same meal if I had known beforehand exactly what carne de cabra meant. But, I'm glad I did. As I said, it was delicious. I do admit to secretly hoping I didn't unexpectedly see carne de cabra again while out on the trail. It was going to be a long march between bathrooms.

After paying for my meal, I put all my gear back on and looked at my watch. It was 2 PM. A pang of anxiety shot through me. Although the meal and a short rest by the fire did me a lot of good, there was still an hour to go before reaching the top of the mountain. Then, at least a two hour hike down the other side to the hotel in Chipude.

The wind was becoming fierce. I took to the trail with my head down in a steady rain, quietly walking through a beautiful laurel forest adorned with hanging moss. I had never seen anything like it. There were overlooks dotting the trail with split-log bench seats along the way. I passed by all of them. I was still in a cloud and all things distant were hidden from view.

I came to a highway near the top of the mountain, crossed the road and headed up the final stretch of trail that would lead to the peak of Garajonay at 1487m (4878 feet). I reached the peak about 15 minutes later.

At the top of the mountain was a large circular observation area, a stone circle with a central stone pier that contained a brass geological marker, a surveyor's strike point for the entire island. At the summit there was a completely unobstructed view of the whole island, even neighboring islands, but I saw nothing except white.

Still, I had conquered the mountain and that brought an immense sense of accomplishment. I sat down on the stone circle for a bit, contemplating my surroundings and the twists and turns my life had taken that had brought me there to sit in contemplation.

A thought popped into my head about all the major pivots and turning points in my life and what had lead up to them. All of them could be traced to a seminal event and for each of them I could remember hearing words which had changed my life forever.

There, sitting at the top of Garajonay on the island of La Gomera, Spain I could feel the power of words heard long ago as the wind pushed hard on my back. It would be a thought I would come back to later on the trip.

I looked up from my brief reverie and found I was still enveloped in a cloud at the top of the mountain. Clouds are funny, so beautiful when they are all puffed out, floating across a sky of blue. Inside of one, it is a completely nondescript, featureless white murk. Perspective is everything.

I snapped some pictures of the observation area and the nothingness beyond and walked on down from the top through howling wind, carrying with me some satisfaction of having won the highest peak on the island. A few minutes later I came to a split in the trail.

This was a new marker and it did not appear in my guidebook. I checked my map. It looked as though it was a longer more scenic route to Chipude. A shorter more direct route lie on up ahead.

It was getting late and I wanted make Chipude before nightfall. Deciding on the more direct route I marched on until I found the right trailhead. I turned onto it and headed on down the other side of the mountain.

To describe the path I was on as nondescript would be an injustice to all things nondescript. The trail turned out to be a logging road, at least for the first several kilometers. The vegetation had thinned out on either side of the road.

This was the southwestern side of the island now and things grew more sparsely here because of the wind and less total rainfall, which I thought was funny because I was still waking in an unrelenting, drizzling rain. They got the wind part quite right, however. Several times I had to hold on to my hat to keep it on my head.

At a bend in the dirt road on the side of the mountain, I watched in amazement as a cloud slipped down from above and poured like rushing water over the edge of the road, flowing on down the mountainside. I thought if time had shape or substance, it might look like that cloud.

The otherwise monotonous look of this portion of my hike gave me lots of time to think. This path I was on, couldn't have been the best choice. It was too late to backtrack and compare this one with the other of the two, plus I still had miles to go before reaching my destination.

Finally, I found a trail sign leading me off the logging road and onto a trail through the countryside. Continuing my descent, I passed through beautifully terraced, picturesque valleys that were being actively farmed. Plodding along, I marched up one ridge and down another, in a descent overall.

The bright white of the surrounding clouds was beginning to turn gray in the gathering gloom of evening. It was 5 o'clock. With at least another 2 kilometers to go I topped what I hoped to be the last ridge before my goal. The wind had transitioned from steady to strong and gusty.

The trail was now grass with large and small stones popping out of the ground making for cautious walking. I was hugging the hillside on my left with a drop-off to the valley floor on my right. As I neared the crest of the ridge the trail began to open up on my left, leaving me more exposed.

When I crested the ridge, a fierce gust of wind hit me like a hammer. The trash bag looking poncho-de-Walmart I was wearing, filled with air and popped open like a parasail. I was completely taken off my feet and pushed toward the edge of the trail.

It felt like I was in the air forever before touching down on solid ground, right at the edge of the cliff but it must have been only for a split second. I let out a full-throated explicative, lowered my center of gravity and just about crawled the remainder of the path over the ridge. As soon as I was about fifty feet below the ridgeline, the wind died down to a warm and supple breeze.

There was a break in the clouds. The last few rays of a setting sun glinted off buildings in the small town of Chipude below. Years ago I had written, "wind and rain come hardest just before the door." What had been figuratively true many times in my life was literally true now.

I walked into the center of town just as darkness fell, reaching the Hotel Sonia Plaza de Chipude tired and soaking wet in spite of the poncho-de-Walmart but feeling triumphant just the same. I had made it.

The hotel owner called my name as I entered the door. My bag was there waiting on me. After a long, long, long hot shower and a satisfying meal in the hotel's restaurant, I sat back in the chair for a long think about my first day's hike on the island of La Gomera.

# A pathway to clarity...

As I reminisced over the day's events I realized just how much that day's hike mirrored my life - this path I am on. Powerful Words were echoing through my head. I couldn't help but reconsider all that had happened and all I had heard in my life which had culminated in my visit to La Gomera. I was overwhelmed with a sense of thankfulness for this adventure.

Two days later I was up on a ridge overlooking the town of Vallehormoso. In just two hours, I had hiked high above the township and was gazing down on it and  the valley far below. It was hard to believe how much ground I had covered in such a short time. At the same time I had been thinking about my march over the mountain two days earlier.

Pulling out my cell phone I recorded the following quote, "It is amazing what one can accomplish physically, mentally and emotionally when fueled by the human spirit and untethered by desire." Those words held power for me because I was feeling somewhat powerful at the time. I felt as though I had accomplished something.

A path, as in a walking path or trail, has been used countless times by countless authors throughout history as a metaphor for life. There is good reason for this. The two concepts, a pathway and life, are harmoniously congruent with one another.

I became keenly aware of this on my hike in La Gomera. My thoughts kept returning to past events as I walked and experienced the journey. It didn't matter if my experience on the trail was good or bad, happy or sad, dull or inspiring, boring or surprising. The trail kept reminding me of constant and analogous events in my past, both recent and remote.

I got a late start on the hike. I got a late start in life. There was a time I didn't feel I could or would accomplish much in life because of something I heard as a child, Powerful Words that would hold me back for many years because I let them.

I really didn't decide on what I was going to do with my life as far as a career was concerned until I was 24 years old. That is when I went back to school to get my undergraduate degree. Again, something I decided based on something someone said to me one day that changed my thinking and then the course of my life. They were Powerful Words which made all the difference, because I was ready to hear them and ready to be different.

After returning to school I was full of enthusiasm and energy, at least in the beginning. Then came graduate school, then medical school, then residency. They were long years that seemed to drag on without much reward, just more degrees, permission slips (think signposts) to continue on down the path I had chosen for myself.

I often questioned the paths I had taken. Medical school was tough. There were many times I feared I wouldn't make it to the end. There were many other times I faced real setbacks, big stinking huge ones. Like the day my residency program director called me into his office and delivered some Powerful Words, "Either go off to treatment for alcoholism or you're fired."

After a separation, a divorce, trouble performing in school and a flirtation with spectacular self-destruction by way of active alcoholism, it eventually hit me. I'm going in the wrong direction! Just like my hike, it had been a rough start and a hard slog. I had walked down many dead end paths.

It was during treatment for alcoholism when I adjusted my course and found a new zest for living. I was in a recovery meeting in Aberdeen, North Carolina, on the third night of my voluntary incarceration in a 28-day treatment program when I heard a woman give her own gut wrenching story of her descent into alcoholism and her subsequent recovery.

She delivered some words that night which I will never forget. Were they powerful? Yes, I would say they were powerful, plain words but powerful. The moment I heard them the compulsion to drink alcohol left me and has never returned. I have been sober since. The years I spent as an active alcoholic were extremely difficult, just like the vertical climb on the first day's hike on La Gomera.

At the age of 37, I began private practice. After completing residency I put my nose down and went right to work as a family physician. Just like my hike, there have been many ups and downs along the way. Just like most everyone reading this book, there have been good days and bad both at professionally and in my personal life.

Patients, friends and acquaintances continuously surprise me and in the most unexpected ways. Over the last 24 years, I have had mighty triumphs and dismal failures. In the practice of medicine, I have seen things and heard things that few people have the privilege to experience. Over the years, I have planned and succeeded, planned and failed, and failed to plan.

All the while, serendipity has lead to both amazing moments and tear stained ruin. Things I thought were going to be great turned out to be a steaming pile of excrement. Things are I thought were going to be god awful turned out to be simply the best and most memorable events of my life.

I have worked feverishly and tirelessly and over long periods of time with certain goals in mind only to be wholly disappointed with the results. Looking back, things I did, which I thought were only half-good, someone would thank me later for being so great.

Periods of welcome relief have been punctuated by seemingly unending boredom or dread. Awesome expectations have been both exceeded and dashed. Surprises and disappointments have popped up daily, mere bumps in the road, something to step over with the next forward stride.

I have sought to try the untested and unknown, some of which I have loved, some of which I liked and some of which I have hated. Just like the path, just like life. Just like life, just like this path I am on.

All the while I have heard the echoes of words from the people who have floated in, out and through my life like the clouds of Garajonay. Powerful Words. I am in large measure, the product of them all.

I am old enough to know even any daily routine that seems boring now, will be missed later when it is no longer possible. I don't like running that much, at least while I'm at it. I keep it up because it's good for me and one day I know I won't be able to run anymore. Then, I will wish I could.

I know I must continue to move forward on this path I am on. The same goes for the path you are on, dear reader. Always moving forward, time's arrow points in but one direction. The path before us has many branches but they are all in front of us. The only choices we have are which direction is forward and what we will do along the way.

What struck me most at the end of my hike was the deep sense of satisfaction and appreciation I felt when I was done, over every bit of the journey, from the beginning, through the middle, to the end. Even the parts that weren't pleasant or were disappointing at the time, seemed beautiful to me when it was all done.

When I was crossing the road just below the top of the mountain, soaking wet, tired, discouraged and anxious about finishing before nightfall, I could have stopped there, hiked down the road to the nearest village and taken a taxi to the next hotel. I chose instead to stay on the path and hike to the top of the mountain which should have provided the best view of the whole island and surrounding islands.

Instead, I was immersed in clouds. For some reason, I decided to linger there for sometime with my eyes closed. I thought, well I've got other senses besides sight, why not use them? I felt the wind on my face and listened to it howl and inhaled deeply the cold misty air which I could almost taste.

It made me feel lighter inside and that made me smile. I could feel and hear the rain which seemed to be swirling and pelting me from all directions and could feel my legs adjusting for the pressure of the wind pressing against my back and frame.

There is where I began to consider all of the Powerful Words I have heard throughout my life and the impact that they have had on me. It was a Transformative moment. The only place all of that could have happened, just like that, was where I was sitting. I had to be there.

If it had been an easy hike that day with a cloudless sky and crystal clear views from the top of Garajonay, I doubt I would have lingered there with my thoughts and had the Transformative moment. I would have been too dazzled by the view, too busy snapping pictures. As cold and rainy and cloudy a day as it was, it was a perfect day. It was the only day it rained the entire week.

If I close my eyes now I can experience it all over again. Some people say that it isn't the destination, it's the journey. Others say it isn't the journey, it's the destination. It is both dear reader. You can't have one without the other. For all of the good and the bad, would you really want it any other way, on this most excellent path you are on?

You are on a different path from everyone else, one of your own choosing. If you like the path you are on then you should stay on it, if you can. If you are on a path you do not like then you should change your bearing and strike out in a new direction. Either way, you have the power to do so. Either way, it is your choice.

# Powerful Words...

DOUBT, MISTAKE, ACCOMPLISHMENT, PATH, DESTINATION, ADVENTURE, LIFE, REWARD, PLAN and APPRECIATION are Powerful Words.

You may consider most of these words as positive and think them desirable and a few of them as negative and therefore undesirable. Which are which? I'm not so sure. I believe the answer depends on your experiences with each of them, the level of emotional connection you have with them and how you use them.

Powerful Words are neither good nor bad. They just are. The emotions they may elicit are neither good nor bad. They just are. It is what we choose to do with them that can be judged as either good or bad.

Powerful Words are tools, tools which can be bent to any great purpose if you are the master of them. Conversely, you will be a slave to them and serve only them if they are the master of you. It is an odd thing, either way only you get to decide which it will be.

We are all walking a PATH toward an uncertain future and unknown DESTINATION. Uncertainty brings DOUBT and fear. The principle of initial position applies. Where and how we end up is determined in large measure by how we begin, the conditions under which we start. PLAN well, begin well and you will probably end up in a much better place and position than if you had started poorly without a plan. Planning reduces uncertainty, which reduces doubt and fear.

That is not to imply LIFE will not throw us curve balls. It is hard to know how to knock a curve ball out of the park if you have never been thrown a curve ball. Guess what else? You must also enter the ball park, walk up to the plate and practice. These are the initial conditions necessary for a favorable outcome.

# POWERFUL WORDS

You have seen them. You have read them. You have heard them all of your life. I'm talking about Powerful Words. You knew they were powerful the moment you read them or heard them because not only did you read them or hear them, you felt them.

You felt them deep inside. Perhaps they caught you by surprise and moved you in ways that were unexpected. Perhaps they served to propel you into some kind of action. Maybe they made you feel angry, or thrilled, or grateful, or maybe they made you cry.

You remember them because they changed you. They left an indelible impression on you. For you, they were Powerful Words.

The powerful words that each of us remembers will not all be the same because most of our experiences are different. Yet, some will be the same for all of us because they are part of our collective consciousness.

Powerful words do not have to be long, or technical or complicated. The most powerful messages are simple, comprised of simple words arranged in a simple way but conveying powerful meaning.

They surprise us. They delight us. They can build us up or tear us down. They can be utilized as tools for good or as weapons of evil.

The effects of simple but powerful words are always underestimated at first. Their strength is always realized and amplified in the fullness of time. Such is their majesty. Such is their power. We love to hear and feel powerful words.

Each of you have Powerful Words within you. If you doubt this is true, by the end of this book you will know that it is true.

# I Have Heard Powerful Words

In 1973 I found myself working part-time at a local Radio Shack out of a love for electronics, when the store manager decided to leave for other work. I asked the District Manager if I could run the store. He took a chance on me. I became the youngest store manager in the country for Radio Shack at the age of 19.

My performance that first year was not great. But, I gained some experience which I was able to capitalize on the next year. My performance improved. Sales climbed. I was given a larger store to run. I did well with that one and was winning sales contests. Later, I was given the opportunity to open a brand new store in Hickory, NC.

I did well with that store too. Confidence in my abilities had risen along with my rise within the company. So much so, I began to entertain the thoughts of doing something more, something different. I began to daydream again, the dream I once had in grade school, of becoming a doctor.

But, was I good enough? Could I do it? I was afraid.

I must have been mulling this over one night at work when one of my regular customers, a Mr. Larry Kahill who sold paper products, dropped by the store. He said, "Clark, you looked perplexed about something".

I told him of my dilemma. I was doing well with Radio Shack but I was thinking of going back to college and possibly on to medical school if my grades were good enough. I told him about my disastrous first year of college and the bad grades I made four years earlier. I told him I was afraid to make such a drastic change.

He asked me about my time with Radio Shack and the successes I had had with the company. After I had given him the run down, that is when he said it. That is when this relative stranger would open his mouth and say something to me that would ultimately change the course of the rest of my life. To me, he uttered some Powerful Words.

He looked at me thoughtfully for a moment, smiled and said, "Clark, based on what you have just told me, it is clear to me you can do what ever you make up your mind to do." With that, he turned on his heel and left the store leaving me standing there blinking.

Right place. Right time. Powerful Words. It was a TRANSFORMATIVE moment for me.

One week later I enrolled in summer school at Lenoir-Rhyne College in Hickory, NC. I did a four year program in three years. Then came a masters program in biology, followed by medical school and a MD degree.

There is just nothing like a good slap in the face with a strong chill bracer of reality. Sometimes it is absolutely necessary in order to wake us up, in order to smell the coffee or get a grip, as they say.

One day in my office 16 years ago and at the age of 46, I was talking to a patient about his overall state of health during a routine physical exam. His was not good. He was middle aged, overweight with several worsening medical problems and no program of regular exercise.

I put on my scary doctor face as I scolded him saying, "You really need to get some regular exercise for the sake of cardiovascular fitness." He stared blankly at me for a second or two before he asked "and what do you do doctor?"

Aaah, wauahh, mmmhm, well you see I, I uhaaa. That was about all I could manage to get out. I wasn't doing anything for myself. Oh, I had thought about it many times. I had the best of intentions you know. But, I was always too busy. I had a lot on my plate, important doctor things to do, people to see, places to go and blah blah blah blah blah.

All of those were just excuses I trotted out so I didn't have to take my own advice. It was embarrassing. The patient had unknowingly uttered some Powerful Words. Right then and there I became determined to make a change at 46 years of age.

I knew I had been neglecting my physical wellbeing. I had gotten sober in 1990. I quit smoking cigarettes four years later on my fortieth birthday (I figured if turning 40 was going to be a crappy day then I would just make it a good and crappy day and add in some nicotine withdrawal).

I had taken steps to improve my spiritual self and I was seeing to my emotional and psychological needs within my program of recovery. But, I was lacking in the physical realm. Sure, I had stopped some unhealthy behaviors but I hadn't fostered very many healthy ones.

This is one realm that is often disregarded by physicians but shouldn't be. It is incumbent for doctors to see that we get adequate rest and sufficient exercise to keep us healthy, so that we can meet the challenges that living life on life's terms has to offer. All four realms must be addressed for total vitality - emotional, psychological, spiritual and physical. I had neglected my physical self long enough. If I was going to ask my patients to do something, I had to be willing to set an example by taking my own advice.

After getting off from work that evening I went to the local mall and bought some running clothes and a pair of running shoes. I promptly went home, donned my new and quite fashionable running outfit and stepped outside ready for my first run. I looked great and

I already felt great. You know that great feeling you get when you JOIN the gym.

I thought, well I used to run some in high school, I'll start out slow and just jog an easy mile. I had clocked off the circle around my neighborhood and it was 1.1 miles once around. I reasoned that my run would be done in precisely 7 ½ minutes. I added a couple of minutes to my high school one mile run time figuring that at my current age I had probably slowed down a bit.

I looked at my watch and I started to run. Everything went well, for the first couple hundred feet. I didn't make it around the circle in 7 ½ minutes. I didn't make it around the circle period. I had jogged a total of 2,000 feet, less than 0.4 mile and you could've stuck a fork in me. I was done! I had to stop.

My heart was racing and pounding and I was so breathless that I couldn't have shouted for help, even if I had wanted to. I didn't know whether to pass out or throw up. I was horrified. Like most people I encounter in my practice, I was in better shape in my head than in my body.

Over time, your stamina for that kind of exercise will steadily fall to accommodate what ever level of activity you employ. As I found out for myself, if you don't do much then you won't be able to do much, even if you have to or want to. It's a good thing most of us don't have to run from a tiger these days because there would be fewer of us and a lot of fat tigers.

As I stood there panting and sweating, on the verge of emesis (vomiting) and syncope (passing out), I made a commitment to get my physical house in order. I made a plan.

I ran that same distance every day for the first week. Then I added 528 feet or one tenth of a mile and I ran that for a week. Then I added

I never felt I knew exactly what to say or how to say what I was thinking, fearing it would sound dumb or I might stumble over my words. That would all change when I moved to Hickory in 1976. More on that later.

## You (Everyone) Have Heard Powerful Words

You have heard powerful words all of your life. They are instantly recognizable because they have left their mark on your (our) collective consciousness.

Thinking about famous speeches from the past, please, fill in these blanks for me...

I

have a

_____.

Ask not

_____ _____ _____ _____ _____ _____ _____

Houston, Tranquility base here.

_____ _____ _____.

Or, words from a song...

She lived her life like a

_____ _____ _____ _____.

With very little context provided these Powerful Words are the instantly recognizable in these statements from Martin Luther King, "I have a dream..."; John F. Kennedy, "Ask not what your country can do for you..."; Neil Armstrong, "Houston, Tranquility base here. The Eagle has landed..."; and words from the song Candle In The Wind, "She lived her life like a candle in the wind." There are countless other examples such as these.

But, Powerful Words do not have to rise to the level of national prominence in order for them to become powerful. Not everyone in your city, state, country or the world must know these words in order for words to hold power for you. There are words that hold tremendous power for you that only you may have heard.

Are you a parent? If so, you have heard Powerful Words. You will instantly remember where you were, what you were wearing and who was nearby when you heard them for the first time. Words like, "it's a girl, it's a boy, I love you mommy, I love you daddy." For parents, the happiest of Powerful Words may have been, or may be, "I'm home" and the saddest, "Good-bye."

All of us have heard Powerful Words growing up. Words like, "Santa Claus is coming." "Would you like to go out with me?" Or, "You won!" Many of us heard other Powerful Words growing up that weren't pleasant to hear. Words like, "I'm so disappointed in you. You're ugly. You're fat. You're stupid. I hate you." We made them powerful because we believed, in whole or in part, they were true.

Powerful Words are not powerful because they are large, complex words you need to look up in a dictionary. They are not powerful because they are colorful, or poetic, or elegant or overly dramatic. They are not made powerful by way of their delivery, whether by a shout or a whisper. As I said, they are often the most modest of words, simply conveyed.

at is it then that makes Powerful Words powerful? I believe I
....ow. I believe there are five common qualities or attributes which
make all Powerful Words powerful.

# #1. All humans are human.

As much as we are different, we are all the same. As much as we are
the same, we are all different.

I believe sometimes we like to feel we are the other, **completely**
different from everyone else. Well, sometimes we are different,
sometimes we aren't different. But, never **completely** different either
way. Each of us have our own set of unique natural talents and
abilities, our own likes and dislikes, our own way of looking at things,
our own way of describing things and how we express ourselves.

So, we say we are unique. Do you believe this is true, we are uniquely
unique?

Okay, let's perform an experiment. One you can do in your home,
right now. With your right foot extended, move your leg in a circular
motion clockwise and at the same time take your right hand and
draw the number six in the air. You will notice your leg or foot
changed direction.

Without exception, the exact same thing will happen to every
human on the planet, every time it is tried. All of our brains are
fundamentally hardwired pretty much the same way. I could give a
hundred more examples of how that is true.

As much as we are the same, we are all different. As much as we are
different, we are all the same. **All humans are human. This is the
basis of our interconnectedness.**

# #2. We all emote.

We all feel and express a range of emotions. No one is completely bereft of feelings or expression.

How much has been written, how many speeches have been given, how many movies have been made, how much advertising has been generated, and how many words have each of us conveyed to others based on feelings? I submit, almost all of it! We all emote pretty much all of the time.

As much as we feel similarly, we feel differently. As much as we feel differently, we feel similarly. This much is absolutely true, **only you know how you feel unless you share your feelings with another human being**.

Two philosophers are sitting by a lake looking at the fish swimming by the shoreline. One philosopher points to a fish and proclaims, "That fish is happy!" The other philosopher responds, "You, not being the fish, do not know that that fish is happy." To which the first philosopher replies, "You, not being me, do not know that I do not know that fish is happy."

I will not know precisely how you feel, unless you can tell me **precisely** how you feel. No one will. Even so, maybe not even then. Feelings can be difficult to describe. If you and I both say we are happy, are we the same kind of happy, for the same reasons and to the same degree of happiness? Probably not. But, that does not make us feel any less happy, together. We both know what we are talking about. We feel a connection based on a feeling we are sharing called "happiness."

Furthermore, the range of human emotions as we describe them is not infinite. My feelings may not be your feelings all of the time. But, they will be some of the time. We do feel commonly concerning common themes.

The impetuses of feeling may be different. The degrees of feeling may be different. But, the outcome **of** feeling is similarly shared. We feel. **Emotions are the strength of our interconnectedness.**

# #3. Words will elicit an emotional response.

How much depends on how closely we identify with them.

Words are the most powerful way we communicate. Whether words are heard, read, or spoken, they are always felt! The words themselves, the context in which they are delivered and their connections to past experience (left brain) determines their emotional impact. The emotional impact of Powerful Words gets assimilated into our consciousness and sub-consciousness.

Context is the most important determinant of the emotional impact words will have on each of us. Although feelings are individual, the context which elicits them can be the same for many. If you have no children and you hear a small child say the words "mama" or "dada" to their parent you might think, "how cute" and you will soon forget them. If it is **your** child saying those words for the first time **to you**, you will laugh, cry or both and you will always remember where and when you heard them. That's context.

If you have ever heard the Powerful Words, "I don't love you anymore, I'm leaving you, there is someone else, I have already spoken with an attorney" then right now, you may be feeling the emotional impact those words convey.

I have heard those words. If you too have heard them then we are connected by how we feel because of the context of our shared experience.

After 19 years of marriage, the day after a completely normal Valentine's Day any husband and wife might enjoy and without any inkling or warning, I came out of my office, opened the door to my Jeep and there I found a letter on the driver's seat. "Uhmm, what's this?"

It was from my wife. "Probably a love letter," I thought. It had been a few months since I had gotten one of those. Or, I knew she hadn't quite been herself for the last couple of months so I thought she might be apologizing for having to work so much lately.

I opened it eagerly and read, "My feelings have changed. I'm leaving. I have already consulted an attorney." The words, "There is someone else" would come later.

Powerful Words! Life changing words. It was as if a bomb had gone off in my hands. In an instant, just as Powerful Words are apt to do, my life was forever changed and in the most profound ways.

If you have ever gone through separation and divorce, and I hope you never have and never will, it would be hard for you to identify deeply with someone who has had the experience. That's okay. There are other divorcees who can, who will feel connected through that shared experience.

If you have never been addicted to alcohol, other substances or struggled with an addictive behavior in your past it would be impossible to feel **what it was like** on the same level as an addict.

That's okay. I know, because I am a recovering alcoholic. I have been sober since January 23, 1990, my sobriety date. There are other addicts both in and out of recovery who know how I feel and I know how they feel because of our shared experience.

But, on anything **you** have experienced, just name any topic, any occurrence, on any subject or any idea, on any triumph or any defeat and you can always find others in agreement with how you feel or have felt because they have felt that way too.

The more closely you identify with someone's words, the greater your emotional response. The more closely someone can identify with your words, the greater their emotional response. **Words are the proof of our interconnectedness.**

# #4. Words that elicit the greatest emotional response are the most powerful words.

They tap into personal and shared experiences, into deeply held beliefs and kindred connections.

Powerful Words take you back to where you once lived, how you once thought, how you once felt when you were greatly impacted emotionally. They can pull you into a future you have not yet known but dream of frequently. Oddly, a future which feels familiar somehow even though you have not yet experienced it.

When I was about twelve and in the sixth grade my parents went to see my grade school principal. I was beginning to have some trouble in school with my grades. I wasn't interested in school anymore.

Well, except for Science and Geometry, which one teacher made very interesting for me. I connected with him. His name was Mr. Clampett and he had always taken an interest in me and encouraged me to do better.

With the exception of his classes all I really wanted to do was sit at my desk and dream of far away places. I loved to daydream. I discovered I could go anywhere I wanted and do anything I wanted to do in my mind. Today, I would probably be diagnosed with a learning disability or ADD. Learning was never my problem. Boring teachers teaching boring subjects was my problem.

I dreamed about being a doctor like Ben Casey on TV (1961-1966). My principal had called my parents in for a talk. About me. Mr. Caldwell, my principal, told my parents point blank that they probably expected too much from me, that I should probably paint houses for a living just like my dad.

I was sitting right there, listening. I heard what I thought were some Powerful Words. I thought I heard, "you're not good enough to be a doctor". After that, my grades did not improve. Go figure. I stopped trying.

I managed to make it out of high school okay, but my grades were certainly nothing to crow about. I spent one year in college right after high school because my parents wanted me to and all of my friends were going. It was a disaster. My heart wasn't in it and I didn't really know what I wanted to do. So, I quit.

I have heard Powerful Words again and again, many times throughout the course of my life. Sometimes there were Powerful Words I did not want to hear because of their emotional impact which seemed devastating at the time. But, it turns out they were words I needed to hear in order to turn my life around.

At other times I have heard Powerful Words, which served as a source of great inspiration and motivation. Words that launched me into action, again, redirecting the course of my life. In each and every instance they were Powerful Words because they initiated an unforeseen sequence of events which caused me to experience the magnificent splendor of change.

Powerful Words are the touchstones of our truest feelings, our truest selves. The more emotional your response to them the closer they are to the real you. Powerful Words will reveal not who you think you are, not who you wish to be, but **who you are**. **Powerful Words are a consequence of our interconnectedness.**

## #5. The most powerful words and messages are remembered, sometimes forever.

They are able to do this because they remind us of who we were, who we are, who we are becoming, who we hope to be.

As I said, I am a recovering alcoholic. My sobriety date is January 23, 1990. Prior to getting sober, my last few years of heavy drinking were spent in near isolation. As I sank deeper into the abyss of my disease I would run home to see my folks less and less as time flittered away, precious time I can now never retrieve.

When I did go home I never stayed very long. You see, I never drank in front of my parents so that meant a short stay. I was always in a hurry to leave and drink.

I was closest to my dad growing up. During those years of heavy drinking my dad and I drifted apart because of my shame over what I had become. I let alcohol get between him and me. Those were years I wasted.

When I went into treatment for alcoholism, I had to call my dad to let him know where I was and what had happened. It was a call I fearfully dreaded to make. I spent an entire afternoon summoning the courage to call.

I finally called and told him where I was, and why, and that he shouldn't worry about me. I told him I would be okay. I hurried him off the phone, I was in so much pain. My own personal pain and I had heard the pain in his voice which made mine so much worse.

After he hung up the phone my dad got in his car and drove three hours to the treatment center where he arrived unannounced. He would not be denied access to see me. At first sight I was so relieved to see him, but I also became scared.

How could I face him, that quiet, strong, but gentle man with the twinkle in his eye? The WWII veteran who worked hard everyday to provide for his family, who always did the right thing, who taught me everything I needed to know, all the good things a father teaches a son about life and living. Although, I did not always heed his lessons.

I was a first year family medicine resident with a promising career ahead and now I was in a treatment center for alcoholism at the age of 35. I felt I had let him down. I felt horribly ashamed and defeated.

We sat down in the cafeteria of the treatment center and I told him everything. As I cried I told him all about the years of heavy drinking, the lies, the mess I had made of my life and of putting my career in jeopardy. I told him of the many times I had tried to quit drinking on my own and had failed. I had never seen him fail at anything.

I told him I felt this was my last chance. This time I was going to try my very best. I promised **him** I would do my very best. He sat patiently and listened. His quiet calm was almost palpable.

After I laid it all out for him, I waited anxiously for his response. What would he think of me? Would I be his biggest disappointment, his biggest regret? The last thing I wanted to hear, what I thought I would hear, was how disappointed he was in me.

I would tell you nothing could have prepared me for his response but, unknowingly, he had been preparing me for it all of my life. If I close my eyes and rest my mind I can still hear my dad's sure and steady voice. He said something to me that day, something I heard him say to me so many times growing up and as a young adult. Never was I happier to hear those words again on that day. He let loose some Powerful Words. He said, "I'm proud of you son."

I had only just begun my race toward sobriety and meaningful recovery. Hearing those words, though, it felt like victory. It was all I needed to hear. Twenty-five years later, I'm still sober. Believe me when I say, even though he is no longer here to hear me, I am so very proud of him.

# Individually All Together Now

Powerful Words. They bind us, one to another. Even in groups, people can be moved on an emotional level, en masse, by central themes or common beliefs. Where none exist, Powerful Words can create them.

Powerful Words like:

*I know not what course others may take; but as for me, give me liberty or give me death!*
~Patrick Henry

*Four score and seven years ago our fathers brought forth on this continent a new nation, conceived in Liberty, and dedicated to the proposition that all men are created equal.*
~ Abraham Lincoln

*We shall go on to the end. We shall fight in France, we shall fight on the seas and oceans, we shall fight with growing confidence and growing strength in the air, we shall defend our island, whatever the cost may be. We shall fight on the beaches, we shall fight on the landing grounds, we shall fight in the fields and in the streets, we shall fight in the hills; we shall never surrender...*
~ Winston Churchill

*We choose to go to the moon. We choose to go to the moon in this decade and do the other things, not because they are easy, but because they are hard...*
~ John Fitzgerald Kennedy

*I have a dream today! I have a dream that one day every valley shall be exalted, and every hill and mountain shall be made low, the rough places will be made plain, and the crooked places will be made straight; "and the glory of the Lord shall be revealed and all flesh shall see it together.*
~ Martin Luther King, Jr.

*General Secretary Gorbachev, if you seek peace, if you seek prosperity for the Soviet Union and eastern Europe, if you seek liberalization, come here to this gate. Mr. Gorbachev, open this gate. Mr. Gorbachev, tear down this wall!*
~ Ronald Reagan

*Blessed are the peacemakers: for they shall be called the children of God*
~ Jesus Christ of Nazareth.

Many individuals can connect with the emotions generated by Powerful Words such as these, not because of "group think" but because of "group feel". Powerful Words can be the solvent that dissolves the barriers between us all and makes us feel as one. **Powerful Words that move us on an emotional level and are remembered describe our interconnectedness.**

# Your Platform for Powerful Words and Messages

**#1. All humans are human.** As much as we are the same, we are all different. As much as we are different, we are all the same. **This is the basis of our interconnectedness.**

**#2. All humans emote.** The impetuses of feeling may be different. The degrees of feeling may be different. But, the outcome of feeling is similarly shared. We feel. **Emotions are the strength of our interconnectedness.**

**#3. Words will elicit an emotional response.** The more closely you identify with someone's words, the greater your emotional response. The more closely someone can identify with your words, the greater their emotional response. **Words are the proof of our interconnectedness.**

**#4. Words that elicit the greatest emotional response are the most powerful words.** Powerful Words are the touchstones of your truest feelings, your truest self. The more emotional your response to them the closer they are to the **real you**. Powerful Words will reveal not who you think you are, not who you wish to be but **who you are**. **Powerful Words are a consequence of our interconnectedness.**

**#5. The most powerful words and messages are remembered, sometimes forever.** Some of the words, the ones you would use to describe your life, your experiences, your truth **are** Powerful Words. They may not seem all that powerful to you but here is the Great Secret about Powerful Words. If your purpose is to help others, sometimes it doesn't matter how powerful they seem to you, it only matters to the people who are waiting to hear your story, the people who need your words to inspire them, the people you are trying to help. **Powerful Words that move us on an emotional level and are remembered describe our interconnectedness.**

# Have You Dreamed of Delivering Powerful Words?

Have you ever dreamed of being able to write or speak Powerful Words?

Imagine yourself writing something which moves people on a deep, emotional level, which proves helpful to them. Imagine delivering a message in a talk, which brings people to their feet to applaud in appreciation of you for a message you delivered that they know has changed their life. Imagine people writing letters to you or sending emails to you expressing their appreciation for how much you were able to help them.

You have the ability to do all of those things and more using your own Powerful Words. You do not have to be a poet. You do not have to be a literary genius. You do not have to conjure Powerful Words up from nothing. They are already there inside of you, right now.

Powerful Words exist in you from every good deed, every surprise, every kind word, every great day, every momentous event when you were impacted on an emotional level. Theses events left you with words to describe how you felt and some of them are Powerful.

Every great victory, every tragic loss, every happiest of moments, every saddest of times, every hurt, every sting, every joy, every hug, every rejection, every high, every low and the impact they had on you and the words you would use to describe them are all still in you. Some of the words, the ones you would use to describe your life, your experiences, your truth **are** Powerful Words.

## Sharing Your Powerful Words Makes It About Them and Not You.

Your words may not seem all that powerful to you but, as I have alluded to, there is a Great Secret about Powerful Words, where they come from and the impact they have on another human being.

Sharing your Powerful Words and stories isn't about ego or self-centeredness if you are trying to help people. The sole point of telling a story to someone is to establish a connection on some level between you and the receiver. The power of story lies only in the telling.

If you are setting out to help others, in any capacity, it doesn't matter how powerful your words seem to you. It only matters how powerful they **feel** to the people who are waiting to hear your stories, who need your words to inspire them, the people you are trying to help. If the emotion generated inside others by your story is strong the connection you establish with them will be strong.

You already have within you Powerful Words that can change the lives of others for the better. They reside within the stories of your own life experiences. You can learn how to connect with them so you can connect better with others on an emotional level.

## Some Words You Have Never Heard Are Also Just As Powerful

Sometimes, just as powerful as the words you have heard are the Powerful Words you have never heard, rarely hear or have longed to hear. Words like, "you're right, you're smart, you're a winner, you can do it, I appreciate you, you are a great person, I love you, I'm proud of you."

Many people reading this book have been told their whole life long "you aren't good enough." Or, maybe you have been telling yourself you aren't good enough. I am here to tell you, right now, you are good enough.

The words you have never heard, but have a need to hear, are just as Powerful to you and need to be explored. Why? Because there are others out there who also need to hear Powerful Words they have never heard before, words they desperately need to hear.

They need to know they are not alone. They need you to tell them. They need your words to inspire them. They are out there, waiting, listening for you to share your story as only you can.

You say I cannot write or speak Powerful Words. Well, I say not only can you but you must! You may say, "I have no Powerful Words to write". I say, you do!

If you feel you do not have Powerful Words to share, or if you feel you do but don't think you can share them in an effective way, I want you to do me a favor right now. I want you to put your hand over your heart and read the following sentence out loud.

*"I know I have Powerful Words within me. I know I have the ability to share them and I am going to find a way to begin sharing them with those I wish to help."*

Throughout the rest of this book, I will show you how.

# Your Core Values

T his is a part of a process of self-discovery! Everyone has a set of core values that are integral to who they are or even to who they profess to be. Our core values may change slightly throughout the different seasons of our life, but they are always with us. When we form an opinion, make decisions or judgments, we are either honoring or dishonoring our core values in the process.

## Your Very Foundation...

I recently took a trip to the Grand Canyon, my first. I was dumb struck at the sight of it. The canyon is breathtakingly immense, truly awe inspiring in its grandeur. It is, in a word, magnificent.

It is mind boggling to consider that a single river, through the slow passage of time, carved its way through 3,000 to 6,000 feet of high plains sedimentary rock to reveal a canyon up to 18 miles wide. Flowing water carrying sand particles abraded away the softer rock to create what we see today. In differing ways, we are similarly shaped and altered by the passage of time.

Although the Grand Canyon will continue to widen over geologic time scales, the Colorado River will carve no deeper into the rock. The canyon is as deep as it is going to get.

You may be asking, why? In many places the river has reached solid bedrock, the very bedrock on which the North American Continent rests. It is ancient stone and much harder. The river moves too slowly to carve into the nearly impervious bedrock.

The bedrock is the foundation and it is upon the foundation all else rests. Your core values are your bedrock foundation.

People can be worn down by circumstances contrary to their core being. Their best qualities can be eroded away slowly over time until they are stripped of passion, never discovering their true purpose. I have seen people give and give and give with little personal reward, thinking that eventually conditions would improve only to find the wear and tear of a non-purpose driven life to be relentless.

But, what remains is really all that matters. It is the core, the bedrock of the individual. What remains are a person's natural talents and abilities along with their core values, their very foundation. These are never worn away. They are always going to be there as long as you are here.

Even if all the extraneous material that has been layered on to you over the years has already been removed by hard circumstances, your very foundation is still there solid as bedrock. On this bedrock foundation a new and exciting life can be built, one of your own design. The results which will flow over the passage of time will be, in a word, magnificent!

# The Core Values Inventory...

It is very likely each of your top 5 core values hold power for you. They will probably be first on your list of Powerful Words, especially your #1 main core value. It will serve you well to determine precisely what they are by performing a very simple exercise. Why is this important?

If you are honoring your core values you are more likely to be happy. If you are dishonoring your core values you are more likely to be miserable. Violating your own core values you will lead to immense dissatisfaction in your personal and professional lives. .

To be a person of honor is to possess and display integrity in one's beliefs and actions. This is most easily accomplished through one's core values. This is why everyone should take a **Core Values Inventory**.

When you are getting ready to make a decision, large or small, do you consider whether or not the decision or potential outcome is in line with your core values?

Have you ever taken an inventory of your core values? Can you name them?

Knowing one's core values will offer crystal clear insight in to who you are. This could be, should be, then used as a guide when making both the large and small decisions affecting your life and the lives of those around you.

We all make choices. All of us will experience consequences as a result of our choosing. If we choose poorly for ourselves the consequences are likely to be undesirable. Alternatively, choosing based on a true reflection of who we are will help to ensure more positive outcomes.

Core value guided decision making helps immensely when choosing a career, a particular job, a mate, friends, associations, even a home or a car. Deciding in this way, in favor of their own core values, promotes synergy between the individual and the life they chose to live; and synergy promotes harmony.

Everyone has been confronted at some point in their life with a situation, decision or request from someone that dishonors or goes against their inner compass or core values. Think back in your own life whenever this has occurred. You probably said or thought something like, "I can't do that" or, "This is not me" or, "That's not who I am."

If you decided in your own favor then you were honoring the core values which were being challenged. Afterward, you probably felt good about your decision.

If you went counter to what you were telling yourself at the time and made the decision to proceed against your better judgment then I am 100% certain you dishonored one or more of your core values.

Afterward, you probably felt bad about your decision. What was the ultimate outcome? How did the decision to dishonor your core values affect your life, positively or negatively?

Deciding counter to our core values can lead to lying, cheating, stealing, bankruptcy, relationship problems and all of the attendant negative consequences. Laboring in a career or at a particular job which violates our core values will ultimately lead to job burnout.

Before becoming sober, I was in opposition to my core values on a daily basis as an active alcoholic and I suffered mightily as a result. Years into sobriety as a successful, practicing family physician I became burned out because the demands of my job began to conflict with my core values.

In both instances, I had to return to my core values and embrace them as never before. When I did, everything changed for the better.

Addictions to drugs, alcohol or some other addictive behavior; self-inflicted or job related burnout; unrealized personal human potential; working at a job you do not enjoy or outright detest; toxic relationships - these are no states in which to live. It is impossible to live a life of purpose and passion under any of these conditions. The best way to avoid them altogether is to celebrate and honor your own core values in everything you do and in every decision you make.

The best way to avoid negative consequences is to celebrate and honor your own core values in everything you do and in every decision you make. When you are getting ready to make a decision, large or small, consider first whether or not the decision or potential outcome is in line with your core values.

No matter what career or vocation you have chosen, when you begin to share your life experience with others you should tap into your core values and seek to honor them. The power of your stories, your personal truth, will be reflected in the Powerful Words of your values. They will resonate with your tribe.

Determining your top five core values and your #1 main core value can be challenging, but very enlightening. Here is a simple exercise to help your determine your top 5 core values.

# The Core Values Inventory (CVI)

**Step #1.** On a piece of paper make a list of all of the values you hold dear, the values you would use to describe yourself as having, the values you honor within yourself. Take your time and be thoughtfully introspective. Do this now or over the course of a day and a night if you wish. Your list might include values such as knowledge, happiness, curiosity, hope, love, friendship, joy, truth, passion, etc. List as many as you can think of that apply to you. Don't worry about putting them in any kind of order just now. Be careful when enlisting the help of others. They may give you values they think you have, or wish you had, rather than values you yourself actually possess.

**Step #2.** In **Appendix A** in back of this book there is an extensive list of common positive human values. Review this list just to see if you feel any of them apply to you. If some of them resonate with you, but do not appear on your list from Step #1 then go ahead and add them. Skip over any that do not apply to you then move on to Step #3 once you have finished running the list. If you can think of some which suit you and are not listed in the Appendix then by all means add them to your list.

**Step #3.** Answer each the following questions on separate pieces of paper:

1.) When I was a kid I used to LOVE to _____ .
Write down all of the things you used to love to do as a child, the things you tried to do as often as possible which brought you joy, happiness and contentment.

2.) My **strengths** are _____ .
List all of the strengths you see in yourself now as an adult.

3.) As an adult I LOVE to _____ .
List all of the things you LOVE to do as an adult which bring you joy, happiness and contentment.

4.) What two or three things or activities make you OVER-THE-TOP happy as an adult? _____ .

Now, for each set of answers for each of the questions above, write down all of the values that are being **honored** in each instance. The values you write down may be the same as some of the ones you generated in Steps #1 and #2 or you may come up with some different ones. It's okay if some of them are the same. You may list more, or you may list less than in the first exercise. Just write down your impression of which vales are being **honored** in the answers to each of theses questions. Write them down on the same pieces of paper as the answer to each question. From this point forward try not to look back at previous value lists.

**Step #4.** These are the last series of questions to answer. These serve to expand the capability of capturing a more accurate picture of your core values. Be sure to answer each question on a separate piece of paper.

1.) How would you answer this question? I am passionate about _____ !

You can list more than one thing, but list only the thing(s) you are truly passionate about in your life right now.

2.) My career(s) have been _____ .
List all of them.

3.) This really, truly, undeniably TICKS ME OFF!!! _____ .
Describe as accurately as possible what gets you maximally hot under the collar.

4.) Describe the worst day of your life that you can recall. As painful as it may be, write down what happened to make it the worst day of your life. _____ .

5.) Describe your perfect day. I mean YOUR PERFECT DAY! What would it look like? What would you do? Where would you go? What would you eat? Who would be present with you, if anyone? Be as precise as possible and write it out in one paragraph.

6.) What is your favorite color? _____ .

7.) Describe the best day you can remember as a child, your happiest day. What were you doing? What were you thinking? Were you by yourself or with someone? What made it so special? Answer this in one paragraph.

8.) Last one. If you could be any animal, which one would you be? You could be a bird, a reptile or a mammal. So, what would you be? _____ .

**Step #5.** Now, go back to your answers to each of the last series of questions. **Choosing only from the lists of values you generated in Steps #1, #2, and #3**, write down the values that were either being **honored** or **dishonored** for each of your answers. There may be just one value or more than one value that is either being **honored** or **dishonored**.

Some values you will use once, some multiple times and others not at all. You should do this for each of your answers, even with the answer to the question of what animal you would be. For instance, as you picture yourself as the animal you chose, what values does that animal represent to you, which would you be honoring as that animal. For instance, I chose my favorite bird, the owl. To me, owls represent wisdom, knowledge and patience.

**Step #6.** Look back over all of the value lists you have generated. You will notice some of them have been used twice, some have been used multiple times and some have only been used once. **Make a new list of values using only the ones that have been used more than once** and write beside each of them exactly how many times they have appeared in your lists. If a value has been used only once, we are done with it so do not include it on this new list. But do not throw them away.

You should now have at least five values that were used more than once. Pick the five values that appear most often in your lists. If there is a tie for the fifth value then choose which of the two fits you best. **These are your top five core values**. They have been your guide throughout your life. Although, you may not have honored or celebrated them as well as you might have. This will not be the case moving forward. From this point on, in all that you do, you should intentionally strive to honor your top five core values.

**Step #7.** Now, just like a table has four legs for support, four of these values are the ones that support you and your **main core value**. Only one of them is your strongest **main core value**. Just as the legs of a table can not stand alone without the table's top, your **main core value** is what binds the other four values all together. Once your top 4 core values are bound together by your **main core value**, they will in turn support it and You. Your **main core value** is supported by the four, and the **MAIN ONE** ties them all together so they become enabled to offer you their support. Think of these five core values as you, your mirror and your reflection. Together, they form a clearer image of who you are.

Now, if multiple values appear an equal number of times in your top five list then you will have to decide which among them is your main core value. You will do this by starting with any two and asking yourself, "If I can only keep one of these two values then I will keep _____." Keep doing this until you get down to the one main core value that you can not set aside. That will be your main core value.

## Your Top Five Core Vales Are:

1. _____ .

2. _____ .

3. _____ .

4. _____ .

5. _____ .

## Your Main Core Value Is:

_____

My main core values are Freedom, Knowledge, Imagination, Creativity, and Teaching or Sharing Knowledge & Experience. FREEDOM is my main core value. If I had to add a sixth core value to my list it would be Curiosity.

Did the results of this exercise surprise you? Or, did you get what you expected?

# How to Use Your Core Values

Place these top five core values on some cards and display them where you live and where you work. Stick them up on your refrigerator, in your car and on the edge of your computer screen. Let your core values serve as your foundation for making decisions for yourself and others.

Honor them as often as possible. Your core values are the first of your Powerful Words. You should use them liberally when talking about or planning for your dreams, desires, and goals for yourself or for your business. They comprise your very foundation on which everything you do will rest.

When you have a success, look to which of your values you honored the most, the ones from which you derived the most strength. When you have a perceived failure, look to see which of your core values were being dishonored and take steps to avoid doing so again while moving forward. In honoring and serving your core values, they will honor and serve you.

# How Do You See Yourself?

Y ou core values are a good reflection of who you truly are but may not reflect how you see yourself or how others see you. It is now time to ask yourself, "How do I see myself?"

Do you see yourself as a complete reflection of your core values or as something different? Do you see yourself as smart and capable or stupid and incapable? Do you feel you are a good person or a bad person? Do you feel like a winner, a loser or an underdog?

If you see yourself as different from your core values, how do you think others perceive you? The same way you see yourself or differently?

The biggest obstacles I have ever faced were the ones I placed directly in front of myself because of how I viewed myself. For much of my life I carried around an attitude that I was incapable of becoming more than I was assigned to be by others.

I desperately wanted to be great in someone's eyes without realizing I had to see myself as great with my own eyes first.

I visited a friend in Washington, DC in the summer of 2014. Nadia and I walked on the mall on a Friday night to the Lincoln Memorial. It was a beautiful evening. The lighting inside the memorial was subdued except for lights accenting the massive marble statue of Lincoln, sitting there, gaze fixed toward the Washington Monument and the Capital building beyond.

The whole dreamlike scene leaves quite an impression. I was reminded of what a great man this servant of the people became. Yet, Abraham wasn't born great. He became great.

He came into this world just like the rest of us; helpless, crying and completely dependent on others. Before he was gone, a nation in great pain came to depend on him. He was sorely tested, rose to the challenge and prevailed. The effects of his leadership are still felt today.

How did this man from such humble beginnings, come to be so great? We would all like to know. Deep down, I believe we would all like to be great like Abraham. I know I would.

Did he choose to be great or was greatness thrust upon him? Did he have special talents and unique abilities more special and unique than the rest of us?

I would like to believe that any of us could be an Abraham Lincoln, that we have in us the potential for such greatness. Maybe not to the same degree, but just as great nonetheless. We can be or are already just us great in the eyes of those around us, the one's who care about us and care for us, and of those for whom we care.

Becoming great means listening, sharing, helping, and healing by whatever means possible using your own unique set of natural talents and abilities. Whether you are able to help one person or millions, your help is felt individually by just one person at a time.

So, I will ask you again, how do you see yourself? Do you think you are great?

I know some people who feel they have attained all of the success in life they could ever want. As a result, they've stopped growing or accepting new challenges. Others I know have retired and have gone on cruise control. They do little and produce less. They see themselves as a retiree so they take on the role.

I see countless others in my family practice who have given up on their dreams and seem to be existing more than living. They have a job, work, earn a paycheck, go into debt, pay bills, raise kids, and live for the weekends which always promise more than they can ever deliver. They feel stuck because they are stuck.

How do you see yourself?

When you hear the word forest, what picture comes to mind? Do you see only trees and nothing more? Certainly, there is more to a forest than trees. But, when someone hears the word forest, trees usually come to mind because they are the most prominent and striking feature of a forest.

In truth, you can not have a forest populated only with trees. You must also have underbrush, insects, birds, mammals, reptiles mosses, fungi, water and rich earth. None of these will exist well without the others, if at all. All are part of a whole, each just as important as the other. Remove one and the entire forest suffers.

When thinking of yourself, do you view yourself in just one way or many? Many people see themselves fundamentally different than what they aspire to be. Too many people see themselves as inadequate, deficient and incapable of greatness.

Even if they are successful there is a tendency for people to feel they can only be successful at one thing or perhaps a few things at most. Why?

All of these individuals have come to feel as though they have few choices. Their vision of self has narrowed to a point where possibilities seem too few, too far away or simply unobtainable. They have become monolithic in their thinking.

They tend to have too large a view of just one aspect of themselves, the one aspect which seems most prominent, usually the one aspect which is suffering the most or the one that is most underdeveloped. The tendency is to focus on this one aspect and try to fix it to the exclusion of all else. This is not only the wrong thing to do, it is 100% opposite of the right thing to do.

If you had just 10 minutes a day to work on YOU, would you spend the time trying to improve what you are bad at doing or trying to improve what your are great at doing?

Would you spend any of the time picking up a new skill(s) or servicing neglected ones?

At one point in my medical career I became burned out as a family physician. Working harder in that role wasn't the answer. I tried working harder and I just felt worse. I wasn't leaning in, I was pulling away. I had to take a long hard look at the other areas of my life, the areas I had left unattended for far too long.

It was if I had nurtured only my life as a physician while letting all other aspects of my life slowly die off from inattentiveness. Also, I wasn't learning anything new. I wasn't stretching. I wasn't exploring, creating, teaching or sharing. I felt trapped in my career. I didn't feel free. (Remember my top 5 core values?) My life was out of balance.

Things began to change for the better when I began to devote more time to the other realms - *mental, emotional, physical and spiritual* - and arenas of my life - *family, community (social), relationships, environmental, intellectual, financial, legal, and moral* - not just to my occupation.

I had to come to the realization that I had let what I did for a living, my job, had become entirely who I was. I saw myself only as a physician. The results were dismal. I had to make a decision to become more of who I was supposed to be. Once I began to take in a different view of myself, new and exciting possibilities began to appear right in front of me.

I was no longer just a physician. I discovered I was also a writer, an online radio host, a coach, a speaker, an artist, and much, much more. I reacquainted myself with my core values and began to celebrate them more in everything I did and every decision I made.

I became engaged, the opposite of burnout. Everything changed, and will continue to change, because I am no longer stuck. When you are fully engaged in living you will go from becoming, to being your better self.

It starts by looking at yourself differently and by asking yourself, "Just what am I capable of doing?" Let me help you answer that one. It is clear to me you can do what ever you make up your mind to do. Every day I have come to question more and more, exactly what is impossible for myself, for anyone?

It is not about becoming complex. It isn't all about the acquisition of new skills. It isn't about getting another degree. It isn't about becoming something you're not. **It's about knowing or remembering who you are by honoring your core values and embracing your unique set of natural talents and abilities while in the pursuit of your own happiness.** I hope you will agree these are Powerful Words of advice.

Do this, and you will never look at yourself in the same way ever again. Or a forest either, for that matter.

## Powerful Words...

CAPABLE, OBSTACLES, DREAMS, STUCK, POSSIBILITIES and HAPPINESS are Powerful Words.

To change, to let your voice be heard, you must **feel** CAPABLE before you can become capable. No one says NO louder than the voice in our own head. Trade "I can't" for "I'm capable." Then, there is no excuse.

OBSTACLES need not be barriers. Obstacles have their basis in fear. Steel away the power of obstacles by recognizing them for what they are - cerebral insecurities without form or substance. Like ghosts they pop up, or we trot them out, when we step outside our comfort zones. Yet, we are the only ones to see them or to hear them and the only person they scare is ourselves.

DREAMS and POSSIBILITIES share power equally and are synonymous as far as I am concerned. Ask someone to share their dreams and you are likely to see them brighten or become more energetic as they passionately describe them to you. Or, they may become sad and lament over dreams unrealized. Either way, they are powerful.

Dreams are most powerful if considered possible, because then and only then do they have a chance of becoming true. More and more I ask myself, what in this world isn't possible? If you are open to infinite possibilities, an equal number of dreams are possible. If your dreams are of all things possible, then the possibilities are endless.

STUCK must be a Powerful Word because so many people are stuck. Who is it that determines who is stuck and who isn't? If you know the answer to the question then chances are you aren't stuck or will soon be unstuck.

One thing is for sure. If you aren't stuck, if you feel capable, if you relish removing obstacles from your path, if wherever you look you can see possibilities, if you dream dreams and endeavor to make them real, you are happy.

The power of HAPPINESS is universal. Everyone wants to be happy. Not everyone will put in the effort to make themselves happy. Happiness, like everything else in life, is a choice. If you are happy, and can passionately share what makes you happy, you will help others choose happiness too. Happiness is a very Powerful Word.

# Your world of words within...

Have you ever been stuck? What did you do to get unstuck? Are you stuck now? What do you plan to do about that? Do you feel capable?

Do you limit your possibilities? Or, do all things seem possible? What obstacles have you overcome? Those are the powerful stories people need to hear.

What are your dreams? Have you realized them? Or, have you given up on your dreams? Why? Did giving up on your dreams make you happy? How can you turn that around?

What is the source of your happiness? Does it come from within or do you look outside yourself for happiness? What stories do you have about happiness?

Write your thoughts down as they come to you. If any of these questions move you on an emotional level then your answers need to be explored. Therein will lie some of your Powerful Words.

What are your dreams? List three dreams you have had for a while.

1. _____

2. _____

3. _____

What would make you happy? Right now. What do you want? This could be different from the list of your dreams. List three things you want right now.

1. _____

2. _____

3. _____

# SELF-IDENTITY

My recovery from alcoholism has become one prism through which I view my life and the world around me. Ask a thousand people in a solid recovery program, whatever their addiction might be, what is the single most important aspect of their recovery and you will get many disparate answers.

Yet, for each and every one of them there is one overriding necessity, a singular imperative that I believe to be absolutely necessary for lasting sobriety. It is absolutely key for any kind or recovery or meaningful change. It is a common objective that lies at the end of many paths. People will attain it without being able to name it, the singular imperative of *self-identity*.

Over many years and with a lot of trial and error, I have come to know more of who and what I am and who and what I am not (just as important). The importance of self-identity isn't just for people in recovery. It is just as important for everyone in the world. Self-identity is fundamental to one's personal freedom which equates to happiness.

Self-identity is a collection of beliefs, notions and realizations about oneself. It is the answer to the greatest of questions, **"Who am I?"** The answer lies deep within each of us and is reached by introspection and reflection. If, we dare to reach inside to know ourselves.

I have heard Dan Miller (48 Days to the Work You Love) tell the following story many times and I have read it in his publications. It is a story about Akiva the rabbi and it conveys a very simple but important lesson. Here is the story in Dan's own words...

*There's an old story about Akiva, the rabbi, who had been in the village to gather some supplies. Walking back to his cottage, he absentmindedly* took the wrong path. Suddenly, a voice came through the darkness: "Who are you, and why are you here?"

Shocked to awareness, Akiva realized he had wandered into the Roman garrison, and the voice had come from the young sentry keeping guard. But being a rabbi, he answered the question with another question: "How much do they pay you to stand guard and ask that question of all who approach?"

The sentry, now seeing that this was not an intruder but a rabbi, answered meekly, "Five drachmas a week, sir."

At that point the rabbi offered, "Young man, I will double your pay if you come with me, stand in front of my cottage, and ask me that question each morning as I begin my day: 'Who are you, and why are you here?'"

So many fail to ask and answer this most basic question. As a result, they never realize their full potential or their place in the world. If you do not know who you are, you will end up living your life according to someone else's plan and not your own.

As we focus attention on ourselves we compare and contrast past and current behaviors to our internal values and standards. Great internal conflicts can arise when our behaviors fail to reflect our own internal standards. These conflicts may induce us to change our behavior for our own good.

Individuals are more likely to change their behavior to comport with their internal values and standards when they are made to be more self-aware by circumstances or by others. As time goes by and we become more self-aware and we develop a more accurate sense of who we are - our self-identity.

This is a process that happens to all of us as we live our lives. We make decisions. Some of them are supremely good decisions, some horrendously and tragically bad. We gain experience as we make them, at the expense of ourselves and of others. It is how we learn, if we heed the lessons life is teaching us.

This endless series of choices, actions, reactions and experiences can change us or constrain us. They will alter our journey to take new roads or seek out the dead ends, compel us to drop old habits or to pick up new ones, cause us to abandon old concepts or to worship the obsolete, force us to embrace new paradigms for living or accept self-destruction. It comes down to choice.

Just like a long journey to an unknown destination, you will never know precisely when you will arrive, the route that will be taken to get you there, or where you might end up. That sums up my foray into alcoholism followed by my recovery.

I did not expect to become an alcoholic. I didn't wake up one day and just decide I would become one. It was much more insidious than that. But, an alcoholic is what I became.

Once I became one, for the longest time I did not know that I was one. Once I knew that I was one, I did not know if I would or could get sober. Once I became sober, I had to come to terms with what had happened, what I had become and what it would take to live a new and different life moving forward.

I was given an opportunity to change by circumstance and by those around me who cared. I took a deep breath and took a leap of faith and gave myself over to a simple program of recovery. I decide I would change.

I became a sober person. I had a spiritual awakening. A new me emerged on the other side of devastation. As far as I am concerned, it was a miraculous transformation.

When I became burned out as a family physician, I made some changes which made me a better doctor and brought me more satisfaction from the practice of medicine. Any scars I incurred along the way have helped me to help others who have been similarly wounded. Now, I work with others suffering from addictions and job burnout.

When I felt I had been shredded into tatters through an unexpected divorce, I began to explore new opportunities to find what else I might be capable of doing. Writing this book is an example. As a result, I have a clearer picture of who I am. It has helped me on my journey of self-discovery. Telling your stories using your own Powerful Words will do the same for you.

All of us will have transformative times and events peppered throughout our lives. Looking back, all of our life experiences are now and forever a part of who we are. There is no sense in denying them. They are very important facets of our self-identity. You can try and deny them but then you would never be fully in touch with the real you.

Everyone should come to terms with who they are and who they are not. Not everyone will. If you choose, you could be on an enlightening voyage of self-discovery with a singular imperative - self-identity. Your eventual destination is FREEDOM and you would be most likely to arrive HAPPY.

## Powerful Words...

SELF-IDENTITY and FREEDOM are Powerful Words.

To find your purpose in life you must first come to know who you are which is SELF-IDENTITY. Everything else flows from this concept of the self - your natural talents and abilities, your wants and needs, your dreams and desires. In knowing yourself, your direction becomes clear and focused.

FREEDOM empowers self-expression. The more freedom people have, the happier they are. The less they have, the more miserable they are. I cherish all forms of freedom - liberty, financial freedom, the ability to travel freely, freedom of expression.

Freedom is my number one core value. This word resonates with me like no other. I have no doubt this comes from my father who I think about and miss every day.

There are many stories about my father which bring very strong emotions up in me. These stories contain Powerful Words. When I talk about my father those words connect me with others on an emotional level. The emotions inside me flow through those words to the listener and they feel my emotion too. We connect. This is the power of story and Powerful Words.

# World of words from within...

Can you answer the question, "Who am I"? What revelations and experiences have you had which helped you to answer the question? If your answer is, "I don't know" are you still searching for the answer? I hope so.

Even I don't know if I have completely answered the question "Who am I" to my own satisfaction. I do know this, I am closer now than I have ever been to the answer and I will never answer the question unless I keep trying, unless I keep searching. This is why this fantastic journey I am on is so fantastic!

If you have discovered who you are and your purpose in life, you have Powerful Words to share. If you haven't, your have Powerful Words to share about your journey thus far. I implore you, if you are still in discovery mode, don't stop. The story of your journey to self-discovery can be of benefit to others who also search.

If you haven't yet begun your journey of self-discovery to answer the question, "Who am I", please START. We are luminous children of the universe. Shine brightly.

When you hear the word FREEDOM, what thoughts come to mind?

Freedom to/from/for _____

This is a tough one. How would you describe yourself? Who are you?

_____
_____
_____
_____
_____
_____
_____
_____
_____
_____

This is can be an interesting exercise. Have some of your friends, acquaintances, co-workers or family members describe you as they see you. Are their descriptions different than yours? Do they see you differently than you see yourself? If so, how so? Is their image of you the one you wish to project?

# YOUR PERSONAL TRUTH

## Rigorous honesty is key...

Here is the straight up truth. If you want to find YOUR own Powerful Words and stories and share them in a way which can benefit others then you are going to have to become brutally honest. Any less and people will look right past you perceiving you are without real substance.

In this regard, there is no holding back. The doors and windows to all of the dark and light places within you must be flung open. Yes, there is risk because it will make you vulnerable. It will also set you free.

When you connect with your personal truth and the emotion behind it, there will be no denying the power in your words.

As you tell your stories, listeners will fall silent as you speak. They will laugh with you, cry with you, rise up with you and fall down with you. All the while they will be in awe of the courageous person standing before them telling their story.

When you are done some people will come up to you with tears in their eyes or a smile on their face and they will thank you for changing their life. If they are reading your stories you will get letters of appreciation for the impact your words have had on them.

These are not idle promises. It has happened to me and I have seen it happen too many times with other speakers to deny that it is true. It will happen to you too. But, you must be real. You must make it personal. You must be vulnerable.

# Time to drop the mask...

Everyone has a fake persona they put on from time to time. It is something we do when we want to hide our true feelings. Ever feel sad, sick, tired, emotionally unbalanced, but smile anyway and say everything is fine when asked? Of course you have. We all do this with the best intentions, of course.

When asked how we feel or what we think about something, we may hide the truth in order to spare someone's feelings, avoid a lengthy conversation, avoid a painful or controversial topic, or to avoid an argument. For a variety of reasons, some people are just incapable of telling the truth when it comes to their feelings. But, we all wear a mask.

Throughout this book I have laid bare much of my life story. It is what must be done in order to connect with others who might be helped by hearing about my experiences. Here comes some more honesty.

I wore a mask when I was an active alcoholic. People like me who were/are addicted to drugs, alcohol or aberrant behaviors are held hostage by this incapacity for truth telling when it comes to stating exactly how or what they feel in a forthright manner. They live a great masquerade. I, too, wore my mask well.

When I was actively drinking and had crossed well over the line into alcoholism, people around me became genuinely concerned. They knew that all was not right with me and they would ask, "How are you doing?" My standard response was "fine" and I would say it with a smile.

People in recovery joke that what FINE actually stands for is Freaked out, Insecure, Neurotic and Emotionally unbalanced. I can't argue with them there. I was all of that and more. The number of times I smiled and said that everything was fine are beyond counting. To masquerade, the mask I donned had many names - feign, make-believe, pretend, obfuscate, misrepresent, lie. That is what addicted brains do.

First and foremost, alcoholics and addicts exist in a perpetual state of denial. Their hair could be on fire and if acknowledging said blaze meant they must admit their addiction, or that using their drug of choice might be curtailed in some way. Then, they would deny their flaming crown and claim the next door neighbor must be having a barbeque.

So, when you ask an active addict how they are doing, even if they share some of their current difficulties, you will most likely get a response that does not include the use of drugs or alcohol. These will not be included because to "addicted brain thinking" these could not possibly be the cause of their worries and problems.

The masquerade is the false outward show that disguises the addiction for fear of being discovered. When I was having trouble in medical school, I said it was because I was having trouble with my marriage.

When I was seeing a psychiatrist in medical school for depression and the problems I was having in my marriage I said it was because of the problems I was having in school. Not once did I allow the common theme of both problems to be explored, my hidden alcoholism. I wore my mask well, at least for a time.

I never felt good the next day after drinking heavily the night before, but I always said I did. I remember saying on more than one occasion, that I never felt hung over even after a night of very heavy drinking. I would put on the mask of happiness and well being, smile and say "I feel great" when I really felt like road kill.

I had to maintain the persona of someone who could drink everyone else under the table and still be okay. To my addicted brain thinking, to admit otherwise would mean admitting to myself and others that I might have a problem with alcohol. The masquerade continued.

I have always maintained that mental anguish can be worse than physical pain. Addicts and alcoholics can be in terrible, crushing, tortuous mental anguish and still effectively function, at least until the latter stages of their disease.

People who say addicts and alcoholics are lazy have never been addicted and have no understanding of the addicted. It takes a tremendous amount of energy to be a functional alcoholic or addict. Living addicted is to experience an unremitting series of losses. One of the last things to go is the job, especially if the addict or alcoholic is a professional.

With great effort addicted individuals will try and hold it together under tremendous mental and physical pressures to protect their great secret. They present the pretense of normalcy when all inside is turmoil. The addicted brain is ever vigilant, disguising the truth at all costs in the face of declining wealth, health, spiritual awareness, emotional stability and psychological well being. This dissimulation continues apace until what is hidden becomes patently obvious to everyone.

Before I got sober my view of the world had narrowed significantly. I was living from day-to-day to drink and drunk. I had constructed a facade, a great mask of invincibility all the while hiding my vulnerabilities. It was all a great masquerade.

I suffered in silence until it was all out in the open. When I went off to treatment it was with trepidation. I didn't know if treatment would be successful and that was a huge fear. I was at a point where I desperately wanted sobriety, but all of my earlier attempts (daily) at quitting were failures.

In treatment, I had to drop the mask. No more masquerading. I had to become a real human being with real feelings that I would no longer deny. At first there was a lot of guilt, remorse, shame. Feelings once relieved only by years of heavy drinking, caused by years of heavy drinking, had to be squared with my new reality - rigorous honesty. It was a quintessential paradigm shift.

In treatment I gave up all of my secrets until there was nothing left to hide. When there was nothing left to hide there was no further need to masquerade. I can't begin to tell you how liberating that was for me. It is the same for anyone who embraces meaningful recovery.

From masquerade to revelation where a new freedom and a new happiness can be found. It is a journey I would recommend for anyone. Without the alcoholism, of course.

That was as honest an appraisal of what it was like and what happened as best I can recall.

# They are in there...

I have given "my story" and other stories of my descent into alcoholism and subsequent recovery numerous times at recovery related events and meetings. I have been told by individuals numbering too many to count, both in recovery and by those still suffering, that my words helped them. As such, they were Powerful Words because of the connections which were established between us.

I have heard Powerful Words from hundreds of speakers over the years whose stories of experience, strength and hope have helped me tremendously and have been able to pass their wisdom along for the benefit of others. Powerful Words can have a life of their own.

You have Powerful Words inside of you, waiting to be shared. People will be helped by hearing them if you are honest, determined and intentional about getting your voice heard. If you are ready, let's begin.

## What it was like, what happened and what it is like now...

We all lose things. I lost my baseball cards in a move once. I still think about them from time to time. I'm sure I have lost countless other trinkets over the years, most of which I don't remember. I can only conclude it didn't matter, because I don't remember.

I've lost beloved pets. I still have pictures of my first dog next to my bed, one on each night stand, a white and brown collie named Lassie, of course. In one picture she is sitting on top of a bench. She would always hop up onto the bench and sit down for me with just a nod and wave of my hand.

In the other picture she is lying on the ground on her side nursing a bunch of puppies. I am sitting on the ground behind her with her head in my lap and my hand on her head. I was about eight or nine years old.

My dad shot 8mm movies as I was growing up. In one of the movies I am rolling around on the ground covered in puppies. Lassie's puppies.

She was my dog from my earliest memory until she died of kidney failure when I was 15 years old. I had never known life without her.

I remember the day she died, vividly, even though it was more than 45 years ago. That evening, I was sitting at a table trying to distract myself by working on a one thousand piece puzzle. I was crying. I had been crying on and off all afternoon.

Then, I felt something unusual. I felt it in my feet at first, a kind of vibration. The vibration grew in intensity until my chair began to shake and then the table. Pieces of the puzzle began to dance off all around the edge of the table. All I could do was watch them fall to the floor to join my tears.

I had just experienced an earthquake in my hometown of Belmont, North Carolina. From what I remember, it lasted a total of about 10 seconds. After I realized what had happened my first thought was, "How appropriate. An earthquake to send my Lassie off in style. Or, maybe it was her, saying goodbye."

I didn't cry anymore after that. I still think about her. Every night when I go to bed I see her picture and I'm reminded of all the joy she brought to my life growing up. I miss her so.

We will all suffer profound loss of some kind in our lifetime, if we live long enough. Worse than the loss of a beloved pet is the loss of a parent, a sibling, or a child.

I do believe there is an upside to every downside. So, where is the upside in these instances?

I lost my sister to pancreatic cancer in September 2010. This left a big hole in me. My mother and father had already passed. I loved them very much, but I knew they weren't going to live forever and they each had a long life.

I didn't expect my sister to die. Not at 64, with an out of-the-blue terminal illness in one of the healthiest people I knew. I would fondly refer to her as the health nut. We would both laugh.

She made it 9 months from the time of diagnosis until she died. The first time I visited her gravesite alone I stared at her marker for a long, long time. It couldn't feel any upside potential for my loss just after she died. I miss her and I think about her every day.

I have her picture on the wall in my office and I look at it every day. She looked so well in the photograph, but she went into the hospital four hours after it was taken and she died just several days later.

Mercifully, her husband brought her home to die after she slipped into a coma. She had stopped taking any fluids by mouth. Her daughter, my niece, asked me how long it would be before she would die. I said, "one day." She asked me how I could be so sure. I told her, "You can live three minutes without air, three days without water, three weeks without food." It had been two days since she had any fluids.

I sat alone on the edge of her bed, holding her hand, sobbing. I kept telling her I was sorry. I was sorry she was dying. I was sorry her life had been cut short. She was 64. I was sorry she was going to leave this world. Mostly, I was sorry she was going to leave me. She passed away quietly the next day.

I hear her sometimes in my head, when I don't know what to do about something, when I am struggling with something or have tough a decision to make. I tell stories about her all the time. I reminisce about all of the fun we had traveling together and at family gatherings.

I get out the old pictures of us when we were small and they make me laugh, and cry. In time, I came to realize that the upside of the downside of losing her was just how privileged I was to have her as my sister in the first place. How everyone loved her. How special she was to all who knew her.

Elaine made me a stronger man. She inspired me. I decided I would backfill the hole she left in me with the choices I would make moving forward.

When we lose, we hurt. Wounds heal and we learn that it feels much better in the long run to be well and to win. If we can. If we choose.

When we lose, we need. We can understand and accept that necessity is the mother of invention, of innovation. If we choose.

When we lose we are sometimes damaged, even broken. We fix what is broken and repair the damaged parts of ourselves and come back stronger than before. If we choose.

When we lose, we grow tired and think about giving up. But then we center ourselves and regroup. We seek inspiration from others, like I do from my sister. We avoid negativity. We reenergize. We get to work. We build. We create. We soar.

I prefer to choose an upside to my downsides. I have found this to be another pathway to a new freedom and a new happiness.

# What of triumph?...

You might ask, what about stories of triumph? Of course, stories of success and triumph are very powerful. In fact, nothing gets me connected on an emotional level more than a story involving triumph. Especially, if it involves an underdog or unlikely hero who fights against overwhelming odds and tremendous hardship, and emerges victorious in the end.

Most people love those kinds of stories. Love for those kinds of stories is as ancient as the stories of myth handed down from generation to generation. Triumph stories follow the general storyline of a descent into darkness where an epic battle or struggle occurs followed by a victory and then a reemergence into the light.

Sound familiar? I'll bet it does. Almost everyone has personal stories to tell which follow this particular pattern of events.

Earlier in this book I recounted the story of speaking before the Optimist Club when I was in grade school. You will remember it did not go well. In fact, it was a disaster.

For many years if more than two or three people were gathered in a group, I was too afraid to speak. So, I didn't. When I decided to go to undergraduate college in 1977 I thought, I have got to get over this fear, I have to speak in public.

So, while I was living in Hickory, NC, attending Lenoir-Rhyne College, I joined Toastmasters International. They are devoted to improving people's speaking and listening skills. It was nerve-racking at first, but I kept at it.

My confidence level speaking in front of an audience, began to rise. I entered speech contests. I won some and I lost some, but I kept at it. In 1981, I entered the North Carolina State Serious Speaking Championship contests beginning at club level and working my way up.

One night in Charlotte, NC, I delivered a speech on Our Greatest Natural Resource - People. I went prepared. I had something to prove to myself.

As I stood behind the podium giving that speech I imagined every woman I saw in the room was my mother because she couldn't be there. I imagined her looking right at me instead of looking away as she had many years earlier.

At the end of my speech I brought 500 people to their feet for a standing O and won first place in the contest at the state level. I have given hundreds of talks since then.

You have stories of great triumph to tell as well. There are Powerful Words imbedded in those stories. Words which resonate with you on an emotional level and will resonate with others.

# Begin to tell your stories...

The Power of story lies only in the telling. Begin to think about and write out some of your stores involving tragedy, loss or triumph. Let the words flow from you as the events unfold in your mind.

As you write your stories down, keep your word usage simple. It isn't necessary to use large words, poetic prose or flowery language. The largest impact will come from an honest recounting of your story, simply told.

If you have trouble writing out your story, have a friend interview you and record the interview. Write out ahead of time the questions you would want answered by someone telling your story just as it happened. Then, take the audio file of the interview and have it transcribed. Elance (at elance.com) is a good resource for transcription and editing services. You can edit the transcribed version later. There you have it, a hard copy of your stories.

When you are writing your story (stories) be sure to include the following general information.

**What it was like.** Paint a picture of the conditions you were living in/ under at the time of "the event", what your life was like at the time. This is setting up the story. It prepares your audience for what is to come. Be sure to include pertinent details, but only if they enhance your story. Include details like the time of the day, what the weather was like, who was there with you, how you were feeling, etc. This the part of your story which serves to capture people's interest.

**What happened.** This is a description of "the event" whether it was a tragedy, a loss, a victory, a triumph, a personal epiphany, a revelation or a transformation. This should be an event which helped to shape you or one which changed your life in profound ways. This is the part of your story which some people will connect with on an emotional level.

**What it is like now.** Here you will relay what has happened to you since "the event", what your life is like now since whatever happened has happened. This is really a description of what the event meant to you and how it has affected or changed you.

Convey what you learned about yourself, others, the world or about life in general? Share the ways in which the event helped you to grow or to become a stronger person? Finally, and most importantly, share how what happened to you can be of benefit to others.

If you are stuck searching for topics to write about then try this theme to get you started.

# Lessons from everyday life...

We find ourselves in situations every day which can teach us something if we are alert enough and open to them as they present themselves to us. Stories are unfolding all around us. Listen for them. The following is an example of something that happened to me during an encounter with one of my patients.

A patient once asked me, "How do you set something down when you don't know how to set something down?" Part of transformational thinking is the ability to let go, to get past being stuck, to move forward. His question concerned this very issue, about his inability to move past a personal tragedy.

I didn't have an answer for his question at the time but I always remembered his question. It would take me nearly eight years and a personal crisis of my own before I could offer him a complete and reasonable response.

My patient shouted "Wait!" to his son who was bounding toward his motorcycle, already late for work. His son stopped and turned toward his father, listening for an explanation. "Don't you be late for dinner again tonight!" he yelled with smile on his face and a hand up in the air waving him off. His son shouted back grinning, "I won't. I promise."

The son jumped on his motorcycle, cranked it up and sped off down a back country road. Less than two minutes from his house he was struck and killed by a motorist who had sped through a stop sign at 60 miles per hour.

Afterward, to describe his father as a broken man falls far short of the mark. He fell into a pitch black depression. He blamed himself for his son's death. He would say to me repeatedly, "If I had not stopped him and teased about being late for dinner he would still be alive. My son would have missed that car at the intersection where he was killed."

Listening to him tell this story was heart breaking because he believed it was true. I would point out to him many times that if his son had made different decisions and taken different actions himself, that also might have saved him.

If he hadn't overslept and been running late for work, if he hadn't stayed out too late the night before which caused him to oversleep, if he hadn't gone out with his friends the previous evening, if he had bought a car instead of a motorcycle, and so on and on and on.

Deep down, my grief stricken patient knew all of this was true. But still, he couldn't let go of the wrong headed assumption that he was predominantly responsible for his son's death. He just couldn't get past that notion.

More than a year after the incident occurred he was back in my office, despondent. I was seeing him regularly for his depression. The medication I was prescribing and the counseling he was receiving weren't helping to lift his depression.

I was telling him that he had to find someway, somehow to begin to put this tragedy behind him. That is when he asked me, "How do you put something down when you don't know how to put something down?"

I had no answer for him. I had no idea why this good man lost his good son at too young an age and why he was left behind to sort it all out. I never forgot that question. I thought it was a very profound question which deserved a response even though I could not give him one.

It was only much later that I was able to offer him any answer at all that made any sense. Something terrible happened to me nearly eight years after he had asked me the question. It was a personal tragedy of my own.

My world, my world view, everything I thought I knew, all my plans, all my hopes, all my dreams were all turned upside down and destroyed in an instant. My faith was shaken. The person I trusted the most in this world betrayed my trust. I felt lost and broken.

I knew I would survive, I just didn't know at what cost. I slept only a few hours a night. I couldn't eat and I lost 41 pounds. For months I cried all of the time, in front of my dog, in front of my friends, in front of my staff, in front of my therapist and, at times, even in front of my patients. I couldn't stop myself. This went on non-stop for about four months.

Everyone was extremely supportive. But the pain continued. I never went back to drinking alcohol. I never went on any prescribed mood altering medications and I took no illicit ones either. I knew none of those would fix what was broken, me.

But, as the months passed I began to feel better. I stopped crying all of the time and began to enjoy some simple things again. I began to sleep better and I stopped losing weight. Still, I relived my tragedy over and over again, daily.

I just couldn't stop thinking about it. It was the first thing I thought about when I got up in the morning and I hated it. I wanted to put it all behind me. I grew weary of thinking about what had happened to my life.

As I walked my dog every morning and I couldn't help but think of her. I got angry, really angry because I was hurting so badly and I saw no sense in what had happened. I had developed huge resentments, which are not a healthy thing to have if you are in recovery.

I was explaining all of this to a friend a few months after she left and they told me that I was going to have to find some way, some how, to put all of that behind me.

Without even thinking I turned to them and asked, "How do you set something down when you don't know how to set something down?" My friend didn't know either.

After a year of separation, subsequent divorce and through a series of happier circumstances, I began to explore some other avenues of expression with great interest and later on with purposeful intention. I began to write more and really began to enjoy the process of writing content for my blog. I started a podcast, The Power of Transformation, and put up a website of the same name.

I attended several of Dan Miller's seminars in Franklin, Tennessee, joined his 48Days.net community and enrolled in his Coaching Mastery Program with the intention of becoming a personal coach. I kept writing, a lot.

One morning while walking my dog I realized that I had gone several days without thinking about what had happened to me a little over two years prior. Whether it was just time or more forward looking that caused this I still don't know but that is when it hit me, the answer to the question for which I had no answer - "How do you set something down when you don't know how to set it down?"

For me, the answer wasn't setting what had happened to me down. You simply can't forget tragedy, not as long as you have a memory. Turns out, I didn't have to set anything down anyway.

The answer for me, dear reader, was to face forward and pick up other things, lots of new, different and promising things. It seems that my arms and hands became too full of the new and different to hold on to the old and familiar. No longer able to hold on to it all, I was simply letting go of what no longer mattered.

You have had learning experiences such as these in your life and you will continue to have them. Remember, how you look at situations, how you experience them and how you deal with them is as unique as you are. The lessons you glean from living can and will help someone else.

# Powerful Words...

VULNERABLE, PERSONAL TRUTH, STORY, LOSE, BROKEN, TRIUMPH, HARDSHIP and GRIEF are Powerful Words.

Your PERSONAL TRUTH is the STORY of you, the real YOU. I believe there is power in everyone's story. Otherwise, I would not be writing this book. If you are an adult, your personal story contains HARDSHIP, GRIEF, TRIUMPH and the circumstance of how you came to be, who you are, where you are and where you may be headed.

When we are BROKEN, when we LOSE, we become most VULNERABLE to the vagaries of our emotions. It is easy then to fall prey to self-doubt. During those times our left brain is imprinted with all of those negative emotions. Suppressing the memory and emotion only stores them for future reference. The only way I know to off-load the emotional pain associated with bad memories, while simultaneously helping another person deal with their pain, is to get the emotions and memories out and talk about them. This is when people heal. This is when people connect.

## World of words from within...

Do you harbor secrets which are causing you pain? In instances where there has been past physical or sexual abuse, which may be too difficult to deal with alone and without guidance, I would suggest getting help from a professional. Otherwise, can you be vulnerable enough to share your story honestly and completely with another human being? What is your personal truth?

What are your biggest secrets?

_____
_____
_____.

People will listen to your personal story. It is how we connect, one with another. Think of all the personal stories you have heard from others during your lifetime. Even if they seemed tragic in the beginning, I'm sure you walked away inspired in the end. That's because the people telling those stories learned how to connect with you on an emotional level through the power of story, their story, using Powerful Words.

## Powerful Word themes...

Here are some additional Powerful Word themes you might wish to explore. All, some, or maybe just one of these themes may tap into long held, deep and strong emotions. Emotions you may wish to explore. They will hold power for you, power which can be shared when you use them to connect with others on an emotional level.

Your happiest of times.
Your best and worst relationships.
An unexpected, life changing surprise.
Your worst nightmare.
Things which make you laugh.
Things which make you cry.
People you admire and why.
A personal tragedy.
A favorite pet.
Your best friend growing up.
Your first kiss.
Your first love.
The feeling you had when you turned 16.
The loss of a loved one.
The first time you got a bad grade.
Your favorite movie.
A horrible divorce.
Your biggest scare.
A near death experience.
A bad accident.
A big win.

Which of these resonate with you the most?_____

Are there other themes which resonate with you? List them here.

_____
_____
_____

# ARE YOU BEING SELFISH?

You are more than likely reading this book because you feel you have something to say. You feel you have a message to share and you probably believe it can help someone. You may have taken other steps to prepare yourself for this eventuality.

You might also have considered making some money as a result of your efforts.

Is this being selfish? In an emphatic word, NO!

There is a fundamental difference between self-interest and selfishness. Self-interest is a rational, healthy, valid concern for ones own well being. Trying to better ones self while helping others is not only noble, I believe it is our responsibility. If you can make a living while doing that, so much the better.

Self-interest is healthy. It keeps us learning, creating, growing, and moving forward. It is our responsibility to foster enough self-interest to identify and build upon our own unique set of natural talents and abilities.

Selfish people, on the other hand, are exclusively and excessively concerned with themselves to the exclusion of nearly all else. The selfish person will want what you have without doing anything to get it other than to ask or demand it for themselves. The selfish constantly seek to pleasure, advantage, or enrich themselves with a complete lack of regard for others and at the expense of others.

Let me give you a sterling example of selfishness. Addicts are supremely selfish people. I think they are the most selfish group of people on earth. I should know, I was one of them.

When I was an active alcoholic, I thought I was a better person in my head than I was in reality. This is true of most people. But, that difference is markedly amplified in the addicted individual. They are supremely concerned with themselves and their drug(s) of choice to the exclusion of anything or anyone. That is selfishness personified.

Take care to heavily invest in one and not the other. Serve the one which will help you to serve others, self-interest.

## Powerful Words...

SELFISH and SELF-INTEREST are powerful words.

I was raised "to share and share alike." I believe most of us were. Some where along the way, looking out for one's self became SELFISH. More politically correct crap, I suppose.

If you do happen to subscribe to this notion, answer the following question. Is it simultaneously both better and easier to give more from a cup not full or one which is overflowing? If your answer is the latter, then you are just going to be the very best you can possibly be and produce as much as you can possibly produce. It is your responsibility to do so. It is in your SELF-INTEREST to do so.

You rob selfishness of its power by being the best you can be at whatever you do and by reaching a state of abundance. Then, attempt to improve the lives of other people. In the service of others you will ultimately find you are serving yourself which will be an unending source of abundance. This will ultimately enable you to live your life as you see fit as you are helping others.

# Your world of words within...

Were you aware of the differences between selfish and self-interest? Can you write out examples of how self-interest has allowed you to help others?

_____

_____

_____

Or, has someone been able to help you out of their abundance? Either way, there are Powerful Words to share within those stories.

What emotions come to mind when you hear the words need, abundance, scarcity, selfish, self-interest and share? The words attached to those emotions are your Powerful Words.

_____

Do you have a scarcity or an abundance mentality? Write down the differences as you see them here.

_____

_____

_____

# REALITY BASED THINKING
# FOR YOUR PREFERRED
# FUTURE

People are by and large hopeful for their futures. If you are not hopeful for your future, meaning you are feeling hopeless, then there is little reason to get out of bed in the morning.

We hope and pray for many things. Commonly hoped for things include love, health, ubiquitous stuff, a fulfilling job, passion or purpose. We hope and pray for these things in order to bring added meaning to our lives.

But many never realize their dreams and never obtain what they truly desire. Why? Is it because of a lack of luck, bad timing, a lack of faith, not the right education, a lack of money, an unsupportive spouse? I do not believe so.

We have amazing bodies with a complex and highly functional brain to boot. Each of us are born with unique talents and abilities. If we feel something is missing we have the wherewithal to obtain whatever is lacking.

I believe we have already been given all that we need to succeed in life. For those who are into reality based belief systems, I submit the following list of suggestions for a more bountiful and successful future:

# SUGGESTIONS for REALITY BASED LIVING

- The is no such thing as luck. It is an illusion. Sustained, persistent hard work with passion and purpose will lead to success. To an independent observer, it just looks like luck.
- There is no magic formula, magic wand or magic fairy dust. There are tried and true formulas for success which are not magical and are available to anyone. That is, they will work if you work them. Magical thinking gets you buttkus.
- Serving the needs, wants and desires of others will bring you your needs, wants and desires. They will come from those you serve.
- If you are full of discontent, unhappiness and discomfiture and are looking for a sign for when to begin to transform your life, your sign is discontent, unhappiness and discomfiture.
- Your preferred future is your dream and no one else's. Translating your life from where you are to your preferred future is your job. No one else will do this for you because they are concerned about their own lives and preferred futures.
- If you say "I can't," I will not believe you even though you will be right 100% of the time. My not believing that it is true will not make any difference, though, until you stop believing that it is true at which point you will again be right 100% of the time. It is the only instance in your life when you will be 100% right either way. Your choice.
- Praying for God to do something for you that you can do for yourself, to figure out something that you can figure out for yourself or to give you something that you can get for yourself is a waste of mental energy, your natural talents and abilities, not to mention the good Lord's time. Get to work with what you have, what you have been given and be grateful for it.
- The road to success passes through the gateposts of failure, every time, always! There is just no easier, softer way. When you come to a point where you can name failure as a cherished

friend you will have both feet firmly planted pointing toward, or actually within, your preferred future.

We are glorious creatures of the universe destined to accomplish, to build, to produce, to create, to innovate. Do you believe that is true, as I do?

# Powerful Words...

LOVE, HEALTH, MEANING, REALITY and GRATEFUL are Powerful Words.

LOVE is without question **the most** Powerful Word out there. You could fill a library with everything written about love. Often said, seldom completely understood and often misunderstood, the breadth and depth of the range of emotions this word represents are breathtakingly complex and powerful. There are four different words for love in Latin alone.

Love represents the one emotion from which we derive so much MEANING from life. To live with out being loved or having never loved someone or something would truly be a sparse and bland existence.

We all have stories of love won and lost in the rich panoply of our lives. There are other Powerful Words within our stories of love. These Powerful Words and stories are the great connectors of people. Get your stories out there about what and who you truly love and start connecting on meaningful emotional levels.

Whether you have enjoyed good HEALTH or currently enjoy good health, we are always GRATEFUL for it. It is often said, "As long as you have your health..." To enjoy life the utmost, one must have the utmost health. I have never seen a patient who couldn't improve their health status, even my patients with profound health issues.

You don't hope for good health. You must work at it with an actionable plan and routine maintenance. You can make yourself healthy with effort or unhealthy through neglect.

Remember, REALITY based living beats fantasy, magical and wishful thinking every time it's tried. I lived a combination of all those ways for years wasting time for sorry results. Take my advice and take up residence in Realville. Read the above list, SUGGESTIONS for REALITY BASED LIVING, everyday for several weeks and watch your thinking begin to change. You will see magic happen.

# Your world of words within...

Do you believe something is holding you back from your preferred future? If so, can you name it? _____

Is there a solution? What did you discover?

What are you most grateful for these days? List 5 things for which you are most grateful.

1. _____

2. _____

3. _____

4. _____

5. _____

Tell the story behind your answer. What has brought the most meaning to your life? To your work? To your relationships? To your play? What stories of self-discovery can you tell which might inspire or motivate others?

Stories of people who have had profound health issues and recovered from them are very powerful and contain Powerful Words that others will identify with. Do you have a story to tell which will inspire others? Are you on a mission to improve your health now and find yourself struggling? There are Powerful Words to share from those experiences as well. Make some notes here.

_____

_____

_____

_____

_____

_____

If you are already living a reality based life then you have some stories to tell from when you weren't and what you learned in the process. They will contain Powerful Words which you can use to your advantage in your interpersonal relationships and in the marketplace with your business.

# Your Future: The Biggest Gamble of All?

Do you gamble? Most people do not. They would prefer to make better use of their money and time. Some do but purely for the entertainment aspect. A sizable minority of the population is addicted to gambling and will gamble away every last cent they have, even money they don't have.

I look around these days and I notice the unhappiness in people. I hear them complain about the daily grind, how happy they are to have a weekend away from work that they must hate. I can feel a quiet sense of despair over lives that have not turned out the way people have planned and yet...

I counsel people everyday who come to my office and complain about their spouse, their significant other, their children, their parents. Toxic relationships abound where people say they feel trapped, alone, afraid, abused, resentful and resented and yet...

I see so many individuals addicted to alcohol, prescribed drugs, street drugs, food, and sloth. They complain about how terrible they feel and yet...

Yet people seem loath to change their circumstances, even dire, dangerous, life threatening circumstances. They stay in situations that exhaust them, rob them of their dignity and take away hope for a better life. Worse yet, they will let these situations rob them of their preferred future. Why?

I know they have heard that it doesn't have to be that way. I know they know there is help just around every corner. Deep down, they have to know that they are capable of changing things for the better. So, why don't they?

I hear them talk about how things will get better with time. By just waiting? I hear them talk about how things will be better next year yet they have no plans to make things better by this year.

I hear them make excuses for the very same people that they feel are holding them back and I have to believe they can't be serious. Yet, they are serious.

They, all of them, are gambling with their futures. They are leaving to chance what should be fiercely, intentionally and boldly managed - their own lives. I should know, I gave a good portion of my life up to the whims of chance.

If you know someone like this, or if this sounds like you, then here are five steps any individual can take right now to stop gambling away their life, their future:

- **Make a decision.** Nothing will change for you until you decide it will change. Figuratively speaking, if you don't like the scenery, change the view. You must decide to decide things **will** be different. You are at the starting line of the rest of your life, so start moving. You might not know exactly where the finish line is just yet but at least you are moving forward.
- **Help yourself first.** Acknowledge your particular situation. Completely and honestly probe the depth and breadth of it. Know that you can be the agent of change in your own life. Stop waiting for outside forces to rescue you or provide for you. Help yourself. Come to depend on yourself and your own actions for your own needs.

- **Ask for help if needed.** I don't mean a friendly ear to bend or someone that will be content to offer words of encouragement. I mean people, agencies, facilities, providers, institutions, programs and groups that will offer assistance with your particular issues. This is not in disregard of the second step above. Asking for help if you honestly need help **is** helping yourself. You may need advice. You may need protection. You may need counseling. You may need treatment. Ask for what you need.
- **Never turn back.** I have seen people extract themselves from deplorable situations only to crawl right back to them in moments of weakness or self-doubt. Protect your weak spots. Develop strategies to protect yourself from the allure of old habits, codependency traps and those that have harmed you. Your preferred future always lies ahead of you, never behind you.
- **Trust in change.** You must come to realize that you are capable of more, that you can be different, and create, and learn, and produce, and build, and grow. We grow by how we change. We all have different natural talents and abilities that will compel us to change if we choose to use them. If you're not changing, you're not growing.
- These steps are just the beginning, to get you moving. They are intended to stop you from gambling away your future, the biggest gamble of all, so you can begin to embrace the possibilities of change.

# Powerful Words...

GAMBLE, DESPAIR, TRAPPED, ABUSED, WEAKNESS and SELF-DOUBT are Powerful Words.

People who feel TRAPPED whether by SELF-DOUBT or DESPAIR but remain that way often cite the difficulties they would incur if they were to make needed change. So, they choose to stay trapped. As such, trapped is a Powerful Word. They have effectively trapped themselves with the underlying emotions those words represent. If only they could realize they hold all the keys to their trap.

People who are ABUSED always feel trapped. Those who eventually break free always look back and wonder, "Why didn't I leave sooner?" They had the power to do so all along. It isn't about WEAKNESS, it is about gaining strength. Strength is found in the Powerful Words of others who have experienced what they are experiencing. The power of story lies only in the telling.

No one should ever GAMBLE that their future will just happen to turn out the way they expect. This is leaving all to chance. Where this one life you have is concerned, it would be the biggest gamble of all.

## Your world of words within...

Do you feel you have been gambling away your future, just getting by on hopes and dreams? Are there other steps you will take, or have you taken, to ensure a more favorable future for yourself? List five here.

1. _____

2. _____

3. _____

4. _____

5. _____

Are you being abused by someone emotionally, mentally, spiritually, physically? Are you feeling trapped? If so, get help now. Your stories of abuse contain Powerful Words which will get someone's attention. You may feel you can't. I say you can. Look how much you have already endured. Seek help now.

If you have been abused and overcame it then you definitely have Powerful Words to share. Those words will encourage others to change their circumstances because you will connect with them on an emotional level and they with you. That is when the power comes. That is when lives are changed. Make some notes for future exploration here.

_____

_____

_____

_____

What are your weaknesses, your self-doubts. What stories do you have connected to those words of power? Have you been desperate, truly desperate? What were the circumstances? What did you do? Write them down now.

_____

_____

_____

_____

Have you been an abuser of others? Did you stop and find your way to healing? How? Have you told your story? How many could you help if you did? There is only one way to find out, begin.

If you answer any of these questions from an emotional level you will unleash some Powerful Words. Words which can help to heal both you and someone else. Share your power by sharing your personal truth.

What Powerful Words came to you in this section?

_____

_____

_____

_____

# YOUR PREFERRED FUTURE:
## WHY CHANCE IS NOT AN
## OPTION.

What does your preferred future look like? Have you thought about it, really thought about it? If you have an exact picture in mind and you are doing what is necessary right now, then there is a higher likelihood that you will have and live in your preferred future. If not, then you are most likely leaving your future to chance.

It is said that every journey begins with a single step, the first step. The journey to your preferred future is no different. However, the first step is not a physical one. It requires a change of mind, of one's mind-set. That is where the hardest battles are fought, lost or won - in the mind.

## Cold Hard Facts...

One thing is for sure, success does not follow or favor chance.

If you happen to have a clear picture of your preferred future in your mind but have not taken the necessary steps toward attaining and securing that future for yourself, your chances of success are nearly zero.

If you are laboring at a job you detest, spending all you make and saving none, stagnating in an everyday routine that offers nothing but variations of sameness, your chances of a bright and successful future are exactly zero.

If you are addicted to alcohol, a substance or some addictive behavior then your chances for a bright and successful future are less than zero.

# Your Preferred Future...

I see too many people who have come to believe that they are what they are, that they are incapable of change. Nothing could be further from the truth! Sometimes you just have to start over and reshape yourself in order to reshape your life. Sometimes you just have to hit RESTART.

The people who do this, they have undergone a profound and meaningful transformation. They discovered a secret that will work for anyone. They have discovered that transforming is a choice and they have chosen to choose better for themselves.

# Developing the Picture...

I believe if we have a clear picture in our minds of our preferred future then we can reshape ourselves, our lives, to make that picture a reality. That picture must come deep from within.

I love movies. There is an old one that debuted in 1984 that I really enjoyed, the original Karate Kid. In the movie Mr. Miyagi (a Japanese karate master and teacher) gets Daniel (his reluctant student) to shape and prune a bonsai tree. Here is some dialogue from a scene in the movie. It is a metaphor for life and living.

Daniel objects to Mr. Miyagi's request to prune the bonsai tree saying, "I don't know how to do this stuff. I may mess it up. I don't want to mess it up!"

Mr. Miyagi insists, "Close eye. Trust. Concentrate. Think only tree. Make a perfect picture down to last a'pine needle. Wipe from mind, clean, everything but tree. Nothing exist whole world, only tree. You got it?", he asks Daniel after a pause.

Daniel nods yes with his eyes still closed.

Mr. Miyagi says to Daniel, "Remember picture?"

Daniel replies, "Yeah."

Mr. Miyagi follows, "Make like picture" and hands him some pruning scissors. He says, "Just'a trust'a picture."

Daniel asks, "How do I know if my picture's the right one?"

My Miyagi imparts his wisdom, "If come from inside you, always right one."

Developing a clear image of where you want to be and what you want to do in your preferred future will give you purposeful direction. It must come from inside you, not from somewhere else or someone else.

# Transforming the Hopes and Dreams into Reality...

It is not enough just to dream. Sure, dreaming is easier than doing. But, your dreams are not reality until you make them your reality.

Hope is not a strategy. Only gamblers hope for success. They lose the majority of the time. Las Vegas was built by losers. Las Vegas is owned by planners and doers.

We can transform our lives with continuous positive change. That image of your preferred future is your call to action. It will take a plan, intentional hard work, passion and perseverance to make it happen.

Along the way you will succeed some, fail a lot, doubt yourself, be tempted to give up, excited one minute and full of dread the next. Straight up, I know of no other easier, softer way. Just trust your picture and start.

# Powerful Words...

FUTURE, PREFERRED FUTURE and CHANCE are Powerful Words.

I believe everyone has a PREFERRED FUTURE in mind. How detailed a picture this might be is probably commensurate with how actively and aggressively it is being pursued. If the image of your preferred future is fuzzy and indistinct, I would question your level of commitment in attaining that future for yourself. Even if you did, who wants a fuzzy and nondescript FUTURE.

> If you do not change direction, you may end up where you are heading.
> ~ Lao Tzu

If the image of your preferred future and how you will reach it is crystal clear, you have a much better CHANCE of succeeding. Leaving your future to chance is the thing to do if you are a fatalist. I have never subscribed to that line of thinking. I enjoy asking fatalists if they would drive their car home blind folded (not suggesting that you do here).

When they say "No", I submit that they would only get hurt or end up dead if it was so fated. No one who has heard this has ever elected to test this theory. Most of us plan to lessen uncertainty. If you haven't planned for your future and acted on the basis of those plans, your future is uncertain. Don't leave your future to chance by choice.

# Your world of words within...

Do you have a clear picture of your preferred future? If not, what is holding you back? If so, are you fully engaged in developing that image into reality? Are you leaving too much to chance?

Describe as detailed an image of your preferred future as you can. Where are you living? What are your living arrangements? What is your day like? To where will you travel? What will you do? Will you be working (hope so and with purposeful passion)? Who is living with you? What interests will you pursue? What is your health like in your preferred future? Write this down now while your thoughts are still fresh.

_____

_____

_____

_____

Leave nothing to chance if you can manage it. This description will contain Powerful Words for you to use along your way. Are your plans compatible with your core values? Do they celebrate them as much as possible or dishonor them in any way?

If you decide these things now, you get to decide. If you wait until later to decide, someone else may be deciding these things for you. One thing I can guarantee, if someone else decides for you, you will not prefer the results.

# LIFE WITHOUT SELF-
# IMPOSED LIMITS

**I can't. That's impossible.** These are also are Powerful Words. They hold people back and down of their own volition. They are dream stoppers and hope enders. The mere utterance of these words destroy initiative, stifle creativity and limit growth. They do not even have to be spoken in order to feel their full force. Just thinking these words is enough. How powerful is that?

The words *I can't* or *that's impossible* form finite statements. What would be, could be, should be begins and ends with those words. After those words, there is nothing left to add. They are declarations of cessation, of complete arrest and of conclusion. They are a barricade to further effort. The end.

I guess there is an upside for those who use the words *I can't* frequently. They are always 100% right, just not in the way they might think. For anyone insisting on employing the *I can't* mentality, let's just get it right from the outset and translate this to what it actually means - *I won't*.

That might sound harsh, but it's the truth. The truth only sounds harsh because it's the truth.

There are numerous antithetical statements to the contrary of *I can't*. Of course, *I can* would be the most obvious retort to *I can't*. Though, not everyone will be honestly able to say *I can* in every given situation. They may lack knowledge, the necessary equipment, needed tools or expertise. Why should this hold anyone back, though?

If you don't know how to do something, does it follow that you could never know how to do it? Have those who subscribe to the *I can't* mentality completely stopped learning anything new? Forever?

With an object smaller that a 3 x 5 index card and not a lot thicker you can have the world literally at your finger tips. I'm talking about a data phone. There is nothing that you can not find on the World Wide Web. Life changing knowledge has become comprehensive, limitless, instantaneous and free. There is no more sacred knowledge available only to a privileged few.

Do you ever remember hearing yourself say *I can't*? Was it last week? Yesterday? Perhaps today? Didn't it shut you down cold? The only outcome possible for *I can't* means I am unable.

Saying *I can* means *I am able* to do something. This increases the potential that you **will** do something. Saying *I can* and taking action means no matter what the outcome, you have already won a different future for yourself.

What about the impossible? *"I can imagine that's possible"*, would be the most likely opposing viewpoint. What I want to know is why some feel compelled to cry impossible before fully exploring what can be imagined to be possible?

The brain is an amazing organ. What it is unable to do, it can imagine doing. What is imagined creates possibilities. Possibilities have a habit of turning into reality with time and effort. Which makes me wonder, exactly what cannot be accomplished? I mean really?

Looking back, wouldn't you agree much of what once seemed impossible is now not only possible, but a reality? It's because someone dared to rethink the impossible.

If you have a goal in mind, is it the best one for you or have you compromised? Have you thought of other better goals but rejected them because you felt they were too difficult or impossible? Why? Why do we limit ourselves so?

Those who have plans for brightening their own futures while brightening the futures of those around them harbor no thoughts of the impossible. Thoughts of the impossible are supplanted by "I have an idea", "Just imagine..." and "What if..."

Every successful person, by whatever metric you wish to gauge success, has faced doubt, hardship, failure, ridicule, and fear. ALL OF THEM! I submit none of them ever brought into their declarations for success the words - *I can't* or *That's impossible.*

*I can, I believe, I can imagine, and that's possible* are all open ended potential realities without limits. They are infinite in scope. They begin as words in someone's mind, mere thoughts, thoughts which will later be translated into action because new horizons are being envisioned, sweeping vistas sight unseen. They will not be held back.

Lately, I have come to prefer life without self-imposed limitations. Don't you? I have come to despise the orderly and unyielding flow of variations in sameness the words *I can't* and *that's impossible* seem to impose.

The older I get, the more I see, hear, read and imagine; more and more I have come to ask myself, what exactly is impossible?

# Powerful Words...

CAN'T, IMPOSSIBLE, INITIATIVE, CREATIVITY, POTENTIAL, IMAGINE and LIMITATIONS are Powerful Words.

It would be hard to fathom how much human POTENTIAL and CREATIVITY have been squelched by the words CAN'T and

IMPOSSIBLE. I used to use the word impossible quite a bit. Until one day when someone said something to me and my eyes were opened. Their words were powerful. I looked around and the possibilities began to seem endless. Today, I am convinced they are endless.

> *If you can imagine it, you can achieve it. If you can dream it, you can become it.* ~ *William Arthur Ward*

Mr. Ward isn't wrong. I can cite too many examples to support his conclusions. In fact, I already have throughout this book. Someone who dares to dream and takes the INITIATIVE to act on their dreams are possibility thinkers. You know who they are. You buy their goods and services every day.

IMAGINE a life without self-imposed LIMITATIONS. Imagine if everyone thought this way. I get goose bumps just thinking about it.

## Your world of words within...

Do you live your life without self-imposed limitations? Is there any other kind? Okay, so we limit ourselves. Or, we listen to Powerful Words from others. We transfer power to those words and allow them to limit us. So, what is the difference? It was our choice either way.

Imagine listening to the Powerful Words of inspirational and motivational speakers for 30 minutes everyday through audio books, podcasts, webinars, or You Tube videos. Imagine reading self-help materials or how-to books for 30 minutes everyday. Do you think your horizons to what is possible, might begin to expand?

What do you feel are your main limitations, some things you feel are holding you back? List three of them here.

1. _____

2. _____

3. _____

For each of those three limitations above, list three things you can begin to do, right now, which will help you to begin to remove these self-imposed limitations.

1. _____

_____

_____

2. _____

_____

_____

3. _____

_____

_____

If you are already doing this you already know what I am talking about because you probably do this or something similar everyday. You already have some sense of what works for you and what won't. Your words can become someone else's Powerful Words. All you need do is share them. If you aren't doing so already.

Do you feel you are a creative person? If you have ever imagined anything, a product or service which doesn't exist, or a product or service which can be offered in a better way, then you are a creative.

Think about your creativity. What is the basis for your creativity? Do you have a story to tell? Do you have Powerful Words to share? Write them down while they are fresh in your mind.

_____

_____

_____

_____

# LITTLE TIME REMAINING...

F ear is a Powerful Word, if we chose. Think about just how much constructive action is stopped before it ever gets started due to fear. We all have fears. Some more than others, some less. Different people will have different fears and some fears we share in common.

Consider public speaking. It has been said people actually fear public speaking more so than dying. But, death is still high on the list and for good reason.

We all know that we will shuffle off this mortal coil (die) sooner or later. But, most of us assume it will be later. If you are reading this I will be willing to wager that you do not expect a visit from the grim reaper today.

Yet, I would also be willing to wager all of those people who died sitting in their offices on 9/11 had dinner plans later that evening. We might all concede life is fragile, tenuous at best and some day we are all going to die, just not today. Right?

Last year I had a patient come into my office complaining of a cough with blood streaked sputum, *hemoptysis* in medical jargon. This is not necessarily a cause for alarm. Patients with an acute bacterial or viral bronchitis (inflammation of the airways due to infection) can often have blood streaked sputum until properly treated or until it simply resolves on its own.

What made her presentation somewhat unsettling for her and for me was her smoking habit, one pack per day for 30+ years and she had lost some weight. A chest x-ray revealed the worst possible scenario, advanced lung cancer. She was not yet 50 years old.

I looked back in her chart. Due to other chronic medical problems I had been seeing this patient every four months for the past seventeen years. At every single encounter I had counseled her on smoking cessation. This was recorded under every Assessment and Plan section of every office note, every four months for seventeen years.

She had plenty of warning. All the warning signs were there. Without exception, they are printed on each pack of cigarettes. Her family had warned her, begged and pleaded for her to stop. I had warned her in the strongest terms, repeatedly. At almost every turn these days there are ads giving smokers food for thought and reasons for quitting. But, she never would consider quitting. It is a powerful addiction.

Then, there we were sitting across from one another in my office. I had called her in to see me as soon as I received the x-ray report. Of course, the news was devastating to her. I could see it all over her face, the shattered look, the fear, her quivering chin below a flood of tears. Her sister, who had come in with her, sat gaunt and pale in grim silence.

In that one clear moment the patient knew there was little time remaining. Unfortunately, she was trapped between feeling sorry for her past and sorry for a bleak and foreshortened future. She resolved to stop smoking that day. This was bargaining, one of the five stages of dying. She had waited until it was too late.

Why do people have such a difficult time entertaining any thought of quitting such a dangerous and self destructive behavior? Part of it is addicted brain thinking. The other part, perhaps the greater part, is no one thinks it is going to happen to them. It is in the same way you think you will not, cannot, die today. It is called denial.

Many people have no warning of their eminent demise. Over the years I have lost patients suddenly to automobile crashes, burst aneurysms, heart attacks, and strokes. I am stone cold certain that none of them expected to meet their maker that day, the day they died.

Now, if all of this seems a bit depressing I do not mean for it to be. I want this to be freeing, enlightening and empowering. I tell you all of this not to despair. It is because I have something I want you to realize - because we simply do not know how much time we have remaining, just consider this - there may be little time remaining and how liberating this realization can be for you right now. This is a call for action!

I want you to embrace the **urgency of now.** Now is a powerful word.

We put off so many things in life, too many things. We have an opportunity to change, to be different, to grow, to be challenged, to learn, to build, to produce, to love, to help others in profound ways. We must strive to set aside our fears. Fear is what holds us in place until our end comes, if we allow it.

I say no more fear. Stop putting off and setting aside what you know you need to do, what you must do. Try to do something today that will move you from where you are to where you want to be. Do that everyday. Make that a promise to yourself.

It is time to fling caution to the wind and set sail. Let's hear it for change while we still live because life is short and there may be little time remaining.

# Powerful Words...

ADDICTION, DENIAL and NOW are Powerful Words.

NOW is a most Powerful Word. The way the word is used most often concerns the apparent scarcity of time. There is urgency in the word now. Is time scarce? Is there more for some and little for others?

Everyone gets 168 hours each week. No more and no less. Time on planet earth is no more or less abundant that it has ever been. Who manages our time, but ourselves? Before you say someone else manages my time I would ask, who ceded power to them to do so?

We all strive for more margin in our life. On the rare occasion we get some, we fill it up with things to do and the go out in pursuit of even more margin. Try to learn and remember these three things about time and the urgency of now.

> ➤ We make time for those things we feel are important.
> ➤ We manage our own schedules by the choices we make.
> ➤ When you say yes to one thing you are saying no to something else.

The best use of the time we have been given is to do our best to identify our purpose in life and to pursue it with passion using the unique set of natural talents and abilities we have all been given. I can think of nothing better. Can you?

If you haven't begun this journey of self-discovery yet, start NOW! If you have already begun an endeavor to discover the purpose for which you find yourself among us, keep going. Use the Powerful Words of others to help you on your quest.

They were once where you are now.

Once you find your purpose and are pursuing it with passion, it will then fall to you to help others on their journey using the Powerful Words you've discovered while on yours.

I am no stranger to ADDICTION, or it to me. I could write another entire book on my descent into alcoholism and subsequent recovery. I may yet do so. I used to smoke and I have recovered from that addiction as well. I have worked with all kinds of addicts throughout my career in medicine and through my volunteer efforts with the North Carolina Physicians Health Program (http://www.ncphp. org/).

I understand addictions better than 99% of people who have never been addicted to a substance or an addictive behavior and 100% as well as anyone who has been addicted or is currently addicted. How would the latter group know anyway? Most of them are in DENIAL which is one of the hallmarks of addiction.

Make no mistake, if your preferred future includes drugs/alcohol addiction you will never have it. If you have and are actively addicted you will never keep it. All addictions end. Either the addicted get sober or they die of their disease. Of course, every addict lives in a place where they are going to be different. As I have already mentioned, the place is called DENIAL.

If you have an active addiction, get help. Addicts rarely make it to meaningful and long lasting sobriety on their own. They need to hear the Powerful Words of others to break through their denial and give them an opportunity to choose to be different.

# Your world of words within...

Have you accomplished all that you want to accomplish? Are you putting things off because you feel you have the luxury of time? What are you waiting for, really? Why not NOW?

What are your fears? Can you write down some stories about the fears you have had to face or are facing? Have you faced them or are you keeping them close on the inside? Have you given them a voice by clearly stating what they are?

List your three biggest fears here.

1. _____

2. _____

3. _____

To list them begins to rob them of their power. They do not have to cause the kind of fear which holds you back. You can use the emotion behind the fears holding you back, to propel you forward, if you choose. It begins by telling stories about your own fears and how you hope to overcome them. All the while you will be sharing Powerful Words, which someone else has had to deal with before. They will help you to deal with yours.

Take a critical look at them. Are they reasonable fears? What part of them is controllable and what is out of your control? Do you need help with overcoming them?

When you have dealt with your fears either by eliminating them or controlling them for your own better purposes, then you will begin to share with others how you were able to do so. These new stories about your fears will help others to deal with theirs. That is what Powerful Words do.

Are you actively addicted? In denial? What are your stories concerning addiction?

_____
_____
_____
_____

Are you in recovery? Do you know your sobriety date? You know the drill then. What was it like? What happened? What is it like now? Those stories contain Powerful Words that can help those that are still suffering. Pass them on...

Notes:

_____

_____
_____
_____
_____
_____
_____

# No Regrets

## No regrets, really?...

I believe everyone has regrets, whether they will admit to them or not. If someone says they have absolutely no regrets then I believe they are either in denial or they just haven't lived long enough yet.

*"We will not regret the past nor wish to shut the door on it."*

Many will recognize this as #2 of the 12 Promises of Alcoholics Anonymous. I must admit, I have some trouble with this one. I get the *"nor wish to shut the door on it"* part. I leave the door to my past propped open so that I can remain in touch with the pain of my addiction.

To forget what it was like would be to close the door on recovery, signaling a beginning of relapse behavior. It is the *"we will not regret the past"* part that I have had some difficulty with. I mean, again, who doesn't have regrets?

I have many regrets from my days as an active alcoholic. How could I not? I am presently thinking with a non-addicted brain that has a conscious. So, when I look back at past behaviors I can't help but wish I had done some things differently.

I was thinking about one of my deepest regrets just the other day. It has to do with my father. Before I tell you what, let me tell you about him.

When I was still in the crib my dad made a toy for me out of a piece of board covered in green Formica with a green tile pattern. It was about 15 x 20 inches in size. On that board he affixed various objects. There were sliding and hooking latches, an old light switch, a bell you could ring, metal numbers I could spin around, bolts with nuts that I could turn but couldn't quite remove and various other metal mechanical contraptions.

Today, it most certainly wouldn't pass anyone's safety inspection or make anyone's list of child approved toys. It had sharp parts, tidbits you could swallow and pieces with which you could impale or otherwise puncture yourself. Well, none of that happened to me.

I loved that toy. Mom said I would play with that thing endlessly until I would fall asleep with my head resting against its contrivance encrusted surface. Small wonder I took apart and put back together nearly everything in the house growing up.

I believe that toy gave me an unquenchable curiosity to know how things work, even animals and people. I was dissecting frogs and fish by the time I was six, grew up trying to care for sick animals both found and purchased and ended up with a career in medicine.

Although some of its original parts are missing, I still have that toy my dad made for me to this day. I wouldn't part with it for a million dollars.

When I was older but still small, dad would come home after work and mom would have dinner waiting. We would all eat together and then my favorite part of the day would begin.

He and I would retreat to the living room where he would bounce me on his knee while reciting, "Rid'em little horsey go to town, rid'em little horsey don't fall down!" When he got to the words "don't fall down" he would suddenly extend his leg and drop his knee and I would nearly tumble to the floor before he would catch me.

I would laugh until I couldn't breathe, and so would he. No matter how many times he repeated this completely predictable sequence of events it would always crack me up. The excitement and anticipation would build and break the same way, each and every time. I don't know where he found the energy to do this over and over again, night

Every now and again the subject of favorite colors comes up as a topic of discussion. I can name my favorite color immediately and without hesitation. It's purple. Not only that, I can tell you precisely why it is my favorite color.

Now, most of you reading this can probably readily name your favorite color. But could you tell me why it is your favorite color? I mean precisely and not give just a "because it is" response.

Although I always knew my favorite color was purple, I didn't always know why. A long time ago while handling some purple ribbon it hit me like a ton of bricks. When I was a little boy, before I learned to read, I would sit in my father's lap and he would read to me. The bookmark that he used was a long, wide, deep purple ribbon.

I don't know what ever happened to that ribbon. I would pay a king's ransom to have it back.

My dad taught me the most growing up about growing up. He taught me manners, to respect women, to respect the law, right from wrong, about God and country, that a man's word is his bond, the value of hard work, the value of money, the utility of saving, the need for friends, how to work wood, how to paint, how to say I'm sorry, how to stand on principle, to be honest, how to shake someone's hand, how to fight for what's right, how to care for people, how to lead, when to follow, common sense, how to spit (don't under estimate the importance of that one), self-reliance and resourcefulness.

There was much, much more of course, too much to list here. Although I have not always emulated my father's lessons for life in every way and at all times to the best of my ability, it wasn't because I wasn't properly instructed or because he somehow failed as a teacher. He was the best because he taught me by example.

My last few years of heavy drinking were spent in near isolation. As I sank deeper into the abyss of alcoholism I would run home to see my folks less and less as time flittered away, precious time I can now never retrieve. When I did go home I never stayed very long.

I never drank in front of my parents so that necessarily meant a short stay. During those years my dad and I drifted apart. I let alcohol get between him and me. That beautiful, strong, gentle man with the twinkle in his eye who taught me so much has left this world.

The times that I could have spent with him but rather instead spent drinking, I will never have back. That is one of my deepest regrets.

How could I possibly not regret wasting the time I spent drinking instead of spending time with my father while he was alive? Since I will never be able to forget my regretful moments, how do I square that with the admonishment from AA Promise #2, "We will not regret the past?"

The only answer I can come up with is, in the context of time and perspective we can and should forgive ourselves our regrets and celebrate them to the extent that they have helped to shape who we are today. If I close my eyes and rest my mind I can still hear my dad say in his own strong voice something I heard him say to me so many times growing up and as an adult.

Never was I happier to hear it the day I told him I was at the Pinehurst Treatment center for treatment of my alcoholism. He said it then, "I'm proud of you son." How could I ever regret hearing that?

# Powerful Word...

REGRET is a Powerful Word.

The word REGRET can forever constrain you or liberate you depending on what kind of power you give it, negative or positive. It is okay to have regrets. What you do with them is another matter. Through context and perspective we can square what we truly regret with what we gained or learned from the circumstances which caused us to regret.

Whether this word has a positive or negative influence in your life is a matter of perspective. What influence it will have on the remainder of your life is a matter of choice.

There is always something to be learned from our mistakes, especially the big ones. If, only if, we let the Great Teacher LIFE teach us and we become willing students.

# World of words from within...

Have you regrets over some of the events in your life? What were they? Write them down here.

_____

_____

_____

_____

What did you learn form those events? What lessons did you, can you, take away? How have those events help to shape you? Can you forgive yourself for past actions which have caused you to have regrets?

Are there amends or apologies you could make which would help you move past any regrets you may have? CAUTION: I would do this only if it wouldn't cause any further harm to you or others.

Recounting those stories will reconnect you with emotions from those events. Some of them may be painful to recall but remember why you are doing this in the first place - to help others through the power of your story and in the process you will help yourself. Let loose your Powerful Words.

What Powerful Words came to you in this section?

---------------------------------------------------------------

---------------------------------------------------------------

---------------------------------------------------------------

---------------------------------------------------------------

---------------------------------------------------------------

# Hope Is Not a Plan

I've been there. Hoping for a future which never happened. Oh, I had plans, great plans, plans a plenty. I would think about those plans and build on those plans with more plans. I would think how great it would be when all my plans were realized and I hoped they would all come true.

I hoped and hoped and hoped. But, nothing ever happened the way I planed. At least not while I was busy hoping.

Hope springs eternal in the human breast...(Alexander Pope, *An Essay on Man*)

Hope is generally seen as a strictly positive attribute. Is it? We all do it. Is that all we should be doing? Can hope or hoping for something be bad? As with all things, it depends on your frame of reference.

We all hope. When we were small we hoped for this gift for our birthday or for that certain present for Christmas. We hoped for ice cream. We hoped to play outside longer. We have all hoped for a good grade on a test for which we perhaps did or did not study properly.

We hoped to get a date with our crush and maybe hold hands or steal our first kiss to boot. We hoped to get into a certain college, buy a particular car, marry the perfect mate. We hoped to have normal kids placed in the best of schools who made the best grades.

How many of our most ardent or trivial of hopes have been dashed along the way. Would that be life's fault? Someone else's? Ours? Yet, round and round we spin on a carousel of hope.

When Alexander Pope wrote the "hope springs eternal" statement in a poem, he was making an observation and a value judgment concerning hope and he was not being kind to hope. Here is the full quote:

> *Hope springs eternal in the human breast;*
> *Man never is, but always to be blessed:*
> *The soul, uneasy and confined from home,*
> *Rests and expatiates in a life to come.*

He was being satirically critical of people who spend time hoping for a great life in the hereafter rather than opting for a good one in the here and now. Whether it's to be sometime later in the future or sometime later in the hereafter doesn't make much difference. Neither one are accessible **now**. We hope for some later happening.

If you look up quotable quotes about hope you might expect them all to be rather positive. That is not the case. Many feel that hope can be a bad thing and offer reasons as to why. Consider the following quotes:

*Hope is the denial of reality.*
~ Margaret Weis

*Never deprive someone of hope; it might be all they have.*
~ H. Jackson Brown, Jr.

*He that lives upon hope will die fasting.*
~ Benjamin Franklin

*Hope in reality is the worst of all evils because it prolongs the torments of man.*
~ Friedrich Nietzsche

See what I mean? To understand why the authors considered hope as they did, you would have to understand their frame of reference, but no matter. What do all of these quotes have in common?

While they all convey negative sentiments concerning hope, I believe their overall merit is motivational and therefore positive. Their underlying intent is to get one motivated to look at an alternative to hope, namely taking action. Taking action eliminates the need for hope.

There are reasons that hope may be preferred to taking action. Hoping requires less energy than to work toward a goal or working a particular problem for a solution. Hoping is 100% achievable. Anyone can do it and at any time. Taking action risks failure.

To hope is to procrastinate, which is easy to do. Almost every hope is for something to happen at a later time. Taking action *a priori* means starting now, or should. Hoping is spontaneous given current circumstances. Taking action may require preparation.

Hoping is instantaneous. Taking action requires time. Hoping is dreaming and sometimes involves magical thinking. Taking action can only be accomplished in reality. People hope against fear. Taking action is a purpose for change.

When I was actively addicted I must have been an eternal optimist. I would get up everyday hopeful that things would be different. They never were. Little wonder, I never made them any different.

Early on in my drinking career, I hoped to find a way to live normally but still be able to drink. Eventually, I went to AA meetings where I would dream of a life lived sober and hope for myself the same sober life that I saw reflected by others in the program.

Rather than taking action or positive steps in that direction, I would go home and drink later that day, sometimes right after the meeting.

I hoped to come into money, find the right relationship, get the right career, surround myself with the right like-minded people, hoping that everyone would discover how wise I was and just listen to me and then all my alcohol induced problems would magically disappear. It was all addicted brain hoping. Nothing changed until I stopped hoping and took action.

When I was burning out as a family physician, I was always hoping something would change and I would love my job again. I would do the same routine at work day in and day out without changing anything. I changed nothing and nothing changed.

I became emotionally exhausted, cynical and came to view my work as meaningless. Until one day, I realized I just didn't have to work under those same circumstances any longer. I chose to be different. I made some changes in both my work schedule and personal life, which made all the difference. I traded hoping for action.

I don't wish to convey the impression that I am devoid of all hope, that it serves no useful purpose. But, I do now try to hope more for what is possible and actionable rather than hope away time and daydream with inaction over the impossible.

Hoping to eliminate all pain and all suffering in all of my patients all of the time may be a worthy ideal, but not a very realistic goal. It can never happen. Hoping to do the very best that I can each day and knowing that I am not perfect is a much better way to hope in my opinion.

If you are five feet tall, you can hope all you want that you will be on an NBA league team, but that is probably never going to happen either. But, you can play intramural basketball or perhaps coach a team. You could start a basketball league for players 5'-6" tall or less. If, and only if, you take the necessary steps to get you there.

We can all hope the dog or the kids won't track dirt onto our nicely cleaned floor. Or, we can hope to hug them kiss them when they do and tell them how much we missed them while they were outside playing and we were inside cleaning. Or, we could hope to be outside playing with them next time, if there is a next time, because they won't always be here, or we won't, but the dirty floor probably will be.

In my practice, I see family members of the addicted neglecting their own mental, physical, emotional and spiritual well-being while pinning all of their hopes and efforts on their addicted family member and whether or not they will get sober. They can and must still hope, but they must also realize their limitations; that there is nothing they can do to make their loved one sober or even desire sobriety for that matter.

The only person they can truly take care of is themselves. We can hope for the best for our loved ones, but taking action on their behalf by expending our time, energy and resources is of no help to them at all, especially if they haven't yet decided to stop hoping for outside help and take real action for themselves.

## Powerful Words...

HOPE, ACTION, PREPARATION, PAIN, SUFFERING and WELL-BEING are Powerful Words.

HOPE is not an ACTION. It is an idea. Between theses two words hope and action, ACTION is the more Powerful Word.

If you want to start a business, grow a business, end a bad relationship, start a new relationship, learn a new skill, get a new job, write that book, start a blog, learn a new language, produce music or create art you can hope if you want. Only action can convert a hope into reality.

It begins with PREPARATION and continues with continuous action. There is no end to the actions taken, only a series of successive approximations (steps) toward your goals. If the goal is a life well-lived, then the goal lines will be continuously reset as you move on into your preferred future. You will have "arrived" or be "done" when you assume room temperature.

We all want to be well and have a sense of WELL-BEING. We want the same for those we love and care about. We can even extend this desire to an entire world full of strangers.

PAIN and SUFFERING cannot always be avoided, not only for those we love and care for, but for our own sake as well. We do our best to control what we can. For well-being, we must accept what we cannot control.

When my wife left me, I cried myself to sleep every night for nearly four months while reciting the following prayer, a prayer I became very familiar with during my recovery from alcoholism. It is by the American theologian Reinhold Niebuhr -

> *God, grant me the serenity to accept the things I cannot change,*
> *The courage to change the things I can,*
> *And the wisdom to know the difference.*

Yes, I still suffered, but I can not tell you how much these Powerful Words helped me to get past my suffering. I know this is true because I am still here, whole, healed and engaged.

I have suffered and you have suffered, we all have suffered. Terribly, I know. Think about this, though. If I am writing this and you are reading this, then we are still here and by God that must count for something. So, make it count.

Your stories of pain and suffering, as difficult as they may be to recount, are the source of Powerful Words. You can tell how powerful they are to you by how much they move you emotionally. One of the pathways to well-being is to get those emotions out. It is the therapeutic basis of many cognitive therapies.

The insult, whether it was a loss or tragedy, mental, verbal or physical abuse, comes from the range of emotions experienced during the event(s). Unless we adequately explore and release those feelings then they are still bottled up on the inside. Make no mistake, they will exert their influence on a daily basis.

Only by getting those emotions out and acknowledging their effect on you will you begin to heal and lessen their power over you and your daily actions. If the emotions are too powerful or raw for you to deal with on your own, them I implore you to get professional help. This would certainly mean getting help for post-traumatic stress events caused by a witnessed tragedy, physical violence or physical abuse of any kind.

For addiction, treatment may be necessary. It certainly was for my alcoholism. Treatment saved my life. After my wife left, I went to counseling and my therapist was instrumental in my recovery from that tragedy. Not only did she help me to salvage my life, she helped me to redirect. In each instance, the help I received made all the difference. I heard the Powerful Words of others and they helped me to heal.

Don't hope for wellness; plan on it and take action. It is a choice. Brains can rewire themselves to think differently. One only needs to start thinking differently.

## Your world of words within...

Do you mostly hope? Or, do you plan and take action? How much preparation have you put into gaining your preferred future?

Can you list up to 5 actionable hopes for which you haven't yet taken any action? Also, for each list at least one action you can take today which will move you from hope toward accomplishment.

1. _____

2. _____

3. _____

4. _____

5. _____

You must begin to explore why you haven't moved off of hope and onto action? There are probably Powerful Words in your past you are using to block your own progress. Rob them of their power by getting them out of the shadows and understanding them.

If you are a planner and a doer and you are seeing results, there are stories and Powerful Words you need to share. Others are waiting to hear them. Helping them will help you in ways which can not be fully known or explained. Make some notes here.

_____

_____

_____

_____

_____

Are you in pain, suffering? Is there something in your past that has a hold on you still? Is it time to set your burden down? Can you talk about it with another human being? If not a friend or a loved one, then a professional? We all most come to terms with an ever evolving and advancing past if we are ever to move fluidly forward toward our preferred futures.

The Powerful Words at the root of human suffering, the emotions those words represent, will help others deal with their own pain and suffering as they are shared.

Emotional connection, this is the power in Powerful Words.

What Powerful Words have come to you in this section?

_____

_____

_____

_____

# ARTIST

////////////////////////////

Are you an artist? Ask most people and they will tell you, no. The ones who do will invariably translate artist to musician, painter or maybe sculptor. I believe everyone is an artist, or can be, because the definition is so much broader than painter or sculptor.

I started out in first grade just as everyone else. I was asked to color between the lines. I would reach for the oversized purple crayon. It was my favorite color. I would do my best to stay within the confines of the drawing that was provided to me as I colored my way along.

Sometimes, though, no matter how hard I tried I would stray outside the borders of the drawing. My teacher didn't like it when I went outside the lines and would tell me so. I would feel bad when she pointed this out.

I am sure there was some purpose for urging us to try to stay within the lines. Probably something to do with developing eye-hand coordination or to better learn to take instructions or to obey authority. All I remember is I felt bad because no matter how hard I tried, I couldn't always stay within the lines.

Looking back, the worst tragedy of the situation was not that we were asked to stay within the lines or the criticism for going outside of them. The worst tragedy was that we were provided template drawings to color in the first place.

It was frustrating. I stopped drawing. When someone asked if I was artistic, I told them I couldn't draw a stick. I held that view for most of my adult life. I was only trying to stay within the lines in life, on whatever templates were presented to me.

I have wondered lately, how much more of an enjoyable experience, how much better a learning experience, would it have been if we were all just handed paper and crayons asked to draw what ever we felt like drawing? Draw what ever made us feel happy all over and on the inside? To explore, to discover, to create.

I wouldn't say the coloring exercise was without any tangible benefits. It just wasn't the best experience for me. Because, the only emotional connection with the exercise itself was criticism for coloring outside the lines with my absolute favorite colored crayon.

I believe the word artist should be redefined for what it does and not by what is produced. Art is created when an emotional connection is established between the art and the artist, the art and the observer, or both.

Art, true art, is creating something of personal significance which moves us emotionally. The medium for this exchange seems secondary.

Each of us have the ability to create using our unique natural talents and abilities. Each of us have the ability to express how we feel through what we create.

When we (you) create something, we connect with it emotionally. Rest assured, someone else out there who will feel that connection too. That is art. As such, we have an obligation to create using our own natural set of talents and abilities.

Your profession doesn't matter. The vehicles or materials you use when creating art don't matter. If you are alive, engaged and can interact and connect with others on an emotional level through what you can create, then you are an artist. For no other reason, people are artists because they choose to be.

My work as a family physician, although based in the sciences, is as much an art as it is a science. I have long acknowledged this, but still did not consider myself an artist, not in any classic sense.

When I was in my 40's, on a whim, I produced a large wall hanging of a stylized weeping willow tree out of hand hammered sheet copper and copper wire. I did it because I had reached a point in my life where I thought I could do more than what I was taught.

It was a big hit. I have had other pieces juried into art shows and all of them have sold. I have been commissioned to produce pieces for private collections and get more requests for sculptures than I have ever had time to produce. I have since discovered other ways to create art by writing, coaching, and speaking on topics about which I am passionate.

When creating art, the only "lines" are in the confines of the mind. There are no real lines you must adhere to when creating your art. So, create something using what you have, know and feel and pour yourself into it.

Don't worry that not everyone will like you art. Not everyone gets or liked Picasso. Many influential people thought Ernest Hemmingway's writing was garbage. You don't want or need everyone to like your art. You want those you connect with on an emotional level to like your art. You know what? They will.

People will take notice and recognize you for what you have shared of yourself because of the emotional connection they will feel when they see it. It will help them in some way and they will thank you for it. They will call you, an artist.

The baker in my town where I buy the most delightful fresh baked breads, is an artist. One look and taste of her products leaves no doubt.

The plumber who installed the plumbing and well at my home, the finish carpenters, carpet layers, electricians, painters, and rock mason were all artists.

The people who author the books I read, the blogs I support and the groups to which I belong are artists.

The school teachers, conscientious professors and instructors at our area schools, universities and community college are all artists.

The small business owners and entrepreneurs I know who innovate and bring new products and services to market are all artists.

You can be an artist holding a regular job during regular hours in the way you perform required tasks and dispatch your responsibilities. If you are serving others with passion and purpose in any capacity using your own unique set of natural talents and abilities, then you are an artist.

# Are You An Artist?...

If you speak in front of audiences, write, produce a product, coach, work in sales, create software then you are an artist, just as much as if you drew, painted, sculpted or did photography for a living. Creating great art requires only one thing.

I am a writer and I make wood and metal sculptures. I guess that makes me an artist. Am I a great artist? Do I produce great art? I don't know. Some days I think my art is good, really good. Some days not so much.

I was just thinking recently about what makes art or an artist great. I came up with more questions than answers. These musings may seem a little weird but herein is a message I want to try and convey.

If I produce a piece of art and I happen to think is great. Is it? Is it enough for me to consider it great art in order for it to be great art? Must someone else, besides me, also think it great?

What if two people look at my art or read something I wrote and one thinks it great and the other thinks it awful. Which is it then, great or awful? Many people consider Ernest Hemmingway to be one of the greatest writers who ever lived. Other people thought his writing was garbage. So, which is it then? It is interesting, he ended his own life thinking he had never written his best work.

If a congregation of individuals considered my art is garbage and a preponderance of the people in the congregation think my art is great, does that make it so, even if but just a few think it is garbage? Are their opinions made null and void by the majority? What if the majority is wrong? How would we know? Who is to say?

If my art is hated by a group of people and all that unites them is their unrelenting and complete hatred of my art, did my art then serve no useful purpose? Does art have to be great in order to serve its purpose?

What makes great art great? I think we can agree that great art makes the artist great. But, here is the most fundamental question of all. Which comes first? Does the artist become great first and then go on to produce great art? Or, does the artist produce what is regarded by the masses to be great art which makes him great in return?

I believe I know. It may seem like a circular argument but I believe great art is made great by, and because of, the artist. If, it is the artists expression of their truest self.

We know some works of art are great because they move us, up or down, and cause us to pause and be changed by it. We connect with it because some other lonely, happy, sad, frustrated, anxious, imperfect, glorious, offensive, flawed, hopeful human being has splattered their heart and soul onto a canvas, a piece of metal, or between the pages of a book.

We laugh or cry with them and celebrate their art with them because we are compelled to do so by what they have created. The great artists would create great art even if it were placed in the woods and no one were around to see it because they must.

I would submit if an artist placed a masterful work of art in the woods and no one were around to see it, it would still be great because the artist made it great. The artist knows they did their best, what they had to do, and that is enough for the artist. Whether they realize it or not, the great artists discovered the key to creating great art requires only one thing - passion for one's purpose for being!

Great art is an artist's passion on display. It is the same, or will be, for you dear reader. Passion for what you do will drive you to produce your best work, like all great artists.

# Powerful Words...

AUTHORITY, ART, CONNECT and ARTIST are Powerful Words.

If you say you are an ARTIST and are producing ART then you are an artist. If you say you aren't an artist and you aren't producing art then you are not an artist. Either way, you will be right 100% of the time. It is a choice.

So many people who do not consider themselves artists actually are artists. They produce art everyday and do not realize it. The term artist is no longer reserved those who draw, paint, sculpt or make music.

If you create then you are an artist. If you can do something extremely well with your own particular style and unique influence then you are an artist. If you can fill a need or a niche like no one else then you are an artist. Saying you are an artist and then believing it will allow you to wield the power this word can convey.

If you can CONNECT with another person through your art then you can speak with AUTHORITY when you say you are an artist. It is every artist's dream to connect with others on an emotional level through the art they produce.

# Your world of words within...

Do you feel you are an artist? Circle one:   **YES**   or   **NO**

If not, is it something you should consider? Or, are you reluctant to call yourself an artist? Why? Is there something standing in your way, keeping you from doing so? Are you really not an artist or is this just something you have been telling yourself for no identifiable reason? Have you explored what you are capable of doing in the expanded realm of art?

If you can not see yourself as an artist, is it because of an impression someone else gave you of yourself at some point in your past. Are there Powerful Words which are holding you back? If so, you can take away their power by taking action in the opposite direction of their push.

If you feel you are an artist, do you call yourself an artist? Don't you think it is time you do? Try to put into words, the feeling you get when you are creating art. Some of those words will be Powerful Words and a recurring theme when discussing your work. Use them to your advantage. If they resonate with you they will resonate with others.

If you feel you are an artist, in what art forms can you, do you, express yourself?

_____

_____

_____

_____

_____

_____

Have you pushed your own boundaries of artistic expression? List three things you want to try or things you think you should try.

1. _____

2. _____

3. _____

Be fearless and list three art forms you are afraid to try or think you can not do?

1. _____

2. _____

3. _____

Now, pick one of these and promise yourself you will try. I mean make a real commitment. I believe the results will surprise you.

I will try _____

# Unfulfilled Dreams

What about dreams, you say? Dream is a Powerful Word. Yes? No? What about unfulfilled dreams? There are Powerful Words behind those as well, the reasons they stay unfulfilled.

One evening not long ago a friend sent me a link to an article about unfulfilled dreams. It was a great article. I will provide the link at the end of this section. It got me to thinking about my own yet unfulfilled hopes and dreams and the ones I let go of a long time ago.

While I enjoyed the article very much, there was one main point with which I disagreed. I may be just quibbling over semantics, but I will let you decide. More on that in a moment.

For arguments sake let's just equate hopes with dreams and dreams with hopes, or wishes for that matter. I imagine if you are not dreaming of having something, anything, then you at least probably have hope of something that you would like to see happen.

If not, that means you are devoid of hope and are therefore "hopeless. "If that is the case then seek help, you are probably depressed and are in need of some. A sense of hopelessness and helplessness is a cardinal sign of clinical depression.

If you are human, and most people are (smiley face here), you are allowed to dream whatever you might. It is your right as a human being. Dreaming is in our DNA. Dreams probably fall into two broad categories, those that are attainable and those that are not. Let's look at some unobtainable ones first.

If you wished to float above the ground and travel by flight wherever or whenever you want then that might not be an obtainable dream. Wait a minute; didn't someone invent a flying machine for that purpose? Wasn't it someone's dream of flight which produced the airplane, helicopter, rocket, parasail, glider, hang-glider, jetpack, hot air balloon, gyro-copter, etc.?

Okay, maybe that wasn't a good example of an unobtainable dream. Let's say you were 5'-3" or 5'-7" tall and you dreamed of playing basketball in the NBA or you were 5'-1" and 100 pounds and your dream was to play football for Notre Dame. Surely those would be unobtainable dreams. Well, not for Muggsy Bogues, Spud Webb or Rudy Ruettiger, the people who tirelessly worked to make those dreams their reality.

I am sure I can think of one dream that would be impossible to fulfill. How about being totally blind, but have a dream to climb Mt. Everest. Darn, wouldn't you know it? Erik Weihenmayer did that on May 25, 2001. Oh yeah, he did the Seven Summits in September 2002 just for good measure. Those were his dreams. Everybody told him he couldn't do it. Turns out he didn't need sight, just a vision.

Okay, how about these dreams:

- to produce a device that you can hold with one hand which can hold the entire library of congress (like the one I am typing on right now),
- to produce an artificial heart,
- to clone a sheep,
- to map the entire human genome,
- to split the atom,
- to transplant organs and have the patients live,
- to produce a set of glasses that you wear that connect you to the world,
- to "print" a wrench, a gear box, a car body, a chassis or a gun and have them work,

- to "print" human tissue with a machine that you can transplant into a human and have the human live,
- to privately fund and build a rocket ship that will take a person into space and to a safe return,
- to privately fund and build a rocket ship that will take passengers into space and to a safe return,
- to build an artificial lens with a built in computer display that's solar powered,
- to build an artificial ear, to build an artificial eye, or to move prosthetic limbs with mere thoughts.

At one time, these were all just someone's dreams. Each and every one of them have been fulfilled.

Some dream of curing cancer. My question would be, which one? Of the 130+ cancers known to humans, we have cures for over half of them right now.

What about dreaming to run a marathon, in your 80's. But, not actually starting to run until you are 70 when you retire from farming. In fact, how about running four full marathons, numerous half marathons and too many to count 5 and 10K races in your eighties and run one of those marathons in 4 hours twenty minutes. Then, run 10K's every year until your late 90's. Too much to hope for? Out-sized dreams maybe? Tell that to the family of Peng Perngsa who was Thailand's oldest runner until his death at age 99. He ran last race in 2012. He left behind his young wife, age 89.

The author of the article that I mentioned asked, "must our dreams be realized, or is the call [just] to dream them in the first place." I take the inference to be that it is a noble cause just to dream and that for most, that is or will be enough.

He supported this view by citing many great dreamers such as MLK, Gandhi, and David of the Old Testament who never saw their dreams fulfilled while they were alive, yet they were the impetus for great change after their deaths. Therefore, to have the dream is enough even if you do not live to see it fulfilled.

I do not agree with his assessment, that having a call to dream is, to its own end, enough. To sit and dream without action is not an end to itself, it isn't even a beginning. For MLK, Gandhi and David, it wasn't just their dreams that catapulted them to greatness, it was their individual struggles while attempting to fulfill their dreams.

Dreaming is only part. I submit that it is the journey that defines the depth and breadth of the dream, the boundaries of which are limited only by the dreamer.

Aren't our hopes and dreams the most ever present and persistent kinds of faith that we express? There are some often quoted references on this very point in the Bible. Now *faith is the substance of things hoped for, the evidence of things not seen.* Doesn't that sound a lot like our dreams?

To dream is to express faith. Additionally, *Faith without works is dead.* It is not enough just to dream. Dreams must be combined with powerful action for them to have any meaning or carry weight.

As I said, dreaming is in our DNA. Honestly, I don't know what I would do if I had to stop dreaming, or if my dreams were taken from me, except to hope and dream for my dreams to return.

I know that most people will give up on their dreams. Most people will give up on their dreams because they, well, give up on their dreams. I don't see it as being any more complicated than that. I think the reason is that dreaming is a lot easier to do than the work required while attempting to fulfill them.

I feel that an individual's dreams, either consciously or unconsciously, will fit within their abilities to accomplish what is possible for them, whether they accomplish them or not. But, a dream is just an endpoint. It is a sign post for a direction only.

All the really interesting work, product, art, writing, science, talent, psychology, philosophy and song will occur along the journey toward that end, toward the dream. I would not discount the journey if the end is never reached.

If someone should happen to die while earnestly pursuing their dreams, I submit that their dreams **were** being fulfilled. The terminal end of a journey is just another signpost, the last signpost, not the journey itself.

It is almost universally accepted that a loving God or Higher Power would want or expect us to be happy using the talents that we have at our disposal. To be the best we can be, to be all we can be. All who believe in God or a Higher Power will pray for guidance for His will and then hope that they receive it in a way that is understandable.

There is that word hope again. You want to know His will? Dream. Then, strike out and do your best to fulfill them.

Here is the link to the article A Candid Conversation About Unfulfilled Dreams, by Donald Miller: http://storylineblog.com/2014/02/11/unfulfilled-dreams/

# Powerful Words...

DREAM, DREAMING and FAITH are Powerful Words.

Have FAITH in your abilities. Everyone is given a unique set of natural talents and abilities. If you have discovered them, you know the immense satisfaction and meaning they bring to your life. You are living your DREAM.

There are Powerful Words associated with your story, your truth, your DREAMS. Set them free in you interactions with others as you pursue your purpose with passion. Let them guide others on their journey to realizing their dreams.

UNFULFILLED DREAMS are a tragedy and a waste of the power of DREAMING. I can't think of a worse scenario than to be at the end of one's life without ever attempting to fulfill one's dreams. Will we achieve all of our dreams? Of course not. But I am not so wise that I can predict which of those I will achieve and which I will not. I would rather dream, try and fail than to have never dreamed at all, or dream and never try. Given a choice, would you choose differently?

# Your world of words within...

What are your dreams? Can you list your top three to five lifelong dreams here?

1. _____

2. _____

3. _____

4. _____

5. _____

Do you have unfulfilled dreams? If yes, why? If you have not pursued your dreams or if you have given up on them there are probably some powerful reasons why. Powerful Words are at the roots of those reasons. They are either words you are hearing from within yourself (self-doubt) or from others in your past or present.

Do you know what they are? Can you list them here?

_____

_____

_____

_____

If you are still interested in pursuing your dreams, those words need to be identified, filtered and set aside. If there are people in your life continuously telling you what you can't do, they are not acting in your best interest. I would surround myself with people who talk more about what is possible.

If there are events in your past when something was said which may be holding you back then those are Powerful Words to you. You can change their meaning by bending their power to propel you forward instead of holding you at a standstill.

This is best accomplished by telling your story, of how you have allowed those words to affect you. You will find there are others who have faced similar struggles, same as you. The will offer solutions, real solutions you can use. By overcoming them you will have a more powerful story to tell. One of your own making using your own more Powerful Words.

# Living Beyond Just Dreams

I f you want to live beyond just dreams, in your preferred future, there must come a time when the dreaming ends and the action begins.

## Passion...

Passion is a Powerful Word. Once you have identified your purpose, you will need passion to be and do your best for your purpose in life.

You have seen and probably admired people with true passion. Perhaps you stood by in envy or awe and wondered about the source of their passion. Perhaps you are one of the passionate people and already know. For most of my life, I was not one of those people.

I spent most of my life thinking it was fate or luck or some rare combination of environment and genetics that lead to the singularity of purposeful action we call passion. I couldn't have been more wrong.

I now know where passionate people get their passion. I now know the source, the resonate frequency they tune to as they joyfully hum their way through their work. Or, is it play to them?

When people are truly passionate about what they do, it is difficult to distinguish between their work and play. Only recently have I found the least difference between the two. I am becoming one of the passionate people.

A little while ago I was standing in my kitchen just as the sun struck the window and pierced a small prism sitting on top of the sill. There, cast onto the counter was the familiar refraction pattern of light, a rainbow.

Prisms have always fascinated me. Take white light and run it through a prism and what emerges are the colors of the rainbow. It is astonishing to me. Just like the rainbows in the sky after a rain, the light refracted by billions of water droplets in the atmosphere.

You probably remember the mnemonic from childhood, ROYGBIV, which stands for the different constituent wavelengths of light and the order they appear - **R**ed, **O**range, **Y**ellow, **G**reen, **B**lue, **I**ndigo and **V**iolet.

It still seems like magic to me. That is why I have a prism on my window sill. Looking at the rainbow of light splayed across the counter top, I had an immediate thought.

I grabbed my camera and moved in front of the prismatic array of light and very carefully photographed each of the elemental colors. I used the photographs in a blog post entitled *How Passion Is Like A Prism*. If you would like to see them, here is the URL to the post: http://www.clarkgaither.com/how-passion-is-like-a-prism/

All of the constituent colors are already present in the white light. It only took the prism to tease them out and put them on display.

This was my thought. I believe it is generally known the secret to successful and purposeful living is finding your true purpose and pursue it with passion. What I believe is not generally acknowledged is all of the components are already there, inside each of us, waiting to be unlocked and displayed. Passion is our prism.

Passion takes the light that shines within each of us and brings forth the best from us - our unique set of natural talents and abilities and puts them on display for the world to see. When it happens, it is astonishing. It seems like magic.

Many will stand by and wonder, where did all of their success, zest for living, innovation, creativity, smarts, and energy come from? Just as I used to wonder. Now I know it was inside them all along. It only took the prism of passion to reveal it.

# Your Purpose for Living...

You can feel the energy in a room full of passionate and energized people at a conference. You can feel it in the lecture hall and in the hallway outside the door. It will propagate from one person to the next, from one room to the next. It is conductive.

You can feel the energy on the inside of the individuals in attendance. You can hear it in the voice of the speakers. You can see it on the faces of the attendees.

The speakers sense the real need in the audience. They adjust their talk accordingly and begin to deliver their message with earnest enthusiasm. The audience soaks up the speaker's message eagerly, happily and with gusto because their needs are being met. They all become connected on an emotional level.

The feeling of this positive energy is, in a word, delightful. Have you ever experienced this? Have you heard Powerful Words at a conference which changed you, your life?

This describes very well my feelings at the Podcast Movement 2014 Conference I attended in Dallas, Texas. There was a long roster of dynamic and successful speakers from within the podcast industry. The audience numbered somewhere between five and six hundred spirited participants.

Everyone in attendance at the conference had a singular mindset – share, learn, grow. I heard some Powerful Words there!

I wish I could bottle the feeling from that conference. I would drink it up daily! Then, I would give it to you and everyone I know. The energy in the room was so upbeat, so refreshing, so exhilarating and so restorative the effects have yet to completely wear off because some words I heard there were powerful.

You know what? I don't want that feeling to wear off. Not for a very long time for the reasons I have already mentioned.

The origin of this positive energy was clear to me from the outset. The conference was populated by entrepreneurs of every stripe. Although everyone had a different business plan, a different focus, different goals or varying amounts of expertise, we all seemed to share one overriding quality - eternal and effervescent optimism.

Find an entrepreneur and you will find optimism and that is when the energy comes. I think we should surround ourselves with entrepreneurs. Better yet, I think everyone should become an entrepreneur.

If you haven't started this noble quest of continuous self-improvement and self-discovery, what are you waiting on? Who are you waiting on? The only one that need show up is you! The quest will provide you with everything else you need. But, you must begin.

If you have already started marching toward your purpose with passion then whatever you do, don't stop. The world desperately needs your optimism, your energy, the results of your unique set of talents and abilities and your Powerful Words.

Don't know what your true passion and purpose are just yet? That's okay for now. Keep looking. If fact, if you are reading this book you already have started looking. You started when you completed the core values inventory.

The bases of some of the questions you answered while taking the inventory were what made you happy, got you excited and captured your interest the most. The answer to what you are most passionate about and what your true purpose in life should be will, perhaps, lie in the answers to those questions.

If not, keep exploring and trying new things. The answers will come to you in time, maybe even before you finish this book.

# Powerful Words...

PASSION, PURPOSE, LEARN, GROW, ENTREPRENEUR, OPTIMISM and BEGIN are Powerful Words.

Someone may work and say, "Look at what I can do." Someone else may work and say, "Look what I have to do." Someone who has found their PURPOSE in life and pursues it with PASSION will say, "Look at what I get to do!"

You watch them work and you begin to wonder if they are working or playing or both. You can tell they LOVE what they do. Passion is all over them. It is their persona. They are eager to LEARN and share as they GROW.

You see this almost universally among ENTREPRENEURS who have found their joy for being. OPTIMISM is rooted in their abundance mentality. For them there is no end, just BEGIN.

# Your world of words within...

Do you feel you have found your true purpose and passion in life? If not, are you still searching? Do you feel your are stuck? What feelings do these words generate for you?

_____

_____

_____

_____

Are you an entrepreneur? Do you want to be? Is something holding you back? Are there some powerful words standing in your way or spurring you on?

Do you find it easy to begin? Or, to stall? Are you optimistic for your future? If not, are there Powerful Words in your way? Or, are there Powerful Words propelling you toward your preferred future?

What Powerful words have come to mind in this section?

_____

_____

_____

_____

Are you excited and anxious to learn, share and grow? No? Do you want to be? Do you feel you have the ability to choose? If not, can you name what is in the way? If you can, there is a Powerful Word which is holding you in its grip. Determining those word(s) will connect you on an emotional level with what is in your way.

If you are still searching for your passion and purpose for living, don't stop. No one is born knowing. It is the search which will uncover it for you. If you completed the core values inventory, you may have found some hints there.

# PLANNING

## The Seeds of Plenty

There is an old Chinese proverb, "The best time to plant a tree was 20 years ago. But the second best time is today." Sowing seeds for future harvesting provides us with a powerful metaphor for living. Transformed living means taking that concept to the next level.

There was a man once who lived in the 1800's, a true American pioneer, journeyman and nurseryman. He was an eccentric but in the best ways imaginable. He was born John Chapman on September 26, 1774 and lived an extraordinary life before his death at the age of 80 in 1845.

You may not recognize his name but his legacy remains to this day. He left his mark across the frontiers of the American landscape. You see, Johnny had a thing for apples and orchards. He didn't just plant apple tress randomly here and there, he planted entire nurseries for much of his adult life.

In fact, he would plant nurseries instead of orchards, build fences around them to protect them, leave them in the care of neighbors who sold trees from them and shared in the profit, and Johnny would return every few years to tend to the nurseries.

He introduced apple trees and built nurseries to large parts of Pennsylvania, Ohio, Indiana, West Virginia and Illinois. One such nursery had over 15,000 trees. He was a lover of all animals, even insects, and would go out of his way to care for them and protect them.

Once he heard of a horse that was to be put down so he bought the horse, purchased a few grassy acres nearby and put the horse on the property to recover. The horse did recover. He gave the horse to someone in need after requiring a promise form them that the horse would be treated well and humanely for all of his remaining days.

He became a legend while he was still living due to his kindness, generosity, and leadership in the arena of conservationism. Johnny was quick to preach the Gospel as he traveled and converted many Native Americans whom he deeply admired. The Native Americans considered him as someone touched by the Great Spirit and even tribes considered hostile would leave him alone to pass by unharmed.

He had few possessions other than land for his precious nurseries. He wore old hand me down clothes and was often found scantily clad. He would make mush in an old tin pot which also served as his hat. You know him, of course, by the iconic moniker of Johnny Appleseed.

Throughout his life he sowed much more than apple seeds and he was able to harvest much more than apples. Few people understood as Johnny did the concept and value of planting seeds now for the greater harvest later, that the fruits of your labor are not seen or enjoyed at the time of the planting, but later on in time. His planning was planting (his present). His planting was planning (his future).

None of us possess a crystal ball to tell us exactly how our futures will unfold. But, I predict that if we are diligent today, if we serve with passion and purpose, if we plant an abundance of seeds using our natural talents and abilities, a bountiful harvest of plenty will follow.

## Powerful Words...

LEGEND, GENEROSITY, LEADERSHIP, PLANNING, DILIGENT and ABUNDANCE are Powerful Words.

Adopt an ABUNDANCE mentality. There are plenty of people to produce for and to serve. There is no end to the products and services which can be produced. There is plenty of money to be made. There is ample room in the market place for everyone.

Be DILIGENT in the PLANNING and execution of your goals. Demonstrate GENEROSITY by giving away some of your time, products or services. This will ensure your ongoing success.

Sure, everyone wants to succeed. What would be next level success? Become LEGEND. Give, give, give before you ask. Produce a superior product or service. Display LEADERSHIP by being the standard bearer in your market for your product or service. This is how you foster and retain a loyal following, your tribe.

# World of words from within...

Have you sown seeds for future harvests for yourself and others today? Or, were you the seed someone else planted who is now yielding a great harvest? Who helped you grow as a person? What stories about how you prepared yourself, or how someone helped to prepare you, do you have to share?

_____

_____

_____

_____

Is there an emotional connection with any of these words? If so, there are Powerful Words which describe those emotions. Write your own Powerful Words in this book and use it as your personal communication repository. Refer to them often. They are your strength.

# Being Through With
////////////////////////////////////////////////////////////////////////////////////////////

## Stuck
//////////////////////////////

Here is a message which is simple and clear. You can refuse to be stuck, to become stuck or to stay stuck. It is a choice. Getting unstuck requires a transformation in thinking. Transformations are powerful.

TRANSFORMATION is a Powerful Word.

I see so many of my patients and friends who cannot move forward in life because they are stuck in the past, holding fast to some prior act or event. It is so easy to let this happen. It is seductive because it is a stance that is effortless to maintain.

I have been stuck before, holding on like grim death to my addiction to alcohol, toxic relationships, a dispassionate existence. There was no way for me to move forward in life, to advance, to evolve or to become something other as long as I was passively stuck. Changing took a lot of effort.

It is no different with a traumatic event like an act of violence, a death, a failure, a betrayal, a great financial loss, a business failure. All of these can result in an individual becoming stuck unless the trauma of the event can be adequately dealt with which often requires a lot of effort and sometimes a lot of pain.

Sad to say that some can actually be taught to become stuck and stay that way. Children will emulate their parents. Even if their behavior is undesirable. I have seen generations of stuck individuals who have never felt that they have had the ability to change their circumstances. It breaks the heart.

Some people get stuck in the present. There are those that start a lot of projects but never seem to complete any of them. They lack clarity and focus. It is not that they don't work hard, they do. But they have no plan for completion as they never complete one thing before they have moved on to something else, jumping from one project to the next.

Others, stuck in the present are biding time for various reasons while they work at jobs that they absolutely deplore. They wait for the right break, the right moment, the right piece of luck, the right opportunity, the right idea, the right audience or for when they have enough money or enough time. I hear "when I retire…" all of the time. It never seems to happen in retirement either. Besides, I think retirement is an odious and deplorable word.

People can also become stuck in the future. These are the frenetic idea generating planner people. They love making plans, dreaming big and laying out future scenarios for their success. The only problem is they never plan to start and so they never do.

Their short term happiness is derived from the idea of becoming successful rather than from the actual work that is required. They literally get high from the brainstorming and making plans, not from implementing them.

It is an addiction of sorts. The moment they begin to think of implementing one of their plans they lose their interest buzz and sober up to reality. Then it becomes time to plan again, over and over again. They are stuck in the future.

The basis for all of these states of being stuck is fear and most often the fear is of failure. If we could only teach our children and re-teach all of our adults the gloriousness of failure and all of the success that it can bring, we would have a much different world. The only useful fear we should harbor is the fear of not trying, of not doing.

Are you stuck? If so, are you stuck in the past, present or future?

Getting unstuck requires a transformation in thinking and staying unstuck requires a certain vigilance. Transformation is not a one-off event. It is a mindset, a new way of living that is intentional and continuous.

It begins with this promise to yourself - I will continuously and relentlessly reassess my situation, set new goals, embrace new experiences, abandon old and ineffective paradigms and tirelessly seek to further my understanding of life and my place in this world. With this step you essentially promise yourself that this will be an ongoing project, a process that will be repeated over and over again as you face life on life's terms and all of the challenges life will present from this point forward.

This step presupposes a lot. It presupposes you have adopted a different mindset and it is this new mindset that will lead you inexorably toward the truer version of yourself. It presupposes that you have let go of the dreary sameness that you wanted so desperately to escape, that you have begun to realize your potentials and you are now fully self actuating, self invested and eager to greet what lies ahead.

It means that you have embarked on a journey of self-discovery to find your true passion and purpose in life. Or, perhaps you already know your true passion and purpose and are now intent on pursuing them to the fullest extent possible.

It presupposes that you have made a commitment to spend a lifetime exploring, honing, using and deploying your natural talents and abilities in order to create, produce, sell, build, contribute, compose or author.

Isn't this the desired outcome for a life changing transformation in the first place? Isn't this what people long to discover - their passion and purpose in life, to find their happiness, peace, contentment, joy and freedom?

If you are successful in finding these for yourself in who you are, what you do and what you become, would you ever want to stop?

# Powerful Words...

TRANSFORMATION and FORWARD are Powerful Words.

I love the word TRANSFORMATION. It not only aptly describes profound change in my own life, the word has a certain feeling to me. It feels like great promise is in store after having been transformed. Do you get that?

I think of the caterpillar which undergoes a transformation through the process of metamorphosis to become a beautiful butterfly. Such promise for its future and future generations of butterflies is unleashed in the process. It leaves me awe struck. This is the emotional impact this word represents for me.

Transformation also means moving FORWARD to me, a positive thing. If you dread change, the word forward my scare the daylights out of you or cause you to be anxious. Some people are too busy looking backward to look or move forward. They remain stuck in the past. Don't be one of those people.

# Your world of words within...

Is it time to change, time for you to transform? Have you already undergone a transformation? Either way, there is a story to be told. Stories of transformation are some of the most inspirational stories told. They contain Powerful Words.

Have you had transformational events in your life? What were they? List as many as you can think of here.

_____

_____

_____

_____

People love to hear them because they connect so well on an emotional level, either with people who want to transform their life or with people who already have. This pretty much encompasses just about everyone on the planet.

Write down or tell someone the stories of your desire to transform, your struggles to transform or of your transformation. Try to identify the words in your stories which resonate with you the most on an emotional level. These are the Powerful Words which will either give someone the opportunity to share their words of power with you or give you the opportunity to help someone else.

What other Powerful Words did you think of while reading through this section?

_____

_____

_____

# WHAT ARE YOUR
## INTENTIONS?

You want to start a business, grow a current business, end a bad relationship, start a new relationship, learn a new skill, get a new job, sell something, write that book, start a blog, learn a new language, produce music or create art but you feel stuck. Okay. So, what exactly are your intentions?

I was hiking recently in Sedona, AZ, and had the rare privilege of making it up to the Shaman's Cave. Many Native Americans, spiritual leaders and mystics make it a point to visit this cave for inspiration. If you would like to see a picture of the cave, here is the link: http://www.clarkgaither.com/the-shamans-cave/

Before it came to be called the Shaman's cave it was known as Robber's Roost. Which name fits best would depend on your perspective and your intentions. This requires self-assessment.

Self-assessment begs this question - Are we what we are, what we say we are or what we want to become? Again, which best fits your view of **self** (self-identity, self-concept) determines your perspective and your intentions and those are based on choice.

No one gets to the Shaman's Cave easily but I was determined and engaged. The trail head is at the end of many poorly marked dirt roads outside of Sedona. It doesn't show up on the usual maps. The last quarter mile of road was more like an obstacle course of jutting, oil pan puncturing stones and axle snapping pot holes. A high clearance vehicle with heavy duty shocks is an absolute requirement.

The trail head itself was unmarked, the Park Service's way of discouraging visitors in order to preserve the site. After a one mile hike, the last 100 feet to the cave entrance can best be described as perilously precarious, with a sharply sloping drop-off to one side along a slippery shear rock wall. Still, I made it there and back without incident.

When I left for the cave that morning I was unsure of the exact location or of the validity of my directions. It took some guess work, persistence and a few track backs to get there. I had no idea how difficult it would be when I struck out. But, I made it.

My rewards were a great view of the box canyon and mountains beyond the entrance of the cave and the special, mystical appearance of the cave itself. The acoustics in the cave, with rounded walls and ceiling were quite something to hear. Sounds inside the cave seemed to surround you no matter where you stood.

Although my path to the cave was unclear when I started out that morning, I knew I would be standing inside the cave before the day was over. That was my intent. By simply making the decision to go, I had all but guaranteed my eventual arrival.

Sure, something could have prevented me from making it to the cave at many points along the way. But, there is no denying that I would have never made it to Shaman's Cave without a desire to go, some sort of plan to get there, and without simply starting.

I believe we are not just representing who we are at any given moment in time but rather an amalgam too of who we think we are and who we want to become. It is the summed difference of these that becomes who we are.

# Powerful Words...

START, INTENTIONS, SELF-ASSESSMENT, CHOICE and ENGAGED are Powerful Words.

When I began the journey out to the cave that morning, in my mind I had already become Clark Gaither standing in Shaman's Cave. It didn't matter I hadn't arrived there yet. Such was my perspective, such were my INTENTIONS. How else could I have done it?

How do we get to where we want to be? We get there first in our hearts, then in our heads and arrive at last with our feet. Each individual decides. For so many years I changed nothing, and nothing changed. Nothing in our lives will change unless we change our lives.

Recognizing our wants and needs, the need for change to get them and taking the necessary actions to secure them are determined only through continuous SELF-ASSESSMENT. If you stop self-assessing, you will stagnate.

If you are nose deep in fully ENGAGED living with passion and purpose (think Shaman's Cave) then you have arrived there with intention. There is no other way to get there.

If on the other hand you find you are stuck (think Robber's Roost, i.e. a place to hide) then the only way you will stay there is with intention. Either way, it is a CHOICE. To become unstuck and get to where you want to be you must have a desire to go, some sort of plan to get there, and simply START.

# Your world of words within...

Who you are. Who you say you are. Who you want to be. How does this all add up for you at this moment in time? What **IS** your preferred future? Have you mapped it all out? Have you taken actions to get you there? What are your intentions?

Circle one: Have you hit the start button for **ACTION** or are you **STUCK**? Do you believe each of those states is a choice?

If STUCK, list three to five items which you feel leave you stuck. Beside each one, list two to three things you can do to get yourself unstuck.

1. _____

2. _____

3. _____

4. _____

5. _____

Have you done this much self-assessment? If not, what is holding you back? Are there stories you can tell? There may be Powerful Words in those stories reflecting strong feelings concerning the answer to these questions. Knowing them and understanding the basis for them, you can begin to lessen their influence.

Once identified, share your Powerful Words and stories with others who have had similar struggles. They will share with you Powerful Words of their own which will help you to get engaged.

If you are already engaged, share your Powerful Words and stories with others. You already know the words which inspired you. You know the words that keep you burning with purpose and passion, the ones which resonate with you on an emotional level. Not just the words and stories of your successes but also of your struggles.

People are waiting to hear them. They need your wisdom, inspiration, experience, strength and hope. You will share with them from abundance, because your cup is overflowing.

What Powerful Words of your own have you uncovered while reading this section?

_____

_____

_____

# IS IT COURAGE OR
//////////////////////////////////////////////////////////////
# SOMETHING ELSE?
//////////////////////////////////////////////////////////////

When people attempt change there is a tendency for most to give up, often just before victory, when the going gets difficult. This quest to find your voice, your message and the Powerful Words to convey your message is no different.

I have seen the following many times and so have you. You see someone get knocked down time after time but they keep getting back up, usually swinging. Then, one day they finally make it big. They win. Perhaps this has happened to you.

But, before that happens people on the sidelines will ask, "So why does he keep getting back up only to get knocked down again?" The answer that most people give, the knee jerk response when there is no other apparent adequate or handy explanation, is **courage**.

Is it? Is it courage or something else? People assume it must be courage to keep you raising up after a beating. What if the person knocked down feels there is no other choice but to get back up. Is that still courage?

The definition of courage is *the quality of mind or spirit to face difficulty, danger, pain, etc., **without fear**; bravery*. Uh, what? I always heard that courage was taking action in spite of fear, not the complete absence of fear.

I am pretty sure if life is beating the essence out of someone then they are probably afraid, afraid to get back up, afraid that they will be knocked down again, afraid they will suffer more loss and pain.

Again, what if the person knocked down had no choice but to get back up?

Or, what if it is not that either. What about **passion, drive, perseverance, determination, dedication, persistence,** and **shear true grit bulldog tenacity**? What if those are the reasons? Those are excellent reasons to get back up when knocked down. Wouldn't you agree?

For those people, the ones who keep getting back up, staying down is not an option. They get back up because they will not consent to stay down. They get back up because they are not content to stay down. In fact, you would never be able to hold those people down.

Yet, many people insist that it is courage that motivates the people that keep getting beaten down and keep getting back up. I don't believe courage is the reason and I will tell you why.

I believe there is a general belief that courage is either something you have or something you don't. So, if you find that you don't have courage, you are not at fault.

If you feel you are not courageous, you hope that it is something which will come to you when it is most needed. If not, then you just weren't one of the lucky ones to have courage.

Many will never explore if they have courage or lack it until they are fully and sorely tested. They will wait for the absence of fear. Unfortunately for them, they will wait a lifetime.

But, the attributes of passion, drive, determination, dedication, persistence, and shear true grit bulldog tenacity, those are all **choices**. As such, they can be made ahead of time, before life knocks you down.

Of course, life **will** knock you down. Life knocks everyone down, multiple times. The question is, will you stay down or rise up? Will you keep getting up until one day you just give up? Will you give in to fear and take up residence on the mat?

You can answer these questions now, ahead of adversity. No matter what happens, no matter how bad it seems, making this choice - deciding fearlessly in favor of passion, drive, determination, dedication, persistence, or shear true grit bulldog tenacity. Now that is courageous!

# Powerful Words...

COURAGE, DRIVE, DETERMINATION, DEDICATION and PERSISTENCE are Powerful Words.

Courage can only show up when fear is present. There is nothing courageous about the everyday, the routine, the day-in-day-out. It is only when we are challenged to step outside of our zone of influence that we begin to fear. Prudent action in the presence of fear is courageous, not in its absence.

But FEAR is also a powerful Word if we lend it the power to hold us back, to beat us down, to steal away our opportunities. It is not about eliminating fear. It is about lessening its influence and robbing fear of its power.

We do this by making other words more powerful than the fear in our minds. Why do aid workers go to Ebola infested countries to serve the suffering? Do think they do so without fear?

No, they do so because they possess DRIVE, DETERMINATION and DEDICATION, the proof of their passion. Those words reflect internal emotions which are more powerful than their fear. They feed the meaning behind those words and in doing so they are starving their fear, lessening the power it has over them. So they go.

PERSISTENCE turns a seemingly hopeless situation into one which is manageable.

# Your world of words within...

Everyone has acted in the face of fear at some point in their life. What stories of courage are in your past? Write them down or have some interview you and record the interview. Embedded in your stories are Powerful Words which you will connect with on an emotional level. Those words will connect you with others on an emotional level.

What stories or courage do you have to tell? Make some notes here.

_____

_____

_____

_____

Do you feel driven with purpose and passion in some aspect of your life? Are you a determined person? Do you feel dedicated and feel you are making a difference in the world? If yes, the universe thanks you. You are fulfilling your mission. Think back to how it all started for you. You will use Powerful Words in your description. These words will help others on their journey seeking purpose with passion.

If you do not feel this way it is never too late to begin or continue your search. This is the great challenge in life as I see it.

Start by exploring again your core values and find some strength in them. Continue to explore your road blocks and barriers to progress. There are stories associated with them and it is in those stories you will find the Powerful Words which are denying you your preferred future. Knowing them, you can begin to rob them of their power as you begin to counter their influence.

Are you now, or have you ever been, on a determined quest to find your purpose in life? Circle one: **YES  NO  WAS  NEVER**

If your answer is any of the last three choices, list any obstacles you feel are in your way here.

_____

_____

_____

_____

# Finding Your Voice

## In the time it takes.....

In the time it takes to blow out a candle, your life can instantly and dramatically change, forever. Everyday we all make decisions and then act on them. Sometimes, decisions are made and actions are taken by others on our behalf that directly or indirectly affect us whether we want them to or not, with or without our permission.

Sometimes other people's actions are welcome, sometimes they aren't. We can not control the actions of others, all we can control is how we react to them. Ultimately, it is only our own decisions and actions that we can directly control.

How much we allow the actions of others to affect us is a choice. We have all, at one time or another, assigned to others our own self-generated, painful, negative emotions in response to something we did not like. We effectively put others in charge of our feelings.

We allow our own perceptions and interpretation of what has transpired to harm us. We lay off the responsibility of our own insecurities to others letting them dictate our feelings of happiness or sadness, success or failure, well-being or disquiet.

It is so easy to do. It is human nature I suppose. Stopping this bad habit is not easy, but not impossible. I have yet to fully succeed with this in my own life. It is a task that seems insurmountable at times. But, I am still trying. I claim progress not perfection.

What we can do, very effectively if we choose, is control our own decisions and actions. This can be the case whether we are acting or reacting. This is particularly true when it comes to the choices we make. If mistakes are made in the course of everyday living, saying "he made me do this" or "she made me do that" is just one great big self-delusion.

In the time it takes to blow out a candle I can either chose how I react to others. I can choose what I will do today to better myself and my life. It could be something as simple and innocuous as whether or not I go here instead of there, say this instead of that, denying this instead of accepting that.

Choices are always mine to make and no one else's. Choosing to blame someone or something else for my feelings and behavior is not accepting personal responsibility for my own actions and feelings. Trying to make someone else responsible would be my self-directed irresponsibility.

So you have to ask yourself, "What will be the consequences of my decisions and actions today." Not only for yourself, but how will the decisions you make today affect others? In the time it takes to blow out a candle you could discourage, ridicule, lie, cheat, steal, criticize, diminish, tear down, disrupt, sabotage, and destroy. In the time it takes to light a candle you could encourage, praise, tell the truth, be forthright, give, compliment, develop, build up, organize, fix, produce and create.

For any situation, any situation, there are only three possible modes for feeling as an outcome - one positive, one negative and one neutral. Which we choose (and yes, it is a choice) says something about us, our mindset, our philosophy, our desires, our wants and needs. It could also say something about our intent.

> "We don't see things the way they are.
> We see things the way we are." ~ Anais Nin

Is it the circumstances of a given situation that, in advance, determines how we should feel, or is how we react to a given situation our choice? Instead of reacting negatively, a clear and conscious action to **choose** a positive reaction can make all the difference in outcome. Everything is choice.

This is a lesson that I have had to learn over and over again with my own struggles toward some sort of enlightenment. But, I believe it is a lesson worth learning, worth the time it takes to get it right.

I try to start every morning now with the premise that I am going to be the agent of positive change in my own life and in the lives of those around me. Again, I am not always successful because I am human and sometimes old habits are hard to break. But, in the time it takes, it is getting easier.

Have you been or are you being the agent of positive change in your own life? If not, you can begin today. It is but a choice.

# Powerful Words...

PROGRESS, PERFECTION and ENLIGHTENMENT are Powerful Words.

I seek PERFECTION in the products and services I purchase and in all things I do. Don't we all? I mean, would you purchase a brand new car with a scratch on the driver's door or a hole in the seat cover, even though that is precisely what will happen over time? No, you would want it to be perfect. At least for a while.

There is just one problem with the notion of perfection. It is a myth. It is a mental construct of the ideal which does not exist in reality. Life will be much more enjoyable and stress free s long as you can accept some level of imperfection in yourself and others. This is a step toward ENLIGHTENMENT.

This does not mean we shouldn't strive for perfection as we offer up our very best efforts on behalf of the people we serve. This is how we make PROGRESS.

# World of words from within...

Do you choose to take personal responsibility for your own feelings and actions? Or, have you put someone else in charge of you? Do you feel you must be in charge of someone else's feelings and actions? What Powerful Words come to mind as you read these questions?

_____

_____

_____

Circle one: Do you claim **PROGRESS** or **PERFECTION?**

How has trying to be perfect hampered you? Where does your need for perfection come from? What stories do you remember which still impact you on an emotional level? Make some notes here.

_____

_____

If you have dreams to fulfill, if you have a powerful story to tell or Powerful Words to share, will you take personal responsibility to see that it gets done?

# TRANSFORMATION

I t is said that every journey begins with a single step, the first step. The journey to transforming one's life is no different. However, the first step to change or transformation is not a physical one. It is a mental step. It requires a change of one's mind-set, a transformation in one's thinking. Win, lose, or draw, that is where the hardest battles are fought - in the mind.

If you are looking to adopt a profoundly different lifestyle, start a new business, publish, create, or reinvent yourself then you must embrace the notion of change or transformation. This is an absolutely necessity.

Before people can begin to fundamentally transform they must become aware of this first and most important step and accept it in principle: **acknowledge that your life is not what you want or desire it to be and change is now needed or necessary.** Any hope of a positive outcome depends on the acceptance of this first critical step.

Some people desperately desire change. Other people refuse to believe that they are in need of change even when it is glaringly apparent to everyone around them that something must or should change. This kind of situational blindness or need to maintain the status quo can be the result of avoidance behavior or outright denial any problems exist in the first place. Many just feel powerless to change.

Powerlessness can take on many forms. It could be a person's inability to separate themselves from someone else in a relationship that is toxic or abusive. It could be overspending. It could be procrastination. It could be an inability to say no, to take a different job, to begin speaking or writing. For most people, their powerlessness to fundamentally change their lives for the better lies in fear.

Fear can absolutely paralyze an individual. It can keep them working at a job they hate, living a life they despise or prevent them from pursuing what might otherwise bring them a fulfilling life. Fear is a severe task master. People starving for change will often serve fear before they ever serve themselves. Walt Kelly once wrote in his comic strip, "We have met the enemy and he is us."

I believe that we are hardwired to want, to try, to succeed. It is but a choice as to whether or not we do. Fear seems to be the biggest obstacle for choosing for ourselves the life we would prefer to lead.

Know there is a difference between fear and caution. It is the difference between paralysis and prudent action. I do not believe we are hardwired to fear to the point of inaction or of feeling powerless. I believe that kind of fear is a learned behavior and as a learned behavior I believe it can be unlearned. Like all things worth while, it only requires effort.

There is also a difference between change and transformation. You can change your hair style, your clothes, your car, where you live, your job and your friends but none of that will change you, who you are.

When I talk about a transformation I am talking about changes on the inside as well as on the outside. Transformation means profound change toward becoming your truer self, transformation as in a metamorphosis.

Transformational change means coming to know yourself in a fundamentally different way and acting accordingly. It all begins with accepting the notion "my life is not what I want it to be and I feel the need to change."

# Powerful Words...

JOURNEY, TRANSFORMATION, and BATTLES are Powerful Words.

TRANSFORMATION denotes a complete conversion, a change in form, appearance, nature and character from what **is** toward what is **desired**. Although transformation is a form of change, it means more than simple change. It is both comprehensive and broad in scope.

The word JOURNEY infers exploration, excitement, the unknown, risk, discovery, and adventure. New journeys, if not foisted upon us, should be actively and aggressively sought. What greater doom than to be assigned a single journey in this life?

BATTLES equate to struggles which we all face. All creatures struggle. Humans achieve their fullest potential though struggle, if we choose. To end a struggle before there is a clear loss or win is to lose twice. If you believe struggle produces tangible benefits, even if you should lose, then to struggle and lose or to struggle and win is to win twice. This is the great secret - when we struggle, we only lose if we choose.

# Your world of words within...

Are you satisfied with your life? Is it as you would have it? Are there changes that need to be made? If you could change anything about your life, anything at all, what would it be?

_____

_____

Are there new journeys you would like to begin? Have you accepted a fate or are you destined to change things? Have you accepted you as the agent of change for you?

What battles have you fought? Did you learn more from the ones you won or the ones you "lost"? What battles are you fighting now?

What Powerful Words do these questions conger up?

_____

_____

_____

_____

If these questions move you on some level emotionally, then there will be some Powerful Words or stories either buried within them or bubbling to the surface. Write them down now while they are still fresh in your mind.

# Is it time to Transform?...

With have within each of us the power not only to change but transform, into the kind of person we want to be, living the kind of existence we want to live. I have already explained the first and most important step – to simply acknowledge and accept that your life is not what you want it to be and change is needed and necessary.

Even if you accept that your life is undesirable or unmanageable and that change is needed and necessary, it is the follow through that can seem most difficult. Many may feel that they can't change and will stop here, never moving beyond this point.

But, there is a second step which is also fundamentally important when seeking a transformation. **You must feel or know that you have the power to change yourself.**

There are many reasons some must acknowledge this. Some may cede their power to another or to something else and feel that they can't change because this thing or this other person won't let them change.

If this sounds like you then you must realize that you have had the power all along. If you gave it away in the first place then you were in control to begin with. If you gave your power of choice away then you can choose to take it back.

Some are loath to feel they can change because of what very little healthy achievement and lack of personal enrichment can do to a person over time. It numbs the mind, destroys the spirit and steals away hope.

This may describe you if you hear yourself saying "I can't" too often. If you try at something, yes you will fail at times and at other times you will succeed. If you say you can't all of the time you will be right 100% of the time. There is no easier way to succeed at failing than never to try.

People are meant to accomplish, to build, to travel, to learn, to teach, to love, to innovate, to design, to create, to experience with our six senses. Yes, I said six. The mind is your sixth sense. It is the source of your dreams and intuition, something that can not be experienced with your other senses. It is the portal to the other senses and the seat of understanding. You must come to understand that you have within yourself the power to do all of these things. It is but a choice.

When I ask people why they don't choose to embark on a journey of self-discovery and seek the change they so desire, many will give me an odd look as if the choice wasn't theirs to make. Others will recite a litany of obstacles that they perceive prevents them from changing their lives for the better. When in actuality the only real obstacle in their way is their own mind-set.

Before you can change, before you can transform, you must adopt a CHANGE or TRANSFORMATION Mind-Set. It is a very different way of thinking, one which may be completely foreign to you at first.

Here is an example of a Change or Transformation Mind-Set. You will, as much and as often as possible, trade "I can't" for "I can" or for some version of that.

For example, if you spoke no foreign language and someone were to ask you, "Do you speak a second language?" Your first inclination might be, "No, I don't." A transformed mind might rather say, "I can! I just haven't learned one yet."

You must come to feel or to know that you have the power to change **you**. Do you feel that way about yourself? Do you feel that you have the ability to change, to learn, to grow, to become a different person? I believe you do.

# Willingness is another unstopper of STOP...

We have come to the next step toward a Transformation, **a willingness to change**. Willingness is a powerful attitude and a Powerful Word. It reflect an openness to possibilities.

Everyone has something they would like to change about themselves or their lives. A person may come to acknowledge that a problem exists and that change is need. They might further surmise that they do have the wherewithal to change. These are the first and second steps toward a transformation.

Yet many will stop here by refusing to change. Instead of "I will" it is "I won't."

The reasons for this are many and varied. One can get comfortable, even residing in a rut. Climbing out of the rut takes energy, energy to research, to learn, to invent, to build, to manage, to work toward meaningful change.

No one will never be able to transform their life into their own preferred future with an attitude of "I won't." Saying "I won't" is a non-starter, a compass without direction, a road without a beginning, a song without music, a book with no words, a canvas without paint.

Clearly stated, you must make a commitment to yourself that you will do what is necessary to change, to transform your life. The "I won't do this" or "I won't do that" must be swapped for "I will do this" and "I will do that" if it means that you will be able to create your own preferred future.

What I am about to say happens with great frequency. I will have a patient in my office who is struggling on many levels. Every sound and prudent course of action I suggest which could help their situation, very simple solutions really, will be rejected outright with "I can't do that."

These patients will give me a list of reasons as to why they can't take any of my advice. In the end, many will just want a pill, something to fix their broken life and make everything better. Medicine or no, I predict their struggles will continue for years to come unless they can manage to profoundly change their approach to living.

That is what I have been talking about here, profound change, a transformative change. It's not about becoming another person, or trying to become someone different, someone you are not. It is about being you but re-defined.

It's about getting back to the real you, the one that got lost somewhere along the way. The you that is able to accomplish anything to which you apply your will and your mind. It's about regaining that child-like sense of wonder, when everything seemed exciting and nothing seemed impossible because the possibilities were endless.

When you transform, you will believe and know these things once more.

How you will think about yourself, how you will look at people and situations will be decidedly different.

When people are transformed through a program of recovery, as I was, we were told this: Your whole attitude and outlook on life will change. You will intuitively know how to handle situations which used to baffle you. You will come to know a new freedom and a new happiness and you will know peace.

These are not idle promises. I have seen them come true in my own life and in the lives of countless others. These promises also hold true for anyone who changes their life in meaningful ways.

Are you ready to say I will do whatever it takes to change my circumstances, my life? If you have acknowledged that your life is not what you want it to be and that change is needed, feel you have the power to change and a willingness to change then you have completed the first three steps of your Transformation.

## Transforming the Mind...

Now you have come to the action phase of your Transformation. This is where the work that is required will separate those who **want** to transform from those who **will** transform. There are four realms each individual must address before your transformation can be complete - the mental, emotional, physical and spiritual realms.

Let's begin with the mental realm first. Here are the fundamental steps needed for addressing the obstacles, challenges, shortcomings, or barriers to a meaningful transformative change of the mind.

**Stimulate and nourish your brain.** These are one and the same. Do this before you even come up with a plan for action.

First, unless you are watching something purely educational, turn off the television. Most of what is on TV is crap and will make you stupid. If you must watch something for mindless entertainment, keep it under an hour a day. But just remember, they don't call it mindless for nothing.

Second, I can't think of anything that will get your idea machine cranking faster than reading great books! Pick your area of interest and read to find out what you don't know. Sometimes, you might not even know what you don't know, or what you need to know, until you start reading.

You could also pick books on topics at the periphery of your interests but are in support your interests. For instance, you might have a great idea or make a great product but you are going to have to eventually market that product so books on marketing are a must.

Dan Miller (48 Days to The Work You Love) suggests reading inspirational and uplifting books for at least 30 minutes each day. This is the best way I know to switch your brain to transformational thinking. This is something I do and wholeheartedly endorse.

Read off topic books and periodicals as well to stimulate your thinking. Foster a hobby. Read poetry and awesome quotes. Listen to a variety of music and podcasts that interest you.

Go out and find the tools that you will need for your success. You simply can't fix something or create anything without the necessary tools. I can't tell you how many people I talk with that complain of some problem that they are unable to solve yet when I ask them what research they might have done in order to solve their particular problem, all I get in return is a blank stare or a "nothing" or "I don't know" in reply.

Good grief. We have the world at our finger tips these days with smart phones, computer tablets and home PC's. Virtually any problem you might come up with has already been addressed by someone else whose answer is posted on the internet. There is more information out there than you could possibly review in a million lifetimes, most of it free.

Years ago I read a Scientific American article about Tunisian throat singers who are able to produce up to six or more distinct and separate sounds using just their vocal chords and mouth while singing a tune. It is an art that might take a throat singer 10 or more years to learn and a lifetime to master.

It was a very interesting article and I thought, I have got to hear some of this. In less than three minutes of searching the internet I found a music store in South Africa that offered a CD of Tunisian Throat Music. In less than 10 days, I had the CD in hand.

There is nothing of interest that I can't find on the internet. I have made this bet countless times with friends. I always win.

It has been said that there is nothing that would prevent you from becoming an expert on any subject within six months through intense study. Josh Kaufman, in a TEDx CSU talk found that when attempting to learn a new skill you can go from gross incompetence to being reasonably good at it in just 20 hours. You might say, well except me, of course. Don't be your first and last barrier to learning whatever it takes to propel you forward.

Are you stimulating and feeding your mind daily? If not, why not? What are the barriers to learning that you perceive? Are they real or imagined?

## Transforming Your Emotions...

If the State of Happiness is a healthy mind, body and spirit then the capital city would be Emotional Wellbeing. If your emotional wellbeing is suffering then chances are your mental, spiritual and physical realms are suffering too. How does one repair damaged emotional wellbeing? What kind of transformation does that take?

None of us are born emotionally damaged, ill or bankrupt yet that will be how some of us end up. People can feel beaten up emotionally by others, by circumstance, by lack of success, by life. Some people display tremendous hardiness and are resilient. They overcome emotional setbacks without long lasting impact. They may even thrive after an emotional setback.

Others languish and may breakdown mentally, physically, and spiritually because of uninterrupted emotional turmoil. Seemingly unable to turn things around they can become paralyzed by their emotional misery. When you are viewing everything through a corrupted and broken emotional lens, everything around you looks corrupted and broken too.

In the worst instances of emotional trauma, professional assistance may be necessary. If that sounds like you, seek professional help as quickly as possible. Know this, under the right circumstances and with proper care, everyone can heal.

But what is the difference between these two types of people, the ones who can seem to turn things around for themselves under the worst possible circumstances and the people who seemingly can't?

A 12 year long landmark study be a leading psychologist, Dr. Salvatore R. Maddi, found that those who thrived in spite of ruinous emotional stress possessed three key beliefs or traits that helped them weather adversity and turn it to their advantage.

It all came down to attitude: the **commitment attitude** that would lead them to act to be involved in ongoing events, the **control attitude** that would lead them to struggle to try and influence outcomes, and the **challenge attitude** that would lead them to view stressors, whether positive or negative, as new learning and growth opportunities. Dr. Maddi termed this **hardiness**.

The operative word here is attitude. Is your attitude something that is handed to you by someone else, dictated by circumstance or something you are born with perhaps? No dear reader, like so much else in life, the attitude you have about anything and everything is a personal choice.

Good emotional health doesn't automatically fall onto you from the sky as you sit and contemplate all that is wrong with your life. Emotional balance is something that can be cultivated and developed. Like anything else in life that is worthwhile, it takes choosing differently for yourself, some effort, some practice, some patience and time.

Some might argue that this is easy to do for people who are successful. It is easy to be happy, hardy and more resilient when you are happy, right? Psychologist Dr. Sonja Lyubomirsky of the University of California, Riverside found that chronically happy people turn out to be more successful across many life domains than people that are less happy. Makes sense. The surprise was that their happiness was in large part a direct consequence of their positive emotions and attitudes rather than from their success.

The people were happy before they were successful. They became more successful because they were happy. Here it is in a nutshell: HAPPINESS = SUCCESS.

It is time to state something clearly and unequivocally here. Everyone is entitled to their own emotions. Everyone should own their own emotions and be wholly responsible for them. It is then, and only then, that one is able to change them.

How do you make yourself happy? Well, I know how to do that for myself. I have no idea how to **make** you, dear reader, or anyone else happy. That is your journey and theirs, not mine.

I have a general sense of what it might take to make happiness easier to obtain for most people who aren't happy.

**Embrace, cling to, and devour the positive aspects of living.** Read poetry, uplifting books, inspirational stories. Improve yourself. Learn! Watch comedies. Laugh! Laugh some more. Laugh at yourself.

Are you hardy, resilient and happy? Or, emotionally unbalanced? Are you thriving or in need of emotional transformation?

**Avoid negativity.** Norman Vincent Peale once said, "Avoid like the plague those who fail to crystallize you to your full potential." He is saying avoid negative people as you would a suppurative, plague induced bubo draining pus. That's pretty emphatic. Surround yourself with positive people. Decide to become, at all costs, a positive person. It is but a choice after all.

A positive Transformation requires positive input. Negativity is anathema to positive change. No one would begin a race while tethered to the ground. Negative attitudes, beliefs, outlooks, forecasting, viewpoints, approaches and positions are just binders that keep us stuck. Whether they come from within or from outside ourselves makes no difference.

Make this pledge to yourself - **I am going to become a more positive person by surrounding myself with positive and uplifting people, exploring and employing resources for positive thinking and behaviors while avoiding negativity like the plague.**

Avoid negativity like the plague because it will poison the well of your soul. This must begin within yourself first. This may take some getting use to if you have trained your brain to think or react negatively to any given situation.

Like any bad behavior which has been learned, negative thinking can be un-learned. It doesn't just happen by **trying** to think positively all of the time. It comes from **learning** to think positively and that means being proactive. Here are three steps to help you accomplish this.

1) Begin to read positive, uplifting, inspiring, challenging and affirming material. In whatever your area of interest, find great books and read them! Go to the websites of people you admire and search their reading list. Most will have one and you will begin to notice the wells from which they draw their experience, strength and hope. Study their sources of inspiration.

If you live your life according to what is presented in the popular press we are supposed to be afraid of something, in dire need of something, or eminently dying from something 24/7. Mainstream news is all about what is deficient, broken or missing. If there is an occasional feel good story it is always used as a hook to get you to watch the gloom and doom forecast and reporting

The internet has greatly expanded out news source horizons. Look for blogs, websites and podcasts full of positive information that will help inspire, motivate and crystallize you to your full potential. Everything else is a distraction and a waste of your time.

2) Surround your self with like-minded, purpose driven, passionate people. Avoid negative individuals wherever possible or at least learn how to filter out their negativity. If some one offers you a negative sentiment or observation don't waste energy disagreeing with it. Rather, try to rev up your positivity generator by countering their statement with a positive spin or comment.

3) Challenge and then change your attitude. Look for the positive in everything. Notice positive occurrences throughout your day and begin to comment on them out loud to others.

Try to go an entire day without making negative or derogatory statements. This does not mean that you are to stop giving or receiving constructive criticism. Honest constructive criticism is positive, good and helpful, not at all negative. You know the difference.

These steps will help you to regain control over any pessimism and cynicism that may be dogging you. Or, maybe your positivistic generator is just in need of a tune-up rather than an overhaul. Either way, taking ownership of this step of your Transformation is sure to brighten your pathway to the future you wish to create for yourself.

Are you a positive person? What additional steps can you think of to increase and accentuate the positive in your life?

# Transforming Your Physical Self...

There is a part of Transformation that is often overlooked when people begin to change their lives for the better and in profound ways. It is the physical realm. Your will never be the best you can be, the best you can become, if your physical house isn't in order.

Completely transforming yourself and your life into the person you want to be, living the life you want to live, doing the kind of work you want to do is going to require some effort. Being physically fit will help you to accomplish the work that will be required to reach your goals. It isn't absolutely necessary but it will make your transformation a whole lot easier and much more enjoyable.

To be more mentally fit you must become more physically fit. You might ask, what has one to do with the other? I have never seen a mentally fit patient who felt as mentally sharp as they were capable of feeling if they felt poorly in their body.

Similarly, I have never seen a patient that was physically fit feel well in their body if they were suffering mentally. We all live inside our heads. What we "feel" is a summation of our emotional feelings and our physical feelings.

Furthermore, the sense of well-being that we all seek is a balance between all four realms - the mental, emotional, physical, and spiritual realms. Care for three and ignore the one and your life will be out of balance. The physical realm is the one most often ignored.

Obesity rates in the US are epidemic. Less than 2% of the population gets the cardiovascular exercise that is recommended. Too many people come to me wanting me to "fix" them with a pill when most of the time life style modifications are all that is required. Even modest walking programs can improve one's health.

Instead, too many Americans get their meals handed to them through a drive-up window, never once considering to enter the restaurant on foot. I have seen cars at Walmart endlessly circling the parking lot in search of a parking space a few feet closer to the door rather than getting out and walking those few extra feet. I ask my patients who need the exercise and are able to park as far away from the front door to the mall as possible.

I have non-handicapped patients come to my office every week for handicap placards to hang on their rearview mirrors so they can park in the spaces reserved for the truly handicapped who never ask me for those same placards. Most, not all, of those non-handicapped patients could, and should, leave their cars at home and walk to the mall. They would live longer if they did.

Once, after finishing a run at a nearby lake front community, I saw a women come out of her house, get in her car, drive to the end of a

100 foot long driveway, retrieve her mail form the mailbox and drive straight back to her house. I can here her now sitting the doctor's office, "Doctor, I just don't feel good and I don't know why."

Here is some free sage advice if you don't feel good and you are overweight, eat poorly, don't exercise, recline in the lazy boy to watch TV in the evening after dinner, drink too much alcohol or smoke and can't hold out to do anything and don't feel good then do this: lose weight, eat healthy, stop bad behaviors, exercise regularly until you can hold out to do anything, burn your lazy boy then your TV and feel better. It's really not that complicated.

Trimming down, eating healthy, and regular exercise makes my patients feel great, like they can conquer the world! They have more energy, more stamina, and they are rarely sick. If you can't manage being totally fit then be as fit as you can be.

Regular heart-pumping exercise gives you a sense of calm and well-being that you can not get from a pill. Exercise boosts the immune system, clears the mind, lifts the spirits, and alleviates depression and anxiety. In short, it enhances your other three realms. Improving your physical health will improve all of them without any additional effort.

If you are going to transform, then why not transform your physical status form unhealthy to healthy? It is never too late to start. Small changes add up and amplify over time.

If you have some health issues or are unsure of your health status then be sure to consult with your physician **first** to see what kind of diet and exercise program is best and safest for you. If you already enjoy the best health you can have for your age then you are one step ahead on your way to Transformation.

Ask yourself, am I as healthy as I can be? If not, what are some ways I can begin to adopt a healthier lifestyle? What can I do today to make myself feel better?

# Your Spiritual Realm...

No self-help assessment or effort can be complete unless you address the health of your spiritual self. If you are to Transform your life, not just change it, then your spiritual realm is just as important as the other three realms. Maybe even more so. It is the deeper part of you.

The spirit encompasses your sense of who you are, why you are here and your place in the world. It represents your connectedness, or lack of connectedness, to other people, to nature and reality. Your spiritual health is reflected in your sense of purpose.

How is your spiritual health? Do you feel connected to humanity, a higher power, nature and the world around you? Do you have a sense of purpose, hope for the future, face each day with excitement, feel optimistic, a sense of peace, a sense of calm and serenity? If so, you are in excellent spiritual health.

Or, do you live in fear under a prevailing sense of dread, feel you walk alone in this world, prefer pessimism over optimism, feel hopeless or helpless, feel empty or apathetic and anxious for the future? Do you feel you know who you are and have a sense of purpose? Or, are you somewhere in between these two extremes? If so, then your spiritual self may be damaged or suffering.

When I was an active alcoholic my spiritual health was very poor. I felt dead inside. I felt it impossible to change my circumstances which gave me no hope for the future. I heard someone once describe how they felt when they hit their rocky bottom with drug addiction. He said he felt "perfectly broken". That is precisely how I felt, perfectly broken.

There are many things that can enhance a damaged spirit or restore a broken one.

Be quite and meditate everyday. Concentrate on the things that you do have rather than dwell on what you don't have or feel you must have in order to be happy. Be grateful.

Get adequate rest! Play! Adults need to play just like children. Finds ways to reconnect with your inner child. Color with crayons (especially outside the lines), draw, play with play dough, run with scissors (okay, blunt ones), get in a tickle fight.

Sounds silly, I know. That's the point. Silly makes people laugh. Silly makes people smile. When you laugh and smile, you feel happy.

You want to feel younger in less than 5 seconds or less? Get up out of your chair right now and skip! It will immediately make you smile or laugh. That is your inner child laughing. The spirit of a child is boundless and free. Your child-self is still inside you. It wants you to come out and play.

Practice mindfulness. If there is something that you really enjoy then really enjoy it. Slow down and savor everything worthy of your time and attention. Practice kindness, patience, the art of grace, empathy and compassion. Be decent and tolerant. Be honest. Tell the truth.

Study art. Start with what you like and then branch out. Take an art class. If you say that you aren't artistic and are of the opinion that artists are born, I will tell you that you are wrong. If artists are born then there are just over 7 billion of them on the planet and you are one of them. Take an art class and prove me wrong.

Listen to uplifting music. Again, start with what you like or are familiar with and branch out from there. If you can make music then make it and then make some more. Make music with others. Make music for others.

Connect with other people. Become part of a community. Well, except the Blah Blah Blah, Nobody Loves Me, Everybody Hates Me Community. That one is off limits. But, look around. There are so many different and interesting communities out there to which you can belong. Pick one that will capture your interest and keep you energized.

Connect with animals. Do you have a pet? Some of most cherished memories are of my pets. There are Powerful Words and Stories which connect people and their pets. Pets can bring out the best in people. They will teach us valuable lessons, if we let them. Do you have stories about a beloved pet?

Laugh. Laugh again. Laugh some more. Especially at yourself. Go to a comedy club. Watch some of the old comedy shows that made you laugh when you were younger. You can find them all on the internet these days. Carol Burnett, Harvey Korman, Tim Conway, and Vicki Lawrence still crack me up. If I am feeling sad all I have to do is pull up a You Tube clip and I am laughing out loud in less than a minute.

Give of yourself to others. Give your time. Volunteer. Help those less fortunate. Open your heart. Open your mind. In all things, try to be positive. Avoid negativity like it will kill you because it will if you let it. Share your Powerful Words with others.

Lastly, love yourself. You are not some pitiful, worthless creature to be loathed and despised, deserving of the worst the world has to offer. You are a luminous being, a child of the Universe. My God, there is only one of you. Laugh, love, live.

Do not deny yourself the wonders life in the world has to offer. You were born with God given talents and abilities which will allow you to improve any circumstance if you will but choose to do so. You may have forgotten this, but I haven't. That is why I written this for you. It's your turn to Transform.

How is your spiritual health? Ask yourself what you can do today to enhance your spirituality?


# Let Everyone Know...

If you are already doing what I'm about to suggest then you are fully engaged in living. I don't have to tell you to keep going because you will never stop.

If, not, will you make this commitment to yourself? **I am going to show myself, God (my Higher Power), and my fellow human beings what I am able to accomplish with the natural set of talents and abilities that I have been given.**

This is a very important milestone to reach. We all have God given natural talents and abilities. They may be identical, similar, or completely different than another's talents and abilities. But, we all possess them.

We all employ different ways of looking at the world and operating within its bounds. We all amass different life experiences. We all choose different paths as we travel through life. We make different choices. Nothing else will reflect our differences more than the choices we make. Nothing will reflect the similarities we share more than...

The composite of all of these different facets of ourselves make us singularly unique in this world. That is a marvelous thing! I am awe struck in the full reckoning of it - that as much as we are the same, we are all different. All 7+ billion of us.

In this step of transformation are the words, "what I am able to accomplish." Now some might consider accomplishment to always mean success. I do not. It means demonstrating your commitment in transforming our life.

It means you have begun to take action. You have crawled out of your comfort zone and you are doing something, taking action on your plans for change. It means that whether your efforts meet with success or whether your efforts are less than successful makes no difference. You will be accomplishing something either way.

We learn by doing. We learn by our mistakes. We have success and we learn from those. We have less than stellar moments when things don't go well and we learn from those.

If you believe struggle produces tangible benefits, even if you should lose, then to struggle and lose or to struggle and win is to win twice. To end a struggle before there is a clear loss or win is twice the loss.

When we lose we should pick up, redress, retool, restart, redesign, redeploy, realign, readjust and we try again and we learn form that. Sometimes we create opportunities for a more positive outcome (my new term for failure) and we learn from those.

If you are learning in this way then you are acquiring knowledge. This is one of the very definitions of accomplishment - any acquired ability or **knowledge**. If you are doing, you are accomplishing.

This step also asks you to show God (or Higher Power), yourself and others what you can accomplish. This is important. I believe it to be our mission in life. I believe it is irresponsible and a universal injustice to squander our natural talents and abilities. We should seek out our talents, polish them, hone them, employ them to the best of our abilities and then put them on full display, as long as we draw breath.

I cringe inside when I hear someone say they are going to retire and quit working. Why would anyone want to do that? If you have found your passion for purposeful work in life then only you can do what you do in the way that you do it. Why would you withhold your talents and abilities from the world in that way?

By helping yourself be what you are meant to be and do what you are meant to do you will ultimately help others, which will ultimately help yourself, which will ultimately help still more others....

Showing God, yourself and others what you are able to accomplish with your natural talents and abilities is not a self-congratulatory exercise in affirmation. It is not showing off. It's showing the world your gratitude!

It is one thing to envision change and then roll it around in your head. It is something quite different to say it out loud to someone. In a way, keeping planned changes to yourself is giving yourself permission not to act on them.

Whether it is, as Dan Miller puts it, "comfortable misery", fear of failure, fear of criticism, fear of rejection or fear of losing control, undisclosed desires or plans for change is a recipe for stagnation and maintaining the status quo.

We need the influence, support, guidance, advice, and constructive criticism of those we care about and those who care about us. The only way that can be of benefit to us is through disclosing our desires, goals and plans for needed change.

The only people you should not share with are those that seem preoccupied with holding you back, the chronic nay-saying nattering nabobs and you know who they are. Avoid them like the plague.

There is something liberating about sharing both your fears and excitement about making needed changes in your life. It is a confession of sorts - I don't have it all figured out yet but there are things not right with my life; I know I need to make some changes; in fact I am going to make some changes and here is what I have planned.

Say that to the people who you care about and who honestly care about you and want to see you succeed. They will offer their steadfast support. Thank them and ask them to monitor your progress. Then, ask them to take a step to the side and watch you get to work.

# Powerful Words...

POWER, ACHIEVEMENT, UNDERSTANDING, WILLINGNESS, COMMITMENT, LOST, CREATE, HARDINESS, BALANCE, CRITICISM, PESSIMISM, CYNICISM, PATHWAY, SPIRITUAL, CONNECTEDNESS, PLAY, KINDNESS, EMPATHY, COMPASSION, HONEST, TRUTH, TALENTS, ABILITIES, GRATITUDE, REJECTION and EXCITEMENT are all Powerful Words.

The biggest POWER we possess, we will ever possess throughout our entire lives, is the power of choice. Only we can decide to wield it.

We can choose to buckle beneath all the CRITICISM, PESSIMISM, CYNICISM and REJECTION which has come our way. Or, we can choose HARDINESS, express a WILLINGNESS to change and make an HONEST COMMITMENT to do so.

We can choose BALANCE in our approach to living. We can choose to embrace TRUTH, EMPATHY, KINDNESS, COMPASSION and GRATITUDE as we walk a more SPIRITUAL PATHWAY. In so doing, we increase our UNDERSTANDING of the world and the CONNECTEDNESS we feel one for another keeps us from getting LOST along the way.

We can choose to use our natural TALENTS and ABILITIES to CREATE products and services for the benefit of others which we feel is our highest calling and ACHIEVEMENT.

We can choose to approach each day with EXCITEMENT, safe in the knowledge that we are being and doing what we were called to do, what we were designed to do. Our work has become our PLAY and our play has become our work. We look at the world and say, "Look! Look at what I get to do!" That is, if we choose...

## Your world of words within...

Have you made plans for needed change and shared your plans with others? Or, have you been stuck "thinking about things" for too long? If you haven't found your passion for purposeful work in life, are you looking? If not, why not? What comes to mind here?

_____

What are your perceived barriers? Was there an event in you past, or are there events occurring in your life right now which seem to be holding you back from pursuing your dreams? What thought did you just have? Write it down now before you forget.

_____

Are there individuals in your life who are too critical, pessimistic and cynical? Do you feel rejected in some way? What story about rejection can you tell?

Are you the bounce back kid or do you feel you lack resilience and hardiness? Are you honest when dealing with others? Are you honest with yourself? Do you feel connected to others and the world? Do you nurture your spiritual self?

Write down three things you would like to change most about each of your four realms along with one idea for each to make the change happen.

Your Mental Realm

1. _____

2. _____

3. _____

Your Physical Realm

1. _____

2. _____

3. _____

Your Emotional Realm

1. _____

2. _____

3. _____

Your Spiritual Realm

1. _____

2. _____

3. _____

Do you feel you are you using all of your natural talents and abilities for maximum achievement? Have you found your calling, your purpose in life? If not, does this frustrate you? How? Write your feelings down.

_____

_____

_____

Are you excited to greet the day when you get up in the morning?
Are you excited about what you do, your work? Do you play? Is there
balance in your life? What part of your life needs the most work?
Take some notes down here.

_____

_____

Can you display empathy, compassion, kindness, understanding,
gratitude? Do you?
What thoughts float to the surface when you read those words?

_____

_____

If you are diligent about answering the questions which interest
you, the ones which grab you on an emotional level, then you will
have tapped into some strong emotions connected to some Powerful
Words. Identifying those words will help write your story and the
emotions behind those words will be conserved and maintained.

When you share your Powerful Words and stories with others many
will connect with you on an emotional level. Those individuals are
your kindred spirits, members of your tribe, and you are theirs.

What words of power emerged for you while reading through this
section and answering these questions?

_____

_____

# Your Inner Sanctum

Everyone needs a place to retreat to from time to time. A place that is private, clam, and safe. To prevent being overwhelmed, to stave off stress or to keep from burning out, this becomes an imperative.

Your inner sanctum is where you will connect with the Powerful Words which have helped to shape you as a person. It will be your source for words to help others. From there your thoughts of excellence will flow. If, you give yourself the time to think.

How can this be accomplished with a high pressure, workaday, phrenetical and frenzied life? By taking up residence in your own inner sanctum and being responsible for what happens in there.

A physical retreat would be ideal when things become too much for us, a safe and quiet room or secluded location away from everything and everyone. A place with no radio, television or cell phone. Your own fortress of solitude, a place without interruptions. Wouldn't that be awesome?

This is not often possible in the way we live our lives today. Not to mention the fact you could be completely alone in a quiet room or at some isolated location while still feeling overwhelmed. That's because we live our lives inside our heads. No matter what is going on around us, what is going on in our heads is all that's going on while everything is going on.

Blissful serenity comes from within, not from physical isolation or a destination vacation. That sense of calm and well-being, that place of placid peace and tranquility can only be attained through introspection.

*Introspection - the observation or examination of one's own mental and emotional state, mental processes, etc.; the act of looking within oneself.*

Introspection is when thoughts are turned inward and the self is being considered. It shouldn't be too surprising that to be at peace you must contemplate peace, to become tranquil you must contemplate tranquility, to be serene you must contemplate serenity. We are, in essence, what we think.

Everyone has an inner sanctum, the place we go in our heads to think and to try to make sense of things. Some people meditate there. Some people pray there. Some people simply hide in there. It is where the conscience of our consciousness resides.

Some inner sanctums get more use than others. Some people, the ones that lack self-identity, almost never venture there. The hole they often feel deep inside themselves, the hole in their soul, is an inner sanctum that's empty or scarcely visited.

Getting there, what you are able to accomplish there and what benefit you may derive from being in your inner sanctum is a function of intentional effort, not innate ability. Controlling or altering your thoughts, feelings, mood or emotions will scale one-to-one with your efforts within your inner sanctum. Practice, perseverance and patience are key, I'm told.

I have known people who are so practiced at getting into their inner sanctum and what happens there that they can lower their heart rate and blood pressure just by thinking about doing so. There are well documented instances where individuals can raise or lower their core temperature, ameliorate pain or completely calm themselves just by connecting with their inner sanctum through mental imagery.

It isn't rocket science. It isn't voodoo. It isn't paranormal activity. It is a matter of training and force of will.

For practiced individuals, things could be literally and completely crashing down around them and they would sit calm, cool and collected if they chose. For them, it is a choice. They didn't get this way overnight. It took a lot of effort, patience and practice. But, they are testaments to what is possible.

I am not that good at what comes from being in my inner sanctum, not yet anyway. Personal need has driven me to spend more time and effort there through quiet reflection or meditation. I can see the benefits of visiting my inner sanctum more often and of putting in more effort there.

# Powerful Words...

INTROSPECTION, PEACE, PRACTICE and PERSEVERENCE are Powerful Words.

Powerful Thoughts, Powerful Words and Powerful Stories reside within, and will emanate from, your inner sanctum. INTROSPECTION will be the means of developing your inner sanctum. Give yourself time each day to reflect on your life, what it was like, what happened, what it is like now and how you want your life to unfold going forward. Write down the thoughts which inspire you.

Self-identity is the key to understanding your place in the world. You can discover who you are in your inner sanctum if you are willing, honest and open. Knowing who you truly are is the pathway to inner PEACE.

Like every new skill, developing your inner sanctum and discovering self-identity requires PRACTICE and PERSEVERANCE. It is hard for to me to imagine what can not be accomplished with the actions twins practice and perseverance.

# Your world of words within...

Are you introspective? Do you have an inner retreat that provides needed benefit in times of stress? Are you able to control how you react to life's stresses, turmoil, upsets, disappointments and tragedies?

If not, I would spend some time and effort on developing your inner sanctum and what happens there. This can be an ongoing part of developing one's spiritual realm. If you are to find inner peace, you will find it there. Remember, practice and perseverance are required for this or any endeavor.

Are you at peace? Circle one: Do you meditate?   **YES   NO**

If no, what is the number one reason? _____

What can you do today which would get you past your objection? If you have questions about the practice, a little research on the internet might be in order.

Do you feel you know who you are? Do you feel you know your place in the world? If not, I can't answer those questions for you. No one can. That is your journey and no one else's.

I can tell you this. If you want to know the answers, it is paramount you ask yourself these questions and often - Who am I? Why am I here? It is estimated by some that only 10% of the population feels as though they have a sense of who they truly are which is self-identity (self-concept).

Knowing who you are, your place in the world, your natural talents and abilities, your purpose for living, what you like, what you don't like and being able to express these to others is everyone's journey.

Most people will live out their entire lives never knowing this about themselves. Since there is only one of each of us in the universe, it is a tragedy of cosmic proportions. If you do not know these things about yourself don't waste another minute waiting to find out. Begin! Sail on in your personal voyage of self-discovery.

# The Upside of My Downside

We all hate loss, of any kind. None of us would choose to lose our money, possessions health, a job, a loved one, our youth, a beloved pet, our reputation, a business, our zest for living, a marriage, a friend. Yet, sooner or later, we all will. It is an unpleasant fact of life.

It is probably human nature to view loss as something to be dreaded or feared or as something to be avoided if at all possible. Is it? Should it be? I am beginning to wonder if the downside of life is really the upside in disguise. Should, loss be something we embrace?

When I hit my rocky bottom as an active alcoholic, almost every direction I looked was up. I mean, I could have fallen a little further down the scale, but from which there may have been no recovery.

From my perspective, at the bottom I found hope, then a peace, and eventually a new happiness. I clung to them as a drowning man would a lifeline. I changed. I had a miraculous transformation. I was lifted up past all of the rot and decay until I could see with clarity what I had become, where I had been, where I mean never to return.

In sobriety the good rained down on me in unexpected ways. No longer stagnant, I recovered. I grew. Then I prospered. What can now be said of my decent into alcoholism? Without the downside, I would not have had the upside.

One might naturally ask, couldn't you have achieved all that you have without the foray into alcoholism? Yes. No. I don't know. It was just how life unfolded for me. Or, that is not the way I unfolded my life.

Life is a series of choices. We choose well, we are rewarded. If we choose poorly, are we also not rewarded by the experience? Do we not gain knowledge and insight? Is our mental metal not tempered? Are we not propelled forward to try again and do better the next time? Isn't adversity our friend?

The answer to all of these questions is yes. If, and only if, we so choose. There it is again. Choice presents itself once more.

Consider this then. If we choose well we are rewarded. If we choose poorly and lose. But, if we choose to learn from failure and grow and come back stronger than before then, looking back, which was the better path for us to take?

If you say the latter, wouldn't the downside pathway of loss actually be your pathway to a higher upside? I can say without hesitation or equivocation that I am better off now than before my great slide into hopeless despair. The upside of my downside has been nothing short of breathtaking.

I had similar results after I burned out as a family physician and after a devastating divorce. In each instance I found my way out of a kind of darkness and into a new and exciting life full of light, fulfillment and happiness. Those paths were unknown to me until circumstance led the way.

## Powerful Words...

LOSS and ADVERSITY are Powerful Words.

I believe at some point all of us will graduated from UA, the University of ADVERSITY. I spent the first two thirds of my life thinking adversity was all downside. I completely discounted the upside of adversity until I kept being faced with it.

Looking back I can see where substantial gains came to me through adversity. They were times of strengthening and growth, points in my life where I was pushed onto different and exciting paths I might not have chosen for myself.

Yes, it is true that as we age life stops handing us things and begins to take them away. Particularly in the later years it can seem like an unremitting series of losses. Geting older isn't just about LOSS. It is also a time of tremendous gains.

How you see adversity and loss is a mixture of choice, attitude, expectations and perspective. The key word here is choice.

# Your world of words within...

Loss is one of the most powerful of Powerful Words. What losses have you had which have changed your life for the better in unexpected ways? List some of them here.

_____

_____

_____

_____

When you here the word loss, what thoughts come to mind? What choices did you make from your loss? What did you learn from them? The power in your story lies only in the telling. Jot down some notes for later here.

_____

_____

_____

_____

What adversity have you seen in your life? Did the adverse event weaken you or strengthen you? Did it steel your resolve or steal you power? What are you thinking right now? Write down your thoughts.

_____

_____

Anyone with significant adversity or loss in their life have powerful emotions that came along for the ride. Those emotions are connected to Powerful Words, the words you would use to describe those events. Get those events recorded or down on paper so you can begin to share your stories in a way which will help others.

_____

_____

_____

_____

_____

_____

# RESILIENCE

A re you a resilient person? One aspect of being transformed means having the quality of resilience which simply means possessing the ability to recover from adversity.

Lacking resilience can leave people stuck, paralyzed to the point of being unable to move forward. Everyone should have this trait because the consequences of a lack of resilience can rob you of a brighter future.

Difficulty, tragedy, hardship, suffering will come to everyone in one form or another if you live long enough. That is just living life on life's terms. We might not have a choice in the bad stuff that may come our way in life, but we do have a choice in how we respond.

Being able to adapt, cope, adjust, confront, carry on, endure, survive, move on or move forward, these are all qualities of resilience. I see too many people who lack resilience get stuck. They suffer the same tragedy or the same trauma over and over again. They stop growing. They stop enjoying life. They stop trying to better themselves. It doesn't have to be that way.

There are several steps you can take in order to become resilient or to strengthen resilience. Just know that what works for one may not work for all and no strategy will work right away. As with any skill, learning to be resilient takes time, practice and patience. But, this is very doable for anyone with a desire to transform into a better way of living.

# Here are 9 ways to build resilience:

- **Build self-awareness.** Stay in touch with how you feel. Suppressing negative emotions is not adequately dealing with them. People often avoid painful feelings because, well, they're painful. But, when you feel ready it is best to face emotional pain head on in order move on. If negative emotions aren't dealt with adequately they will just keep reappearing and leave you stuck.

- **Hold on to the big picture.** Whatever happens try to put things in perspective. How many times has something bad happened to you in your past and you thought, "My life is over"? Yet, more often than not those unwanted episodes in your life turned out to be the best thing for you at the time. You just didn't realize it when the bad times were happening.

- **Let time be your friend.** I had a terrible tragedy happen to me a little over two years ago. It was worse than bad. It was mind numbingly, shockingly devastating. But, I knew that I wasn't going to feel that way forever. Just knowing that offered some relief. It would have been easy to continue to wallow in self-indulgent pity but there is just no future in that, and I knew it. Time does heal all wounds, if we allow it to happen. Allow time and perspective to work their magic for you.

- **Get moving.** I tell this to patients every day. Your legs are connected to your brain. If your legs are moving you forward that means your brain is moving forward. Whenever you exercise there are neurotransmitters that are released like dopamine, endorphins, encephalin, epinephrine and others. These make your brain feel good which will make you feel better. They help relieve anxiety and depression. Exercise works as well as our best medicines for treating mood disorders.

- **Learn acceptance.** You may as well. You can choose to deny what is happening or what has happened to you but that will not allow you to live in Realville. Acceptance is giving your self permission to move forward. Acceptance will be a biter pill to swallow at times but just like any medicine, it may be bitter at first but then you get better.

- **Set goals and move toward them.** I believe this is one huge factor in letting go of tragedy. Setting goals and moving toward them requires forward motion. Early on, this provides the distraction the brain needs in order to move forward. In the fullness of time, attaining goals that were set during tragedy provides the context necessary for closure. This has worked in my own life.

- **Be optimistic, avoid negativity.** It easy to talk down when you are down. Talking up will lift you up, even if just a small amount. When things seem to be crashing in on you, be as positive as you can be and reach out to the positive and uplifting people in your life. They will help hold you up even when you don't feel like standing. You are as you think.

- **Have a strong social network.** I don't know what I would have done were it not for family, friends and colleagues when my life seemed to implode. Having a strong social network makes all the difference in being resilient. Also, as you draw strength from others you will be in a better position to one day return the favor to those you know that are in need.

- **Be kind to yourself.** No, you aren't perfect. No one is so allow your self that. If you're feeling broken, become whole again by taking care of your four realms- the mental, emotional, physical and spiritual.

These are just some of the many ways to build and strengthen resilience. Can you think of others?

# Powerful Words...

RESILIENCE, PATIENCE, ACCEPTANCE and STRENGTH are Powerful Words.

RESILIENCE and hardiness are learned behaviors. We are not born with these attributes, we acquire them. If we lose them, we can reacquire them. If someone has never acquired them and has poor coping skills it is more difficult to develop them but not impossible. It would require a transformation.

Slowly, reluctantly, I have come to view adversity as my friend. I have found if I am PATIENT and head the lessons which come from adversity, I find STRENGTH, opportunity and personal growth. These sound much better to me than crumbling into a heap and taking up residence there.

ACCEPTANCE can be a powerful positive or negative influence in one's life depending on one's choices. Is accepting defeat a bad thing if it prompts you to abandon what isn't working in favor of what will, if it moves you on toward growth or greatness? Is acceptance good if you accept you are less than you really are based on someone else's definition? Is it powerful to accept life as infinite source of possibilities waiting for you to experience?

Acceptance of life's lessons taught on life's terms is perhaps the hardest lesson of all. Acceptance of this lesson does make for a smother ride which conserves time, energy and resources. I suppose one could spend time, energy and resource railing against the consequences of poor choices, events one can never control or blaming the universe for how it is constructed. I choose the pathway of acceptance.

# Your world of words within...

Do you feel resilient? Are beaten down by adversity or have you bounced back from adversity? Where do you find your strength to persevere in the face of adversity?

Are you a patient person or do you lack patience? How has this affected your life? What lessons have you learned from acceptance?

Answering these questions will unleash Powerful Words. Either the words which may be holding you back or words which will propel you forward. You should focus on the words which resonate with you the most on an emotional. These are the words to share for healing and to heal.

Powerful Words encountered or uncovered in this section are:

_____

_____

_____

_____

_____

_____

_____

_____

_____

_____

_____

_____

# TIME
/////////////////

## Einstein Was Right...

E instein was right. How time is perceived and measured depends on one's frame of reference. Time seems to fly by when times are great, as if it were compressed. Doesn't it? Conversely, as we lose themselves in our troubles time seems to stand still and never end, as if it has been dilated or expanded.

Everyone has used the phrase, "I don't have time." Sometimes we don't. Sometimes we do. It is an easy thing to say when we just really don't want to do something. They are Powerful Words everyone recognizes because everyone uses them and the message they convey is universal.

We all prioritize our daily lives. We make time for those things we feel are important. Everyone has a mental list of things which need to be done on some timeline. Some are more important than others. As time goes by we edit the list, removing items we feel have become less important and adding others we feel have now become more important.

We make choices when editing our list of priorities. Sometimes, we suffer consequences as a result of the choices we make. Sometimes we like to blame others for the choices we make by putting them in charge of our list of priorities.

Others take full responsibility for their list and conduct their lives accordingly. They have learned the truth. They accept they are the only one in charge of their list of priorities.

If you hear yourself saying, "I don't have time", you aren't taking responsibility of your own priorities list. You are making those words more powerful that they actually are. Remember, we always make time for those things we feel are important.

Here are two more Powerful Words than those - "I can."

# But what if.....?

*Yesterday is history, tomorrow is a mystery. All we have is today and it is a gift. That is why it is called the PRESENT. - Alice Morse Earle*

But what if I, or he, or she, or you, hadn't done that? How much better would my life be? I should've done this, I should've done that. She or he should've done that but not this. He or she should've done this but not that. You should've done this and that, but you shouldn't have done that or this.

Did you hear that?

But what if I run out of money, don't get that job, don't get that promotion, don't get that person to love me, don't get that vacation home, don't get that bass boat, don't get that new purse? What if I get sick? What if I don't get sober?

Well wait just a minute! I'm going to get sober, some day. Just not today. Even before I get sober I'm going to make a bunch of money and become famous and then you'll be sorry! You'll all be sorry! I'll get perfect revenge on all the people holding me back (everyone I know).

I'm going to get out of this hell hole and find someone who appreciates me. ME! I'll move to a big city, get a big house and a big shinny new car. I'll be able to sing and dance and I'll be the life of the party. I'll learn a foreign language and write a book. I will meet the woman/ man of my dreams who will never leave me and see to my every need.

The wonderful caring, compassionate, loyal, all knowing, all seeing, self-sacrificing, totally lovable person that I am and everybody will love me. LOVE ME! And when I fart, it will smell like cotton candy and pink butterflies are going to fly out my butt and.....

There it is again. I know you heard it this time. It's the universe saying "blah blah blah blah blah....."

I don't know how many atoms there are spinning around and round in the universe right now. But outside of ourselves, none of them care very much about you or me. The only person in this big old universe that can simultaneously care about you and can control what you think, how you think, how you act, how you react, and what you feel, is you!

It is a sobering fact. If our lives are going to improve it must come from within ourselves. Not from our past, not from our future, but from the here and now and from our inner self.

Referencing the quote at the top of the page, I think Alice Morse Earle

was a pretty smart woman. What she was referring to is our tendency to focus on what is behind us that has already happened and is therefore unchangeable.

Or, on what is ahead in our future that hasn't yet happened and is therefore also unchangeable rather than focusing on what is right in front of us in the here and now. What is doable now? What can be changed now?

In his brilliantly insightful book, Choose Yourself, James Altucher describes obsessing over past or future events as "time traveling". He writes:

*"Most people obsess on regrets in their past or anxieties in their future. I call this time traveling. The past and future don't exist. They are memories and speculation, neither of which you have any control over. You don't need to time travel anymore. You can live right now."*

He is absolutely right. Everybody does this to some extent but certain conditions will further amplify this time traveling effect. A bad relationship, a toxic work environment, economic worries, an unfulfilling life. Those of you that have been addicted, whether or not you are in recovery, will also know what I am talking about.

When I was an active alcoholic, I would drink over regrets which only served to entrench and reinforce them. Or, I would drink and dream up make believe magical thinking scenarios where life was wonderful. Of course, in all of those scenarios I was still able to drink while having an inexhaustible supply of alcohol.

I made grand plans but never stopping drinking long enough to make any of them happen. With one foot in the past and one foot in the future, it is impossible to live any semblance of a normal life in the present.

I scuba dive and divers are always looking for clear blue waters in which to dive. There is always much discussion about visibility for a particular dive site. People will ask, was the visibility good? How many feet of visibility did you have?

It ranks high on the list of concerns that a diver has in mind when considering a dive site. So much so that visibility is often the deciding factor when considering a dive destination. If the visibility is poor people will often reject the site outright.

I felt the same way until I took a Low Visibility Diving course. The course's focus was diving in low visibility circumstances where because of silt or particulate matter in the water sometimes all you can see is just what is in front of you. I took the course mainly for safety purposes so that I would know what to do and what not to do in case I found myself in low visibility conditions.

In the first lecture the course instructor said something surprising, something that I hadn't considered. He said that low visibility diving is often the most interesting form of diving. This was 180° opposite of what I felt to be true.

He explained that when the water is crystal clear divers tend to scan around haphazardly, darting their eyes from one field of view to the next without taking the time to look for the small things that are easily missed and right in front of them. But when visibility is low it forces you to look at what is directly in front of you.

The end result is that you are able to capture much greater detail. He was absolutely right. Putting on blinders might not be that bad after all if they help us exclude what we can never control - the past and the future.

If you currently feel stuck in your current circumstances then I am 100% certain you are time traveling. If you are time traveling, you can choose to stop. It might be difficult at first but it is possible. You can free yourself from the bondage of the past and future by focusing on what is directly in front of you and living in the present. Accept it as the gift it was meant to be.

Do now what is doable now. Enjoy now what is enjoyable now. Fix now what is fixable now.

# Powerful Words...

TIME, RESPONSIBILITY and CONTROL are Powerful Words.

Concerning TIME Delmore Schwartz wrote, *"Time is the fire in which we burn."* If we can stick with this metaphor, which I think is brilliant, then we should all strive to burn as brightly as we can without burning out. I never want to just smolder. I doubt you would either, dear reader.

If you are smoldering and haven't yet caught fire or if you are burned out and need to reignite with passion and purpose, just remember you are in CONTROL. It is the RESPONSIBILITY of every individual to control their own destiny to the extent we can. It is the only destiny we can control.

# Your world of words within...

Are you time traveling, living in the past or in the future, spending little time between in the present? Do you feel you are in control of your time? Have you given up that power to someone else? Have you taken responsibility for your own destiny?

Powerful events and forces in our lives can cause us to squander too much of precious time. I have often said, I have spent the first two thirds of my life figuring out how best to live the last third.

Are there stories or events you can recall from your past which stand in your way. If so, there are powerful words associated with those events. The emotion underlying those events is probably continuing to dishonor your core values. It doesn't have to be this way. Get those stories out and begin to share them. In doing so you will find the strength from within yourself and from others to make needed change. Make some notes here now.

_____

_____

_____

_____

If you have taken responsibility for this one life you have been given, if you have learned to control your time in a way which is beneficial for both yourself and others, if you are burning brightly with passion and purpose then share the stories of how this came to be. Your stories will contain the Powerful Words others need to hear so they do not waste their life just smoldering. You can help to ignite them. What Powerful Words can you share with them?

_____

_____

_____

_____

Write down the Powerful Words which hold special meaning for you. Look for them in what you read, listen for them in conversation. You will resonate with them and they will strengthen the core of your being.

# Don't Worry About Being A Pro (for now), Unless You Already Are

## What is holding you back, technical difficulty or mental barrier?...

**M**any of us have given up on ideas or dreams in the past because the work involved seemed too difficult. I know I have. But, was the subject too difficult? Was it really technical difficulty we faced or was it just a mental barrier we placed

in our own path?

Many people may shy away from a subject simply because they feel it to be too technically difficult for them to master even though they may feel drawn to the subject or carry some affinity for it. Should we feel justified in doing this?

In 2014 I attended the Podcast Movement convention in Dallas, Texas. I heard many great speakers and one remark stood out in my mind. If you happen to have a passion for a particular subject and you read, fully absorb and understand two or three books on that subject then you will know 90% more than 90% of people who have just a passing interest in the subject. By definition, that makes you an expert.

In his book Mastery, Robert Greene recounts the tale of a self-taught groundbreaking linguist who discovered what prevents people from learning is not the subject itself *"but rather certain learning disabilities that tend to fester and grow in our minds as we get older."*

He goes on to state what everyone who has a mind should already know but too few remember, *"The human mind has limitless capabilities."*

People may also feel inferior when it comes to mastering a subject because they do not have some sort of degree in their area of interest and feel they have no right to declare themselves an expert without one. Are degrees necessary in order to become an expert in a particular topic or field of study? Where do these self-doubts come from? What gives rise to them?

This sense of inferiority could actually work in your favor as long as you don't give up when attempting to master new knowledge. Mr. Greene explains why in his book.

Small children lack the ability to care and provide for themselves which is why they depend on their parents for survival. As a result, they feel inferior. Rather than a negative, this is a positive inducement for learning.

This feeling of inferiority is what drives children to learn. Instead of avoiding a difficult subject or task and labeling it too difficult to attempt, they remain open and hungry for new knowledge. They pay greater attention, experiment, adapt and learn quickly and more deeply at a young age.

As adults, we set aside our child-like sense of wonder and curiosity in favor of other more grownup (or so we think) concerns like jobs, rent, bills, status or money. We feel superior, become smug and rigid with minds that are closed off and filled with hubris.

We feel we already know what is real and true and possible. This closes our minds off to other possibilities. We become indoctrinated with a fear of the different or of the unknown.

There is hope for this stagnating and soul sucking condition. Humans have an inborn trait called neoteny which are the mental and physical traits of immaturity and we all carry these traits into adulthood. In other words, we can become child-like again in our approach to learning. These traits can be called upon at anytime. It is a choice!

We have within each of us the ability to return to a child-like state with a sense of awe and wonder, to reacquaint ourselves with the spirit of out inner child. We can become curious again. When we do, we can learn whatever we set our minds to learn.

Reuniting with our inner child, and no longer happy with the status quo, we will boldly acquire new knowledge with adventuresome abandon. We will learn more deeply and completely, even master, the subjects that interest us. Why, because children know there are no barriers and everything is possible.

# Powerful Words...

BARRIER, EXPERT, MASTERY, LEARNING, ADAPT, CURIOSITY and WONDER are Powerful Words.

There are is no longer any real BARRIER to LEARNING, becoming an EXPERT or MASTERY of a subject or discipline because of the World Wide Web. The Internet has changed everything. All knowledge is there, just a mouse click away.

If you have an abiding CURIOSITY and sense of WONDER about you then there is no end to what you can learn. What is now possible for anyone was nearly impossible for nearly everyone just 50 years ago. Curiosity and wonder can set people on fire with a fever to innovate.

Use these words to your advantage when considering your next steps. If you have any hurdles in front of you check to make sure you did not put them there and whether or not they are real or imagined.

# World of words from within...

Have you boldly gone after your goals, acquiring whatever you have needed to succeed? Are you curious about the world and your place in it? Have you retained your sense of wonder? What Powerful Words or stories can you share to help others who may have stalled?

_____

_____

_____

_____

# Perfectly imperfect...

*Perfect is the enemy of good. - Voltaire*

Perfectionism is a quality often ascribed to physicians of a certain common personality type. It kind of goes with the territory. I'm a physician. I don't think I am perfect although, I would like to be. It would be nice to avoid making mistakes when dealing with patients.

If a physician or other healthcare provider doesn't ascribe to perfectionism then it is certainly foisted on them by the medical establishment lest they should make a mistake. Who doesn't want to give or receive perfect care? Never mind that it is impossible.

We should all have a desire to succeed with excellence. Having high standards can bring out our best and push us to grow our capabilities. But reasonable expectations and standards should be applied when considering the notion of perfection. If being a redneck is a glorious lack of sophistication, as Jeff Foxworthy suggests, then being human is a glorious lack of perfection.

There are two types of perfectionists. There are those with a healthy amount of perfectionist tendencies and then there are the neurotic perfectionists. Normal perfectionists will set realistic goals and standards for themselves and then obtain pleasure from the work needed to achieve them. They are not easily discouraged by failure which does not compromise their self-esteem.

Neurotic perfectionists will set unrealistic goals for themselves while demanding an unobtainable level of performance. Either their goals are outright unachievable or the effort involved is extremely difficult. Either way, they will view their efforts and performance outcomes as unsatisfactory.

Near continuous disappointment with their efforts will lead to overwhelming feelings of failure. At the same time, they will look down on others who do not subscribe to their level of perfectionism. It is very easy for the neurotic perfectionist to be critical of others. They will even blame others for their failures reasoning that they some how got in the way of their success.

Procrastination often becomes a tool for the perfectionist in order to prevent future disappointment and further feelings of failure. Been there, done that, bought a T-shirt.

Perfectionists walk around in a constant state of anxiety. As unrealistic expectations, failure, fear of failures, incomplete tasks and never begun tasks mount the anxiety worsens. Little wonder that many will seek relief or escape through spending, an endless string of relationships, drugs, alcohol or some other addictive behavior. Of course, the effects are only temporary and life never gets better, only worse.

Do you think you are a normal perfectionist or a neurotic one? Ask yourself the following questions. Do you have trouble meeting your own expectations? Do you often feel frustrated, angry, anxious, depressed or inadequate when trying to meet your own expectations? Have you ever been told that you set expectations too high for yourself?

Do the standards and expectations you set for yourself get in the way of your activities of daily living like starting or finishing tasks, meeting deadlines, being spontaneous, relaxing, etc? Have you experienced negative consequences from perfectionist behaviors?

If you answered yes to one or more of these questions then you are expressing neurotic perfectionism. If you answered yes to all of them, get help now!

If you are too much the perfectionist it will slow your growth and stifle progress. Whatever you are trying to produce, sale, create, or provide, forget being perfect. You won't be. It is okay to make mistakes, learn form them and continue to move forward.

The biggest impediment I see to progress due to perfectionism is inability to start. Arrested development can be the only outcome. The perfectionist senses they will not be able to perform perfectly so there is a failure to begin, to take risks. This is not only the wrong thing to do, it is the exact opposite of the right thing to do.

There are things you can begin to do to mitigate and ameliorate the negative impact of neurotic perfectionism. Of course, I'm not talking about trying to be perfect in one's work. We should always strive to produce the best product or provide the best service we can at all times. I'm talking about in everyday living.

All of the following suggestions are just a starting point. Most are more easily said than done, just like stopping a bad habit or an addiction. In the extreme, professional help might be necessary but small changes now can add up to big changes over time.

Begin to step back and look at the big picture of things and ask yourself these questions.

- Whatever task you may be obsessing over doing perfectly at the present time, will it really matter if you don't do it perfectly?
- What is the worst that can happen if you don't?
- If the worst does happen will you perish or will you survive? Survive right?
- Will it matter next week, next month, next year, or a generation from now if you don't do something perfectly? Will anyone notice?
- One year ago today, what bit of perfectionism were you obsessing over then? Don't know, do you? That is my point.

Begin to compromise with yourself and lower your standards for certain tasks. Accept some level of imperfection that you can tolerate. Begin to be less critical of others. Realize that if you can't always be perfect, neither can anyone else.

Begin to face what makes you anxious. If crooked pictures make you anxious, go over to a wall and nudge one until it is visibly crooked and leave it that way. After a while, notice that the world did not spin off its axis, nobody died, nobody left you and nobody called you worthless, stupid, inept, ignorant or incompetent. Those were always just our own voices inside our own heads calling us those names.

Move something out of perfect alignment on your desk, throw a piece of paper on the floor in your office and leave it there for an entire day. Wear something wrinkled or with a stain on it. Don't comb your hair for a day. Misspell something you typed on purpose and don't correct it.

One by one we will take on the constraints of perfectionism and stop the self-inflicted pain. Then, you will come know a new freedom and a new happiness. It is a better place in which to dwell where I am 100% sure we are all perfectly imperfect.

## Powerful Words...

PERFECTIONISM, EXCELLENCE, SELF-ESTEEM, PERFORMANCE and EXPECTATIONS are Powerful Words.

PERFECTIONISM is the bane of the imperfect. If you let it, perfectionism will strap you down and keep you stalled behind the start line. You can be great without being perfect. In fact, you can be excellent. EXCELLENCE does not mean perfect nor has it ever.

All perfectionism does is dent our SELF-ESTEEM. For our best PERFORMANCE we shouldn't set our EPECTATIONS too high for perfect. Of course, we should in all our endeavors strive to do our very best. At the same time we can accept we are human and allow our imperfections. It is the human thing to do.

## World of words from within...

Have you dealt with perfectionist tendencies? Have you overcome them? If so, do you have a story to share? If you are still battling perfectionist behavior, could you share how this has affected your life and what you plans are to change?

_____

_____

How would you rate your performance at work? In your relationships? Has low self-esteem been an issue for you?

Are there Powerful Words associated with powerful emotions you can feel as you answer these questions? Write down any thoughts you may be having about this right now. You may need to explore them further later on.

_____

_____

_____

_____

# CHANGE

*W*hen it becomes more difficult to suffer than to change... you will change. -
Robert Anthony

## Nothing Stays the Same...

*He who rejects change is the architect of decay. The only human institution which rejects progress is the cemetery. - Harold Wilson*

Nothing stays the same, ever. But most people want things to stay the same forever. Why? Where does that come from when it is completely outside of the human experience? I don't know.

Change is inevitable. Since it is inevitable, I believe it is better to try and choose our changes rather than have change choose us. It is a matter of planning and being proactive and intentional in our actions.

It is always nice to have options or choices. They are branch points on the decision tree of life that allow us to exercise some measure of control over our destiny. Sometimes options are numerous and we can pick our direction leisurely and without a lot of attendant anxiety.

Sometimes, our options are severely limited and we are forced to make hard choices. We have all been in the undesirable position of having to "choose the lesser of two evils". But, wasn't it a series of option choices that put us there in the first place?

Ideally, it would be best to have more and better options most of the time and fewer instances where options are wholly constrained in scope with only frighteningly dreadful choices remaining. We can choose to act and be different, everyday.

*You must be the change you wish to see in the world. - Mahatma Gandhi*

# Variations in Sameness...

Do you sometimes feel that you are just going through the motions, existing instead of living? Are you doing the same things over and over again yet expecting different results, finding that over and over again nothing ever changes? Isn't that the definition of insanity? Or, does it feel like the new normal?

Ask yourself; are you what and where you want to be? If not, do you know what and where you want to be? If so, how do you translate from what and where you are now to what and where you want to be? In other words, how do you transform yourself into the desired difference?

These are the questions I have struggled with many times during my life. I spent a great deal of time stumbling through life trying to do what was expected of me by others. As a young adult, I never fully explored my full potential. I played it safe for so long that I became accustomed to the variations in sameness.

I rebelled and broke out of my state of variable sameness only once, by becoming an alcoholic. That didn't work either. I became locked into the variations of sameness of my addiction. Wake up, promise myself I would not drink that day, drink myself into oblivion by that evening, get up and do it all over again the next day. Insanity!

I eventually became sober and so I was forced to begin to work on myself. I began to care for my mental and spiritual realms right away as part of my program of recovery, in order to stay sober. I addressed my physical and emotional realms much later but never to the same degree. But, I was at least headed in the right direction.

Somewhere along the line though, I stopped progressing. Oh, I stayed sober but I stopped developing as a human being. I never kept at improving myself beyond doing what was necessary to ensure my sobriety and to meet my responsibilities and obligations. I stopped exploring.

I stopped learning new things and picking up new skills. I stopped pursuing any course of action that could have taken me to the next level in my development. I became stagnant and stuck.

I slipped back into a life, no, an existence of variations in sameness. Everyday I went to work, did my job well, came home, was a good husband, earned money, bought stuff, got up the next day and did it all over again. All the while, I never felt my work to be a perfect fit for me. I was doing but I wasn't creating using all of my natural talents and abilities.

In February of 2012, something happened. Something terrible that I thought I could not survive. It shook me to my very foundation. I didn't go back to drinking but that only meant I felt all of what I was going through. Every bit of it and it was all painfully and poetically toxic. I felt perfectly broken.

Things are much better now but because of what I went through, something changed. It wasn't one moment of clarity or some kind of instant epiphany. No, it was a slow realization that life was trying to tell me something. I began to pay attention. It was time to break free of variations in sameness.

I heard the message loud and clear – Clark it is time to learn, time to grow, time to aspire, time to explore, time to develop, time to give, time to transform, time to discover your true passion and purpose in life using the set of natural talents and abilities that you have been given.

This is now my mission in life today, tomorrow, day after day after day. I have traded variations in sameness for the permanence of change – a transformation.

Are you experiencing variations in sameness? Has something happened to you that you have begun to question your life and what you want from living? If so, maybe life is trying to tell you that it is time to change, time to transform.

## Change is a constant...

Change is everywhere. Isaac Asimov once said "the only constant is change." Sometimes change is welcome. Sometimes it isn't. No one has a perfect life.

Change is often out of our hands, out of our control. It is how we react that determines how we will be affected by change going forward.

Rapid dramatic change is often easier to deal with than slow change over time. Rapid change forces us to react quickly. With slow change we can become complacent or comfortable, even when the change is undesirable. We allow ourselves to be fooled into thinking that this is just the way things are for us. We stop growing. We stagnate. We become stuck.

# I Can't Change This...

It is then that we fall into the trap, the **I Can't Change This** trap. These are Powerful Words, if you choose. The can hold sway over you, dominate you. They can turn into the ultimate arbiter for decision making.

We can reach a point where we feel that we are incapable of changing our circumstances or ourselves. Have you ever felt this way? For most the basis for this is fear.

However, that is just symptomatic of the development of an unfortunate mindset, a mindset that has forgotten how to dream, to welcome challenges, to consider the potential for dynamic growth, to open up to new possibilities. It is very easy to stay in that trap. It is familiar. We know what to expect from it, no matter how undesirable it may be.

So, caught in the trap we get by. In the trap there is no living. We just exist. It takes a tremendous amount of effort to get free of this mindset, this trap. It grips us and holds on to us like grim death. The thought of getting free of the trap brings to mind a single word – impossible. That is how tightly it grips us.

This is why people will stay in dysfunctional homes, loveless marriages, an abusive relationship; hated, despised, dead-end jobs, stop dreaming and pursuing happiness. This is not unlike the alcoholic or addict feeling trapped by their drug of choice. The task of freeing oneself from the trap is just as difficult for the non-addict as the addict freeing themselves form drugs, or the alcoholic freeing themselves from alcohol.

The solution for all that are caught in the trap is simple. But, as I have said many times before, simple doesn't always mean easy. It isn't easy. What it requires is a transformation and I will spell out what that means. It all begins with a willingness to change and a single step.

# The 2%.

No, I'm not talking about a milk product or a socioeconomic segment of our population. I am talking about the percentage of people in my patient population that will radically change their lifestyle in ways necessary to profoundly improve their health.

The percentage of people who are willing to completely TRANSFORM their entire life into something that is more meaningful and purposeful to them is about the same percentage, 2% or less. Tony Robbins says that 70% of those who by his products will never use them and those are the people at least motivated enough to go to his seminars.

Why? What are the reasons for this? You are probably familiar with many of these 10 reasons although, there may be a few you haven't considered:

- **Fear.** Fear of failure mostly. I believe this to be the largest impediment to personal progress. There is no obstacle that anyone can place in front of you larger or more imposing than that of self-generated fear.
- **Procrastination.** This is a form of anxiety over starting or completing a task, especially new or difficult tasks. Ironically, procrastination creates more stress in the end than it alleviates.
- **Lack of Focus and Clarity.** These twin attributes are crucial to begin a transformative change. They supply us with orderly direction, a list of current needs and a defined audience to serve. Focus for clarity, clarify to focus.
- **Lack of self-awareness.** Having this helps define priorities, provide an understanding of an individuals current status and identify areas where change is most needed in order to progress forward. Lacking this leaves you stuck.
- **Improper planning.** Setting goals is absolutely imperative, both little ones and big ones, short-term and long-term.

Most often, people will stall out of the gate because they fail to build in some easier wins that can be obtained in the short run which provides needed momentum.

- **Lack of personal responsibility.** Individuals who look to blame others, including God, for their lack of success or look to others, including God, to provide them with personal success will be forever stuck in Nowhereville.

- **Avoiding accountability.** Accountability keeps us motivated, honest and moving forward toward our goals. Avoiding accountability is a form of self-sabotage.

- **Lazy.** Defined as an aversion or disinclination to work; indolent. As a practicing physician I can tell you with absolute certitude that there is no pill to fix lazy. But, this has never stopped some people from asking me for one.

- **Progress is not measured, acknowledged or celebrated.** All of these need attention. Are you moving forward? Yes? How do you know if you don't measure for progress or have a means for measuring progress? Also, it is not enough just to know from whence you came. Periodically assessing how far you have come provides valuable context. No points are subtracted from success if you dance in the end zone a bit after a win. I think we are supposed to feel good about a success. Don't you?

- **Conventional Inertia.** I coined this term as a substitute for "same'ol same'ol" or "stuck in a rut" descriptions of merely existing rather than living. A rut is like a grave except it is open at both ends. This is the realm of the comfortably miserable, a state of intentional, low expectation stagnation. This condition is perceived as a lower risk environment in which to be but in actuality it carries the highest risk of all. Upwards of 98% of the population suffers from this condition.

Most people want to be part of the 2% but 98% will never work this list in any actionable way. Breaking free of conventional inertia and overcoming the rest of these barriers is certainly possible. People do it everyday. It requires TRANSFORMATIONAL thinking and action.

If you are in the 2% who have transformed your life already, you know this to be true. You have pursued your passions and overcome these barriers one-by-one. You have discovered happiness through the purposeful work of your choosing. You have stood in defiance of fear and conventional inertia and have redefined your life using your natural talents and abilities.

# Powerful Words...

CHANGE, CALRITY, EXPLORE, DEVELOP, CIRCUMSTANCES, LIFESTYLE, FOCUS and ACCOUNTABILITY are Powerful Words.

I have never met anyone, patient or acquaintance, who could not move beyond their CIRCUMSTANCES. LIFESTYLE is a choice. Ones current lifestyle is the culmination of a series of past choices. Ones preferred lifestyle will be the culmination of a series of present and future choices. It is never too late to choose differently.

CHANGE isn't just something which happens to us, is a force we can apply on our own behalf. When deciding on change, it is important to EXPLORE and be open to all options. We arrive at our preferred futures only with CLARITY and FOCUS based on the choices we make.

Personal ACCOUNTABILITY is the only way we advance toward our own goals. Holding others accountable for the choices **we** make as individuals is useless and a waste of mental energy. People quick to blame others for bad outcomes from rotten choices are the last to let someone else lay claim their success. Accountability works both ways in this regard.

DEVELOP a plan to break free of sameness, of convention, of stagnation. Strive to continuously develop yourself. There is a big old world out there to explore and the possibilities seem endless from where I'm standing. Be curious. Ask little and big questions. Learn. Share. Grow.

# Your world of words within...

If you are in the 2% group, which of these attributes were most critical for your success? Which of these did you use best to your advantage? Are there others? What stories come to mind? What Powerful Words of your own choosing concerning change can you share?

_____

_____

_____

_____

If instead you feel you are in the 98% group, the question you have to ask yourself is which of these barriers to transformation are holding you back? Are there others? What has been the most difficult part of change for you? What stories come to mind?

Write them down now. There are Powerful Words holding you back embedded within those stories. They represent emotional barriers to your progress. Don't wait any longer.

_____

_____

_____

_____

Procrastination is a Powerful Word for you if it is keeping you from your preferred future. If fear is keeping you procrastinating, try to identify the source. What actions can you take today to set these aside, to transform your life and join the 2%? What can you do to hold yourself accountable? Are there stories you can tell about any internal struggles you may be having right now?

List five ways you procrastinate along with a strategy to prevent it. Don't wait.

1. _____

2. _____

3. _____

4. _____

5. _____

# THE 800 BILLION POUND
# GORILLA IN YOUR MIND -
# FEAR

## My fears...

Individuals who become physicians (or other healthcare providers) like me live their lives in fear. It starts as soon as someone makes up there mind to become a physician. The first fears are over grades. Are they good enough?

Then college entrance exams. Did I score high enough? Then collegiate fears. Will I get in the right school? Then on to fears over grades in college. Are they good enough? Am I going to pass this test or that course? Then the MCAT exam. Will I do well? Were my scores good enough?

Then fear over getting accepted to medical school. Then fear over grades in medical school, assessments in clinical rotations and scores on board exams. Then fear over the Residency Match. Will I get my first choice in a residency program?

Once in a residency program, that's when the real fear begins. I'm talking sheer, abject, teeth clenching, heart pounding, flop-sweat terror. This can occur during any or all of the following scenarios:

Being unprepared at rounds and getting pimped (questioned) by the  attending.
The first Code Blue you are responsible for running.

The first baby you deliver at three in the morning when there is no one around to help and you're having trouble delivering the shoulder.

Being asked a question for which you have not a clue in grand rounds with all eyes in the room on you.

Being asked a question that you know the answer to in grand rounds except that it's the wrong answer and everyone in the room is staring at you relieved it's you and not them.

Making a mistake that harms or kills someone.

Having to tell a spouse that the love of their life is gone.

Having to tell sons or daughters that their parent is dying or dead.

Having to tell a parent that their child is dead.

If that's not enough, right after the fears of residency begin to recede in the rear view mirror, all of the fears associated with private practice begin to amass. There was always the fear of making a mistake in training but in private practice there is no back-up.

All of the responsibility of diagnosing and treating patients rests squarely on the shoulders of the provider now. Then there are fears that your patients won't like you or your treatment decisions, the fear of chart audits by the payers or the Fed, the fear of OSHA, the fear of government interference and over-regulation, the fear of going bankrupt and the ever present fear of being sued, just to review a few.

Does anyone seriously believe that a person can walk around in this much fear without consequence? This will take a toll on even the most psychologically intact, emotionally balanced and well adjusted mind. Most healthcare providers, hell most humans, aren't that well put together.

Unrelenting fear contributes to physician burnout which has become epidemic. The hallmarks of burnout are emotional exhaustion, depersonalization and a lack of personal accomplishment. Burnout rates among some physician specialties is approaching 70%.

One recent survey showed 45.8% of physician respondents reported a least one symptom of burnout. Suicide rates among healthcare providers is six times higher than the general population and climbing. Throw in a full-on addiction and conditions can go from bad to worse in a very quick hurry.

I should know. As you have learned, I am a recovering alcoholic and I've been burned out as a physician which is why the subject job burnout has become a specialty of mine. I knew from what I learned dealing with my own burnout, I could use to help others.

Although, burnout rates may be different for other professions, the hallmarks, interventions, treatment and prevention strategies for job burnout are the same.

For more information on job related burnout and what can be done to alleviate burnout, go to Dr. Burnout at clarkgaither.com.

Now a little bit of fear can be healthy. It can keep us on our toes, motivated and moving forward, keeping us prepared, watchful and vigilant to our mutual good advantage. Too much fear can be paralyzing.

When I was an active alcoholic I had even greater fear. Like all addicts, I had a fear of being discovered, that the covert activities surrounding my addiction would be laid bare. I can tell you first hand the addicted brain is a tragically odd contradiction. It is a beast running wild while caged, stealthily cunning and stunningly obtuse, immensely intelligent and bafflingly stupid, supremely powerful yet delicately fragile. That was me prior to getting sober over 25 years ago in January of 1990.

There are proven strategies to deal with unreasonable fear(s). There is a mountain of good advice and proven methodologies just a mouse click away on-line. For individuals that are already paralyzed by fear or those that have developed significant phobias there is no need to suffer. I would suggest professional counseling.

Many people carry a whole subset of fears in addition to the usual ones, the unreasonable fears. Their unreasonable fears will keep them away from help and in harms way. Unreasonable fears include thoughts like no one can or will love the real me, I am worthless and no good, I am dull and boring, I can never have a good time again, I will die without my alcohol or drug, I can not live without him/her in my life.

These aren't the musings of a sane mind. This is the insanity of fear. As much as people can suffer, the person suffering somehow convinces themselves that living with the cause of the suffering must be better than living without it. Change is therefore viewed as less desirable.

The sufferer holds out hope that somehow, someday, someway they can keep one foot in the cause of their suffering and one foot in normal and everything will work out okay. There is just one problem for the one who is suffering and living with fear, there is no normal.

Fear is a state of being, not an action. You could be courageous and still be afraid. So, what is the state of being opposite of fear? It is a state of mind we all seek, whether we can name it or not. It is the place in our mind where all is calm, content, quiet, tranquil, restful, and peaceful. It is called *serenity*.

When times are tough, I am most fearful in the still darkness of the night in the last few hours before sunrise. Not of the darkness itself but of the many doubts that wake me. That is when I feel most vulnerable, indecisive and helpless.

The darkness is home to those feelings. Old tapes and new tapes will play over and over in my head. It is always around 4:30 in the morning, I don't know why. When my wife left me in 2012 I would lie in bed at that hour crying, wondering why this was happening to me, how I would survive and what I should do.

Then I would hear it, at first in my mind. A small voice inside would begin, that would gradually grow in strength until I would repeat it out loud. Over and over again I would repeat it until I could get back to sleep. I was asking my higher power to *grant me the serenity to accept the things I can not change, courage to change the things I can, and wisdom to know the difference.*

I never turned to alcohol. Things got better. I became stronger. Not all of my fears have left me but neither has my steadfast resolve to embrace serenity. Our fears will never leave us but we can have power over them.

# When Weakness Is the First Sign of Strength

We have all had moments of weakness. I have certainly had my share. Especially, when I was drinking. It was so easy for me to give in to the desire or the compulsion to drink alcohol. Thinking with an addicted brain at the time, it was the path of least resistance.

It's different now that I am sober. Now, it's ice cream and the path of least resistance is a direct line between me and my refrigerator freezer where I keep my stash of Blue Bunny old fashion vanilla. But look here, I don't have a problem with it. I can quit at any time. :-)

Seriously, we all have our weaknesses. Most of time when you talk about weaknesses you are talking about something that a person does or some trait that they possess which is undesirable, something they would rather do something about or do without entirely.

Whether is bad relationships, procrastination, inability to complete tasks or projects, exercise, ignorance, overweight, temper, distrust, envy, lying, irresponsibility, drugs, alcohol, food, take your pick, they are all things that we can do something about.

But far too often, the path of least resistance is to maintain the status quo and avoid needed change. At one time or another we have all taken part in what I call functional insanity. We do the same things over and over again and expect different results. Further, we may chose not to change while expecting everyone around us to change. I'm not talking just about addiction here, just bad traits and behaviors in general.

I think part of the reason for this is that people just forget that they CAN change. Secondly, I think people too often tend to feel that they are some how different than everyone else in the world. Lastly, it often takes time, commitment and a lot of energy to change undesirable behaviors or traits.

Before we go any further, let's just all agree on one overriding principle about humans which I introduced in the first chapter of this book. ALL HUMANS ARE HUMAN. All humans can change if they want to, or not. It is a choice.

Just because something worthwhile might be time consuming, require an earnest desire, or some work doesn't make it impossible. In fact, those difficulties are what make something worthwhile in the first place.

Can you remember one thing in your life that was worthwhile that you truly appreciate and of which you are so very proud that was either given to you or was simple and easy to acquire? Probably not.

Now, can you remember something you worked for, sweated over, bleed for, struggle with, conquered and obtained through shear determination, force of will, and hard work? Was it something about which you now care little? I doubt it. It is probably something for which you are very proud.

So, what of our individual weaknesses? Do you know what they are? Do you care? Is it possible to rid yourself of them? Do you want to? Would eliminating them be a worthwhile endeavor? Are you satisfied with the status quo?

The great philosopher, Lao Tzu, said *"if you do not change direction, you may end up where you are heading"*. Do you feel you are headed in the right direction?

I am certain that we are not doomed to live our lives in a certain way. I believe that if we want to change, we can. I know that we have the power inside ourselves to overcome that which holds us back, namely fear.

Nothing about us is immutable, unchangeable, inevitable. I didn't believe that when I was an active alcoholic, before I got sober. I didn't believe it when I became burned out as a physician. I didn't believe it after my wife left me in a mangled heap. I sure do believe it now.

I have seen my life change in amazing ways and I have seen countless other lives change as well. It only took me to become a willing participant in my own recovery, in my own miraculous transformation. There were some things I had to overcome.

Recognizing one's faults and weaknesses and realizing the need for change is not a sign of weakness. It is a sign of strength. So while your first thought might be, "Look, I have this weakness. I'm no good." Or, "I'm not good enough." This is just you getting in the way of you.

Worse still would be denying you have any problems, or refusing to recognize them, or refusing to change them once they are recognized. That is powerlessness personified.

A full and ongoing self assessment for signs of one's weaknesses and a willingness to change for the better is the path to enlightenment, miraculous transformation, a new freedom and a new happiness. It is on this path where we find weaknesses to be our greatest strength.

# Powerful Words...

FEAR, BURNOUT and RECOVERY are Powerful Words.

FEAR is one of the **most** powerful words. The emotional power behind the word fear can be overwhelming, destabilizing, destructive, paralyzing, painful, and ruinous. Or, it can be motivational, self-preserving, transforming, actuating, incentivizing, persuasive, and provocative.

Who gets to choose? I think you know the answer to this question by now. That is, if you didn't know already. You do, dear reader, you do.

So much human behavior is dictated by fear. Our center for fear is deeply buried in our primitive brain. We can't escape it, nor would we want to escape it completely. It serves a useful purpose in keeping us from harm. However, left unchecked, fear can be paralyzing. We should allow our fears to watch over us, not rule over us.

BURNOUT, in any realm of one's life, does have a redeeming quality. It can serve as the impetus for needed change. RECOVERY form burnout can lead to magnificent transformational change. Like most things, it is a choice.

If you want more information about job related burnout, check out my website at drburnout.com or clarkgaither.com.

# Your world of words within...

What is your biggest fears? It helps to name them. It does lessen their impact, especially if you share your fears with someone else. You will find you are not alone.

List one to five of your biggest fears now.

1. _____

2. _____

3. _____

4. _____

5. _____

What steps can you begin to take today to help you move past your fears? Notice I said 'lessen the impact' not 'eliminate'. It isn't necessary to eliminate fear if you can learn to live with it, lessen its impact or learn to bend it to your own purpose.

If you are at a loss for where to start, there are many good sources of information on the internet for dealing effectively with fears. If you have potent phobias then I would suggest professional assistance. The point is, start addressing your worst fears, the ones holding you back, as soon as possible. If you want some things to change you're going to have to start changing some things.

Mine worst fears are rejection or the thought being alone in life. Those terrify me. If I happen to wake up in the dark stillness of the night and think about them, I can't get back to sleep. I believe I know why these two are my biggest fears. Do you know the reason(s) for your biggest fears?

I deal with mine by practicing mindfulness. How do you deal with your biggest fear(s)? What stories come to mind when you consider your fears? The emotions tied to those fears name Powerful Words. The best way to lessen their impact is to name them and talk about them. Share you stories about your fears. Make some notes here.

_____

_____

_____

Have you ever been burned out at your job? Are you burned out now? What is your plan for change? Do you have one? What do you think is the cause of your burnout? Have recovered from a bought with job burnout? Did you undergo a transformation? Write down your story if these questions connect with you on an emotional level. They will invariably contain useful Powerful Words.

_____

_____

_____

Do you have a recovery related story to tell? One involving yourself, a family member, a friend, a co-worker, a boss, a client or customer? If so, I know without much doubt there are Powerful Words associated with those experiences. Jot them down in a list here for later reference.

_____

_____

_____

_____

_____

_____

_____

_____

_____

_____

# FAILURE

The road to success will always lead through the gateposts of failure. No doubt, failure is a Powerful Word. We all fear failure. I am going to ask you a really strange question. Why?

Failure is one of the first lessons we learn in life. We try to sit up and we slump over. We try to stand up and we drop back down onto our butts. We try to walk and we stumble and fall. We try to speak and nothing intelligible comes out of our mouth. So it goes.

People fail. People will fail repeatedly throughout their lives. This does not make us failures at living. It is how we learn and grow. Life challenges us so we can be more than a resource absorbing waste producing lump of tissue.

What about success? Are humans born a success? No. Are humans born to be successful? Yes, I believe we are. But, success comes at the price of failure. Does any one get to be a success in life without failure?

Choose someone who you feel is successful, anyone. I don't care whose name you might mention, or by what measure of their success you might choose, I can rest you assured and without hesitation their road to success was pot-marked with bungle, blunder, and bust and passed through the gateposts of failure on multiple occasions.

The road to success is never straight. There are no signposts pointing the way. There is no route to get there that works for everyone and the last stop before Successville is FAILURE CITY.

It is the same for everyone on planet earth. If that is the case, why do we hate and fear failure so much when it ultimately leads to success if we so choose?

As if the road to success wasn't hard enough to travel, I see so many people place road blocks in their own path, reverse course, veer off the road altogether or just give up for no explicable reason other than fear of failing. It is a self-fulfilling prophecy. What they don't seem to realize, what I didn't realize for so many years of my life, is that failing is the only way we succeed.

Do you fail and accept defeat? Or, do you use failure as a springboard to propel you forward toward your next success?

# Redefining Failure...

Turning away from fear based thinking requires a fundamentally different mindset, a new and better way of thinking. No where is this more needed that when it comes to the use of the word failure.

I don't believe in the way this word is used any more. I believe the word failure should either be redefined or eliminated from our vocabulary as it is currently used.

So, try this - **I am going to either eliminate failure from my vocabulary or redefine the word in a more positive way that works for me.**

Look up the word failure in the dictionary and you see defining words such as unsuccessful, nonperformance, insufficiency, deterioration, decay, bankrupt, insolvency with synonyms such as breakdown, decline, deficiency, wreck, and defeat. It is all so negative.

Really? Is this the terminal end result for failure 100% of the time? Is this all you get from failure, less or nothing at all?

A less than expected or negative result does not automatically mean failure. I submit that it **never** means failure. A negative result is still a result and therefore has positive value or potential. Each time we say we fail at something we learn something valuable, if we so choose. Our "failures" are a form of payment for learning those valuable lessons.

Repeating what is taught, is learning what is already known. Where is the risk in that? Where is the mystery in that? Attempting to create something new and failing in the attempt is a voyage of self-discovery, something you won't learn in a classroom. A classroom is where learning takes place. Life outside the classroom is where your education takes place.

Ask any successful person if they have ever had to confront failure and they will probably tell you that their past is littered with them; hosts of them, long strings of them. They will also probably tell you that were it not for those failures they would have never achieved their successes.

So, do successful people actually produce failures or construct springboards for success, or proving grounds for progress? Do they make mistakes or create opportunities for more positive outcomes? Do they under-perform or establish long-term trend lines for successful growth? In this sense, doesn't FAILURE + EXPERIENCE = SUCCESS for them?

I believe it is time for you to redefine the word failure in a way that works for you and eliminate the word failure from your vocabulary. It will change your mindset.

If you rename failure something like "my avatar for arrested progress" then it is time to run toward your avatar for arrested progress, embrace it, extract knowledge and experience from it, then rip it up and use the pieces as building blocks for your next attempt at a more successful outcome. All successful people will do this.

*If you learn from defeat, you haven't really lost.*
*~ Zig Ziglar*

*It's fine to celebrate success but it is more important to heed the lessons of failure.*
*~ Bill Gates*

*Every adversity, every failure, every heartache carries with it the seed on an equal or greater benefit.*
*~Napoleon Hill*

How or what will you rename failure? How will you use this to your advantage?


# When Stop Means Go!...

We have all heard this certain voice say this certain word. I know I have. You are getting ready to embark on a new adventure, start a new business, learn something new, try something new, meet someone new, or begin a new project and then you hear it. It wells up inside of your head. A voice that says STOP!

STOP is a Powerful Word. We can use it to our benefit unless we too often use it on ourselves. If we tell ourselves to stop, it will be the loudest voice we hear and sometimes the only voice we hear.

Whether from fear, anxiety, feelings of inadequacy or whatever you wish to call the cause of it, we hear the voice inside us say stop. Sometimes it is shouting STOP! Why?

I believe I know. It is a means of protection. A long time ago, when life was very difficult and dangers abounded, you didn't leave your cave or your hut until you had looked out or around a bit.

Those who cavalierly wandered about didn't survive very long. There were always other creatures lurking around for their next meal. We had to spend a lot of time and energy making sure we weren't on any menus.

If way back when you ran up on a member from another tribe, you would not know at first whether they were friend or foe. It was beneficial to be wary of strangers.

Sure, we may not have to run from actual tigers these days but those kinds of dangers still exist. Even today we have known by heart and we teach our children those familiar words stop, look and listen before crossing the street. When out walking about, cars have become the tigers we fear.

We also tell our children, just as we were told, don't talk to strangers or to be vigilant around them. Strangers come from the tribe of the Uncertain, and should be treated as such until they are fully known to us.

Initially, even if you are extremely outgoing, you will still have your guard up when meeting someone new. We all have a mask that we wear to protect our secret self.

A long time ago, in lands far away, attempting to learn something new could be dangerous. If it were something new that meant there was no experience to pass down to guide you. Ever wonder who first figured out what fruit was okay to eat and which one would kill you?

One thing is for sure, all of the survivors knew which fruits you could eat safely. Trial and error way back when was a one shot deal for many.

From this point of view, STOP is hardwired into our brains as a safety switch. It's natural. This helps to protect us from things that might harm us. It gives us pause to reflect on what we are about to set out to do so that we might stay out of harm's way.

For this reason, STOP does not mean QUIT or END. On the contrary, it simply means STOP then PROCEED WITH CAUTION AFTER FULLY ASSESSING THE SITUATION. Just like the road sign, it doesn't mean to stay stopped forever.

If STOP actually meant STOP, we would have never left the cave or the hut, organized into communities or learned anything at all about our physical world.

I submit that in this context STOP really means GO! Especially when you are about to step outside your comfort zone and you hear that voice saying stop. Just know this is just the way your brain is wired.

Here's the thing. That kind of wired thinking can be rewired. Hearing that voice should now become your signal to pause and then GO, learn, build, produce, develop, invent, innovate, create, and grow. I believe that too is naturally hardwired into all of us once we get past stop.

## Share Your Strengths or Your Fears?...

Which do you share most often in everyday conversation, your strengths or your fears? Your answer will depend on your state of mind. If you are burning out, burned out or still smoldering you are most likely sharing your fears because that will be your mindset.

If you are fully engaged in life, living each day with passion and purpose, not only are you displaying your strengths you are freely sharing them. This is always the case with fully engaged humans.

If the statement "you are what you eat" is true then, moreover, you are what you think. What you think is entirely dependent on how your brain is wired. How your brain is wired is entirely dependent on what you think (with your own genetics thrown into the mix). It sounds circular. I know, so let me explain.

Richard O'Connor, author of *Rewire: Change Your Brain to Break Bad Habits, Overcome Addiction, and Conquer Self-Destructive Behavior,* says we are constantly having a running conversation with ourselves in our heads while thinking about this or that throughout the day. This is our conscience thinking which controls about 1% of what we do.

But, 99% of what we do and how we live our lives is controlled by our unconscious thinking. Most of this control is exerted by way of habits which we repeat over and over again without even thinking about them.

If your habit is to be too self-critical, too negative or too pessimistic your brain will form new synapses which will further promote this line of thinking. Or, if you are a habitual procrastinator you will create new connections and pathways in your brain which will increase the chances of more procrastination. These connections are not destroyed. With repetitive use (habit), they become hardwired.

If, on the other hand, you intentionally practice positive thinking you can amass new synaptic connections and pathways which will facilitate more positive thinking. With practice this will become the natural way for you to think and act.

When it comes to computers we often hear the phrase, "garbage in, garbage out." Fundamentally, there is no difference between the human brain and computer in this regard. Negativity in, negativity out. Positive in, positive out. Fear in, fear out. It is no more complicated than that.

No one is born to be a negative thinker. Although, to listen to some people you might think so. Negative thinking is a learned behavior. As such, it can be unlearned and replaced with a new way of thinking. This demands forming new positive thinking habits to change ones mindset.

Norman Vincent Peale knew this very well when he wrote the book *The Power of Positive Thinking* and so did Napoleon Hill when he penned *Think and Grow Rich*. Countless other authors have espoused this notion, before and since. This is now established fact, backed by sound science.

This leads me to the profound albeit somewhat simplistic conclusion - **If you want to change your thinking you're going to have to change your thinking**. Here are three ways to rewire your brain which will positively work.

1. Start by correcting yourself out loud each time you make a negative comment or statement. Reframe the thought in a positive light. If you are in the habit of talking about downside risk, foster a habit of upside thinking instead.

2. Exchange each negative thought for three positive ones. Avoid negative people if you can. If not, counter every negative comment from someone else with a positive one. Trade discussions of the impossible     with what is possible.

3. Sharing your fears with someone you trust is sometimes necessary for growth. But, if this has become the daily beef about "what's wrong" with and about everything, then I would definitely consider the source – you.

These are just three simple ways you can use to work toward more positive based thinking. Can you think of others?

# Powerful Words...

FAILURE, DEFEAT, STOP, UNCERTAIN and INNOVATE are Powerful Words.

You can use the word STOP to your advantage by saying STOP to old behaviors and attitudes which only serve to hold you back. Say STOP to self-defeating choices and self-fulfilling prophecies. Say STOP to "I can't" and "that's not possible".

DEFEAT is never defeat and FAILURE is never a failure if, (a.) you learn something from them and (b.) if you never quit or give up. If you believe struggle produces tangible benefits, even if you should lose, then to struggle and lose or to struggle and win is to win twice. To end a struggle before there is a clear loss or win is to lose twice.

No matter how much we plan, the future is UNCERTAIN for all of us. Granted, those who plan will be better prepared for contingencies. You have heard the English Proverb, *"Necessity is the mother of invention."* It is by way of the unexpected that much innovation occurs. People INNOVATE out of necessity. Necessity = Innovation

# Your world of words within...

What unique way would you redefine the word FAILURE?

_____

_____

_____

Have you ever heard that little voice inside of you say stop? Has it become a blockade to your progress? If so, what has been your experience? Can you share a helpful story where you found a way to use the word stop to your advantage?

How do you view failure and defeat? Is the view all negative? What favorite stories do you have about failure or defeat? How many failures were there before a success? Are there powerful emotions connected with your stories of failure and defeat? If so, there are Powerful words which connect you to those emotions. Those same words will connect you with others. Make note of them here.

---
---
---

Is your future more uncertain than it needs to be from lack of planning or goal setting? What seems to be in the way? In a few words can you describe how you feel about the future? Some of those words will hold power for you.

---
---
---

Do you think you have it in you to innovate? Have you been innovative? What are those stories? What words come to mind to describe your innovation?

---
---
---

# KNOWLEDGE

## But, I don't know how to do that...

It is time to gather together the resources and knowledge necessary to help you achieve your goals for sharing you stories, your Powerful Words. Many people do not even make it this far before giving up. Many others will stall here because they discover they lack critical information or the tools that are necessary for their success.

Rather than go out and get what might be missing or needed, some simply give up. After making helpful suggestions to patients or friends I will too often hear, "But, I don't know how to do that." I have said those very words many times in my own past before I transformed my thinking.

Part of transformative thinking is realizing that you can learn any subject or acquire any skill that may be necessary to perform better or to achieve a particular outcome. All it requires is a do-whatever-it-takes commitment and that, dear reader, is a choice.

If you have a data phone or a computer, you literally hold the world in your hands. Information that was once reserved for a privileged few is now available to anyone, at anytime and usually for free. There simply is no sacred knowledge anymore.

Once I wanted to learn how to splice the end of a braided rope back into itself to form a strong loop at the end without tying a knot. I went online and found a YouTube video that taught me how to do the braid in less than two and a half minutes.

Another time I wanted to learn calculus. I had never taken calculus as a course in college. I was completely intimidated by calculus and I was afraid I would either fail or do poorly in the course. I let fear rule the outcome. For years afterward I would look at differential equations, realizing I would never understand them, and that always bothered me.

Many years ago, after I had begun thinking with a transformed brain, I ordered an introductory course in calculus from The Great Courses and proceeded to learn calculus over the next year. The only thing that had changed was me. Calculus was still calculus, but my mind set had changed. I decided that there was nothing I couldn't learn or understand if I put in the effort.

A change in mindset is all that is required. For instance, let's say that English is your only spoken language. Then, someone approaches you and asks, "Can you speak Spanish?" Your first inclination may be to say, "No, I can't." A confident transformed mind, one that is filled with nothing but potential and sees endless possibilities, might well respond "Yes, I can! I just haven't learned it yet!"

That doesn't mean that you must rush out and learn Spanish. It just means that you will go for a more positive response to any question of this sort because you now have a transformed mind. A transformed mind develops a no boundaries attitude when it comes to learning or acquiring new skills. It is the way you will learn to think. It is a choice. It represents a Transformation in your thinking.

# Powerful Words...

KNOWLEDGE, INFORMATION and SKILL are Powerful Words.

I value KNOWLEDGE highly. It is second on my top 5 core values list. It was Sir Francis Bacon who said, "Knowledge itself is power." He wasn't wrong.

If you are going to write, speak, produce, sell, or serve you will only be successful in doing so from a position of authority. Knowledge will give you authority. Some say experience alone is sufficient but what is experience other than practical knowledge?

I am not necessarily talking about university degrees here. The entire world's panoply of knowledge **is** the Internet, our 21st century codex. All knowledge is available to all people, all of the time, everywhere. There is more INFORMATION out there than you could consume in a Thousand lifetimes, most of it free.

With desire, patience and perseverance you can learn any SKILL you have a mind to learn, or even master. Just remember, you can do all of the marketing you want but a quality product will speak louder than your own words, no matter how powerful they may be.

# World of words from within...

Do you feel there isn't anything you can't learn? Yes? My next question to you would be why? Has anyone proved that to be true other than you?

List five new things you would like to learn or skills you would like to acquire.

1. _____

2. _____

3. _____

4. _____

5. _____

What steps will you pledge yourself to take to begin acquiring this new knowledge or learn these new skills? Is anything holding you back other than deciding to decide to move forward and then doing it?

Are there powerful words from within telling you that you are incapable of obtaining new knowledge or skills? What are they? What are the stories and emotions behind those words? What stories or Powerful Words come to mind when thinking about what you know? What experiences have you had in learning new skills?

_____

_____

_____

Write these down as they come to mind. Look for recurrent themes as you work your way through the chapters of this book.

# THE UNKNOWN

*There are known knowns; there are things we know that we know. We also know there are known unknowns; that is to say we know there are some things we do not know. But there are also unknown unknowns – the ones we don't know we don't know.*
*~ Donald Rumsfeld*

That quote makes me chuckle every time I read it. Yet, the unknown can be a source of great fear, anxiety and depression, if we so choose. Unknown is a Powerful Word. It gets more power than it deserves.

Being stuck, paralyzed or otherwise affected by the unknown is a choice. Life's unknowns are something we all must deal with and to varying degrees. It is a daily struggle in my own life. My biggest fear is of living or dying alone. It always has been. I have long suspected why.

Many of our anxious moments have their basis in things that have not yet occurred, future events that have not yet come to pass and may never come to pass. These make us anxious. Why? Is it human nature to worry over things that may or may not happen, unknown outcomes with anticipated negative consequences?

Why is it not the opposite? Why do we not rather instead anticipate and celebrate, in advance, the possibilities of future happiness and victories that may or may not happen? Early in human history it probably had something to do with survival, anticipating dangers that might cause us harm thereby making us very cautious creatures.

Truth is, whether we anticipate a negative or a positive future outcome, both will tend to make us anxious. Every day we each make choices and we plan. We construct mental scenarios built around possible outcomes of future events but we act accordingly now based on the plans we have drawn.

We dive headlong into the unknown. Then, we commence worrying about the future outcomes of our decisions. We try to control all variables as much as possible for a certain desired outcome and then we worry if things will go our way or not.

But, it may not stop there. We may even worry over circumstances and situations completely out of our control when bad situations present without our consent. And that may be the crux of it all – control, another Powerful Word.

We would all like a crystal ball to help us navigate through life so we can avoid the pitfalls and the dangers, the mistakes and the mishaps and in that way we could control our destiny by the decisions we make in the present. I would certainly like to have my very own crystal ball. Who wouldn't?

Worse still is the emotion we generate over past events of known and unknown cause(s) - "Something bad happened and I don't know why so now I'm afraid to move forward, to let it go. It has ruined my life. I don't have what it takes. I'm no good. I can't be happy anymore or ever again." - It is down right depressing.

These days I wonder if actually knowing why bad things have happened to me would, in any way, make a difference in how I choose to live my life now or make me feel any better about myself? I doubt it. It is probably just up to me either way.

Sometimes the results of our choices and plans are naught, the outcomes are bad or very bad. Our worst fears are realized. Disappointment sets in, perhaps crushing disappointment. Did worrying about the outcome in advance make any difference in the outcome?

We think, if I had only known I would have acted accordingly and the outcome would have been different. Why did I say yes instead of no or no instead of yes? Why did I choose her or him? Why did I trust this person instead of that person? Why didn't I ask more questions?

I have found such ruminations to be a complete waste of time. The answers are, well, unknowable. They all reside in the past - unknowable, unreachable, unfixable, unchangeable. The extent to which our past decisions affect us today are to whatever extent we let them affect us today, negatively or positively. As I said, it is a choice.

So, what will it be – to fear a potential unknown negative outcome or hope for a potential unknown positive outcome? Must it be one or the other? How about neither? It is okay to make plans for the future and to work toward goals. But is it the goal or the journey?

If we concentrate only on the goal we are living in the future with an uncertain outcome. We become anxious and miss a good bit of the journey. If we concentrate on the journey, we are living in the present and our goals will be there waiting on us when we arrive.

We could remain stuck in the past, depressed over past events we can no longer change. We could forever emote over the loss of this and the loss of that, the "we never had this" or the "we never had that" and the why oh why of days gone by.

Isn't lamenting in the present over a past life we desired but never had, causing us to miss out on the life we could have now, but will lament over later in the future? It makes no sense. But, I have spent much of my life doing just that. As I said, it's depressing.

Which is why **dwelling** in the past should be abandoned. I am not suggesting we shouldn't visit the past from time to time. It is where all of our experience is kept. Gaining experience is the way we learn and the way we grow. But, actually living in the past and getting stuck there is no way to live a life in the present.

In deference to Rumsfeld's quote, the known knowns belong to the past and the known unknowns belong to the future. The unknown unknowns that we may discover today are all that matter.

> *If you are depressed, you are living in the past.*
> *If you are anxious, you are living in the future.*
> *If you are at peace, you are living in the present.*
> *Lao Tzu*

# Powerful Words...

UNKNOWN, ANXIETY, DEPRESSION, CONSEQUENCES, PLAN, EMOTION and GOAL are Powerful Words.

I have treated a lot of patients with ANXIETY and DEPRESSION in my practice. You can be anxious without being depressed but anyone who is depressed is almost always anxious. If you have either of these conditions which have lasted longer than six weeks (the definition of chronic), go see your doctor.

I find many, if not most, of my patients who from suffer chronic depression have lives which are out of balance and have been for a very long time. There are in a catch-22. In order to feel better in the long term they absolutely must make changes in their life which require mental and physical energy. In order to get the necessary mental and physical energy to make those changes they must make the changes.

Tragically, most of them believe the notion that they are incapable of change. Yet, the only one convincing them of this, the only one who believes this, is themselves. They are steeped in negative EMOTION. As a result, they become medical cripples and continue to suffer the

CONSEQUENCES of a long series of bad assumptions and choices. I have found the best way to avoid this state of permanent stagnation or decline is to avoid it altogether, if you choose.

If you are addicted to a substance or a destructive behavior, I don't have to tell you about consequences. You are likely seeing them everyday. You can set the following statement in concrete. They will become more numerous and more severe as time goes by unless you become sober and in meaningful recovery. Either way, you have some Powerful Words and stories to share.

Most humans fear the UNKNOWN. The best way to combat fear is to PLAN and execute your plans. This imparts a large measure of control. Goal Oriented Active Living (GOAL) wastes little time, provides for continuous growth and maximizes the opportunity to live a life of passion and purpose.

In short, it maximizes human potential. With goal oriented active living there is no lack of direction or passive "wait and see" approach to living. It is all about the choices we make.

## Your world of words within...

Are you living the life you want? If so, how did you achieve it? If not, what do you feel is holding you back? In each instance, there are stories to tell which contain Powerful Words representing strong emotions. Write them down.

_____

_____

_____

_____

_____

_____

These stories are your living legacy thus far. Thing is, an undesirable legacy can be changed but only as long as you live **to** change.

Circle one: Are you a **NEGATIVE** person or a **POSITIVE** person? With either one, where does that trait come from? Is there a story to tell there? What Powerful Words do you associate with the words positive and negative?

---
 

---
 

---

Do you have a story of struggle or triumph over an addiction? What were the consequences of your addiction? These contain Powerful Words which will resonate with so many people. Write them down and begin to explore the powerful emotions behind them and then begin to share them.

---
 

---
 

---

Do you have short, medium and long-term goals? Yes? Write them down for clarity's sake.

What are your one year goals?

---
 

---
 

---

Your three year goals?

---
 

---
 

---

Your five year goals?

_____

_____

_____

Your ten year goals?

_____

_____

_____

Your 15 year goals?

_____

_____

_____

And beyond?

_____

_____

_____

Are they in alignment with your core values? Are they complete enough? If you have not set goals, why not? What is holding you back? Is it fear? Ask yourself these questions until you have the answers. Talk to others about this. They may share Powerful Words with you which will catapult you off in new and exciting directions.

# Procrastination

## Endeavor to DO...

Change, profound change as in a transformation, requires perseverance. But, before perseverance comes begin or start. Failing to begin or start is the result of procrastination but it is not often the cause. Fear and perceived difficulty are more often the cause.

Sometimes we can get so bogged down or overwhelmed with the enormity or difficulty of a task before us that we either fail to start or give up along the way. There are perseverance strategies to help prevent that from happening.

Once, I asked a friend to help me fill a ditch with gravel. It was a trench with a corrugated pipe laid in the bottom that had to be covered with stone to form what is called a French drain which serves to transport water away from a structure.

I ordered a dump truck load of gravel which was delivered promptly at the appointed time, all 14 tons of it! It looked like a mountain sized pile of gravel. I grew tired just looking at it.

Now fourteen tons of gravel equals 28,000 pounds. To put this in some perspective, a 2014 Chevrolet Tahoe weighs 7,100 pounds so we were looking at moving the equivalent weight of just under four full sized Tahoe's. We had a shovel each and a rickety shallow wheel barrow. The ditch was sixty feet long. The task at hand seemed so daunting.

Dennis thought it would take all weekend. I was a little more optimistic and thought it would take the entire day. Reluctantly, we started to shovel. One wheel barrow load at a time, we began to move gravel.

We both learned something that day which has had application to many daunting tasks I have had to face since then. When faced with a mountainous task here are some steps that will help get you through to a successful outcome, namely task completion:

1) Dig in. Just beginning is the thing with most seemingly difficult tasks. Procrastination is a tool we often use to forestall our efforts due to our anxiety over starting which is a form of fear. Just beginning offers some forward momentum and will immediately relieve the anxiety of starting. Haven't you felt that before, the relief of starting?

2) Stay on task by avoiding getting caught up in unanticipated distractions or, worse yet, by looking for them. This is an old trick of the mind, to look for ways out of doing what you need to do by finding things you would rather do. Unless we are vigilant the mind, just like water, will always look for the path of least resistance. Is this something you have had to deal with at times?

3) Focus on slow and steady progress which is key. Some tasks you just can't rush. Rushing creates mistakes. Mistakes take time to fix which delays task completion. In your experience, does hurrying ever help?

4) Remember, there is no such thing as multitasking, if there is one thing you must do well. Being able to do multiple things all at once and do them all well is an illusion, a myth. If there is one thing you want to excel in doing then just do the one thing until it's done. Have you found multitasking to be the pathway to true excellence in all things or just a dead end for many?

5) Give yourself the gift of time. Set aside adequate time to complete a task. Avoid waiting until the last minute to begin. Avoid the trap of underestimating the time required which will just add pressure on you until you're finished. That is never a comfortable feeling. When it comes to completing your work, is this something that sounds familiar to you?

6) Keep your eye on the prize. It will always pay off in the end. How many times have you finished a large and difficult project, stepped back and thought, "That wasn't that bad" or "That wasn't as bad as I thought it was going to be?" Probably more times than not. It will help to remember that when headed into your next big project, or even a small one you've been dreading.

Oh, how long did it take Dennis and me to move that 28,000 pounds of gravel? Just 4 hours, one shovel at a time, one wheel barrow at a time. It surprised and delighted us both.

# It's a game we like to play...

If you have transformed into a highly motivated, self-actualized individual doing what you love with intention and passion then procrastination is probably not a work strategy you use very often.

However, everyone procrastinates to some degree. We all have tasks that may be difficult or we might not care to do but must do anyway. If not driven to complete a task we may leave it for another time. Whether that means procrastinating, stalling or a logical and judicious use of our time depends on many factors.

One thing is certain, if we voluntarily delay an intended course of action despite expecting to be worse off for the delay, then that meets the currently accepted definition of procrastination (Piers Steel 2007). This type of forestalling can impair you in that it is counterproductive, needless delaying.

Procrastination may be due to or a coping mechanism for:

- **Anxiety.** Over starting or completing a task, especially new or difficult tasks. It is a form of fear.
- **Impulsiveness.** Deciding to put off the task with little or no forethought.
- **Perfectionism.** I can't do it well enough for my standards so I'm not even going to start.
- **Low self-esteem.** I'm not good enough to complete the task.
- **Depression.** I don't have the mental or emotional energy to start or complete my work. This needs attention from a mental or other healthcare professional.
- **Good Judgment.** I have assessed all that I have to do and I am going to put this task(s) off for now because it is less important.

All but the last one of these can lead to decreased productivity and inability to progress. The consequences of procrastination may include:

- **Stress.** Pressure to perform mounts as deadlines approach. In the end procrastination creates more stress than it alleviates.
- **Guilt.** From avoiding what must be done.
- **Crisis.** Too little time remains to adequately complete the task(s) at hand.
- **Stigma.** The chronic procrastinator becomes know as unreliable.

Try these 7 steps to help you stop procrastinating:

- **Remember who you are.** Knowing yourself and what you are likely to do when faced with a new project or task is insightful. Vigilance against old behaviors can serve to usher in needed change.

- **Establish a routine.** Generate a schedule, road map, outline or strategy for handling a new task and try to stick with it. Practice will make it work.
- **Be realistic.** Know the limits to what you can do. Don't try to complete everything at once. Set attainable goals. Don't over promise and under deliver. Do just the opposite.
- **Scale down tasks.** Break up large projects into more manageable portions or segments. Work through them one at a time. Avoid jumping around from piece to piece. Forget multitasking. There is no such thing. It is a myth.
- **Ask for help.** Good grief, nobody knows everything about everything and none of us are super human. If you get stumped or if there is too much for one person to handle, ask for help. It is not a sign of weakness or ineptitude. It means you're human. All humans need help from time to time. If you uncover a weakness, work on it. That is how we grow and how we grow is how we know. You can also set a weakness aside if it is unnecessary to accomplish your goals. The time may be better spent working on your strengths instead.
- **Deadline with a cushion.** Build a pre-deadline cushion into your schedule that will offer some leeway for the unexpected. This margin of safety is not to be used up because of stalling. The actual deadline is the hard limit for project completion. A self imposed pre-deadline cushion is set before the actual deadline and affords some usable margin if needed due to circumstances outside your control.
- **Auto reward.** When the task is completed or the project is shipped on time, take time to rest, reflect and reset for the next project. Oh, and have some fun. If you have worked this list to your advantage, then you've earned it.

These 7 steps can also apply to the other realms of your life. An area were I see patients procrastinate all of the time is on beginning a regular program of exercise. Physical, mental, emotional, and spiritual vitality depend on balanced efforts within each.

Procrastinate is a Powerful Word if you choose to let it hold power over you. It is a roadblock to so many. You are the only one who can place it in front of you and you are the only one who can remove it.

Are there areas in your life where you procrastinate often? Which of these solutions might you use to your advantage? Are there others? How have you dealt with procrastination? Was there one time in particular where procrastinating cost you a great deal? Someone may need to hear or read your story.

# Intentionally intentional...

If you mean to change something about yourself, or even transform your life into something completely different, then you must act with purposeful intention. Attempting to change without being intentional during the process will not meet with much success.

When we say we will act with intention, what actually does that mean? It seems that on the surface of things we act with intention everyday, even for the same activities day in and day out.

We intend to set the alarm to get up and go to work. So we do. We intend to pick the kids up from school. So we do. We intend to watch this TV program or read that magazine. So we do.

There are also many other things that we intend to do that we never do. We intend to have the neighbors over for dinner. But, we never do. We intend to help out at the local charity. But, we never do. We intend to leave that life-force sucking job that we hate and move on to something better. But, we never do. We intend to get sober, or end a soul-crushing relationship, or start a new business, or begin writing that book. But...

If we intend to change but do not, then it would seem that we are actually intending **not** to change. Remember, intention is just a mental thought process. What's the difference between the two intentions - to intend to do something and do it on the one hand, and to intend to do something but not do it on the other? Is there a difference? Yes, I believe there is.

These days when someone is energetically and emphatically talking about taking positive action(s) for change they may say they are going do so "with intention" or they are "going to be intentional" about it.

I know what they mean. I know what they are inferring by those phrases. So do you, I'll wager. But, I submit that there is no difference between the kind of intention that results in a positive outcome and the kind that leaves someone unintentionally stuck. Both are gray matter constructs, cerebral conjuring without fabric or form.

I believe that what people actually and precisely mean by "acting with intention" or being "intentional" is that they are proclaiming to be *intentionally intentional.*

The definitions of *intentionally* are - **Done** *with intention or purpose; intended.* That, dear reader, means **action** on a plan, goal, ambition or destination. Compare that with the definition of *intention - an act or instance of determining mentally upon some action or result.* That means, "I'm going to think about it."

Literally, to act with intention means to act with thought only. To act intentionally means to act on purpose. To be intentionally intentional means to act with purpose on your intentions.

This is not just word play or philosophical meanderings. Words matter. This is your key to unlock unbounded personal potential energy. After that, nothing will seem impossible.

Someone who is intentionally intentional not only has intentions, they intend to carry them out. Here is how it is done:

1. **Set a goal.** If you are about to run a race it always helps to know where to find and how to recognize the finish line.

2. **Develop a plan.** Without a plan you literally have no idea what you're doing so get that straight.

3. **Start.** Good intentions mean diddlysquat. Being intentionally intentional means taking action on your intentions.

4. **Build in accountability.** Pull people into your plans and have them monitor your progress, or lack thereof. This will keep you motivated and self-assessments will be more honest.

5. **Never quit.** Quitting is never an option if you are intentionally intentional. Regrouping, course corrections, redesigns and reboots are not quitting. Stopping=Quitting=Failure. No one fails until they quit.

Fully implemented, these steps will ensure that all of your intentions for positive change will take place. That is, if you are intentionally intentional about it.

# Useful Word Substitutes and Phrases...

If you have ever tried to get a new business off the ground, start a blog or a book, change careers, find a new job, begin speaking, create art or make some necessary changes to improve your situation, then you have probably used some of the following words and phrases I am going to review here.

I know I have used every single one of them at some point, repeatedly. Perhaps you have too.

I still use them on occasion, when I am less vigilant. Although, I have recently endeavored to avoid using them in favor of more constructive and useful substitute terms. It isn't easy, but it can be done if you are intentionally intentional about it.

What am I talking about? Consider the following words and phrases, their more likely true meaning along with some highly recommended substitutes.

**"I'm too tired."** Too tired? Really? The true meaning of these words 98% of the time is "I am just too lazy to do that right now" (sloth), "I really don't want to do that" (whining) or "I would rather do that later" (procrastination.) Okay, 2% of the time you may be too tired.

When I'm feeling too tired to do something I feel I should be doing, I like to ask myself this question, "If Bill Gates promised me a million dollars to shovel a dump truck full of gravel **right now**, would I say yes?" I think we all know the answer to that question - "Where's the shovel? Get out of my way!"

This newfound heretofore untapped reserve energy just tells me what I was really saying to myself was, "I'm not sufficiently motivated to do this thing that needs doing." Motivation, it would seem, is a choice. A choice subject to bribery at that. Which brings me to my universal substitute for "I'm too tired" - "Give me a shovel and get out of my way!"

Think back to a time when you said "I'm too tired." If your washing machine sprang a leak could you have mopped up the floor? If your dog had run out the door could you chase after it to retrieve your pet? If your child needed you would you have responded?

Most of the time when we say we are too tired, it is because we are tired in our heads more so than in our bodies. So be it. If you need rest, get some. But, when you hear yourself saying "I'm too tired", stop and ask yourself if you are really too tired or is it something else.

**"I can't, it's too hard."** You have to ask yourself, as I have to ask myself, hard as opposed to what?" Harder than having or raising a child, graduating from college, the soul sucking work-a-day grind you loath but keep doing anyway, being a responsible adult?

Is learning Word Press, finishing a blog post or developing a new product really more difficult than any of those challenges? The true meaning of the words 'I can't' at least as I used them, is "I quit" (easier to do), "I'm afraid" (okay but fear is manageable), or "that seems too much like work" (I choose to be lazy.)

The substitute response to "I can't" should be something like - "If I can work a job, start a business on the side while taking care of my family, juggle-juggle-juggle things all day long some of which I really don't care about that much, then I believe I could learn  calculus while I am doing the dishes if I must. So, yes I can!"

**"I don't have time."** Bahahahaha!  This is the best one of them all. Of course you have time, if it is important to you. We all get 168 hours each week. While we cannot have any more hours, we all make time for those things we feel are important.

When I trot this excuse out what I am really saying is, "This is just not important enough for me to do (low priority)." Even though I may feel that it is a high priority. Which means I just wasn't "all in" as they say.

In looking back to those times in my own life when I said I didn't have time, there were items I could have taken off my plate and made time. I was making a convenient excuse for inaction.

If something is really important to us we will rally around the concept or task and give it top of list positioning. That's what successful people do. The people who buy their stuff or make their stuff for them are the ones who say "I don't have time."

When I said I didn't have time, when I could have made time, it was precisely because I was content to remain comfortably miserable. The truth is, I wasted time every day. Most people do.

The better substitute for "I don't have time" might be "I am going to create some margin so I will have time if I feel it is important to me. I know I no longer have time to waste!" Now, what did I do with that shovel?

# Sound familiar?

Have you heard yourself saying, "I'M TOO TIRED", "I CAN'T" or "I DON'T HAVE TIME" too often? There are no new horizons in these words. There is no exploration in these words. There is no art, product, change or hope in these words. See how powerful they are? But, only if you cede your power to them. You are the one to decide on how much power they will have over you.

# Don't Wait!...

I have said it before and I will say it again. I have spent too much of my life waiting. Waiting is a form of procrastination. In my case, it wasn't to avoid work. I have always worked hard at whatever interests me. Rather, for me, it was more of a form of delayed self-actualization manifested by **waiting for just the right time.**

I have waited until just the right time to start new projects. I have waited until just the right time to take trips to far away places. I have waited until the absolute, ideal, just right time to begin or launch a new product or service.

At least, that is what I told myself. I now know this behavior was just an excuse to circumvent fear, anxiety, lack of commitment, poor preparation or perceived inadequacies. Although, looking back, lack of commitment seemed to be the impetus behind most of my waiting for just the right time.

The problem with this is far too often the right time never comes. The new project doesn't get started or completed, the grand trip or adventure is never taken, and the new idea or product is never launched.

I convinced myself I was waiting for inspiration. I have negotiated with myself to wait until I felt more rested. I have argued with myself I should wait until I have more money on hand. Or, that I should read another book or take another class or purchase another instructional webinar series. You know, until the time was **just right**.

There were times I needed to do some hard work on me, personal work. There were times I needed to leave a toxic relationship or make changes to an atrocious work environment where I was burning out. But, I chose not to do so because it just wasn't the right time.

By waiting for just the right time, I effectively forfeited having new learning and growth experiences. I denied myself the potential pleasure of glowing success and the valuable lessons of glorious failure. Ultimately, I missed out on golden opportunities to be of value to others.

WAITING FOR JUST THE RIGHT TIME are also Powerful Words. They are seductive in their rationale and extremely efficient at inaction. There is no inertia, no movement in these words. Although they are powerful blocks to progress, they are also easily, too easily, lifted and laid into place.

Besides, what does the "right time" mean anyway? Do the things we wish to do come with a checklist that must be completed before we can begin? Or, is it just some nebulous construct of a notion we generate in our own heads to temporarily make ourselves feel better for not taking immediate action?

How do we know when the right time becomes available other than another feeling? Is that our supreme and infallible test for the right time, when we feel like it? Or, is there a popup sign that appears somewhere in our visual field displaying the word GO? Does the man behind the curtain shout BEGIN? Or, do we simply reach a point where we have exhausted all of our excuses?

Worse yet, how many times do humans just forget about their high hopes, sterling ideals, trailblazing ideas, amazing potentials and possibilities because it never was just the right time?

How much innovation has been lost but for waiting for just the right time? How much pain and suffering would have been eliminated but for waiting for just the right time? How much individual joy and pleasure would have been created and conveyed to others but for waiting for just the right time?

Let's be honest here. Each of us already know just the right time to bind with happiness, secure our families, rise up, use our voices, tell our stories, alleviate suffering, heal the sick, comfort the lonely, feed the hungry, eliminate injustice, innovate, create, inspire, teach, learn, grow, and know using our own God given unique set of natural talents and abilities.

It is NOW!

*Don't wait. The time will never be just right.*
~ Napoleon Hill


# Powerful Words...

PROCRASTINATION, DIFFICULTY, RESISTANCE, INTENTIONAL, IDEAL, VALUE, IDEAS, JOY, WAIT and WAITING are Powerful Words.

DIFFICULTY and RESISTANCE are met by everyone, everyday. They are universal and burdensome companions. They always show up uninvited, especially when stepping outside of one's comfort zone. PROCRASTINATION is the easiest avoidance behavior with the least fruitful results. If you are INTENTIONAL in dealing with procrastination, it will become your least favored inaction plan.

Be through with WAIT and WAITING. There is no progress and no future with these two. Besides, you've already waited long enough, don't you think?

Being of VALUE to people, in whatever capacity our unique natural talents and abilities will allow, should be our highest IDEAL. I believe this would be **the** source for JOY in the world. At least, it would be for me.

# World of words from within...

Do you remember times when you were paralyzed by fear and procrastinated as a result? Have you had difficulty with starting because of procrastination? What strategies have you found helpful? When you are met with resistance, do you find it easier to procrastinate than to push through? How have you grown or what have been your successes as a result?

Write down one to five ways you have managed to deal with procrastination.

1. _____

2. _____

3. _____

4. _____

5. _____

Do you find that some of your good intentions never make it out of the box (your head)? Will defining what it means to be intentionally intentional help with your future plans? Have you thwarted your own intentions in a way that has cost you?

"I'm too tired", "I can't", "I don't have time." - Do you find yourself saying these words too often? Have you been able overpower them? If so, how? Do you have a story to share which involves these words and the effect they have had on you? Make some notes here.

_____

_____

_____

"I'm waiting for just the right time" or "Wait!" - Have you used these words before? If so, how have they impeded your progress? Have you overpowered these words in your own life?

_____

_____

_____

If any of these questions cause you to pause and feel something, then strong emotions are tied up with them. You should try to unravel the stories and meaning behind those emotions. Your emotions will be represented by some Powerful words. They will be contained in the words you use to describe your feelings.

List some of the Powerful Words you have encountered or uncovered in this chapter.

_____

_____

_____

_____

_____

_____

People need to hear your stories. Someone needs to hear your words. Get them heard.

# STRUGGLE

Throughout our lives we are presented with all types of struggles. Some are relatively benign, such as passing a particularly challenging test. Others may be profoundly impact filled, such as a devastating personal loss. One thing is certain, if you were presented with a great struggle and overcame it then you were more than likely better off for it in the end.

Think back to all the worst occurrences in your life you can recall. There were probably some events you thought you could not survive. But, survive you did. Not only did you survive, there were probably many positive benefits and rewards for having made it through the greatest challenges you have ever faced.

Consider something great which was handed to you in the past without any effort on your part. Did you appreciate it as much as something you struggled with and obtained only with determination, perseverance and hard work? Where was the reward greatest?

Sometimes in life we make bad decisions and suffer negative consequences of those decisions. As a result, we struggle. Sometimes, destructive and calamitous decisions are made by others on our behalf, decisions we have little or no control over, and we struggle desperately as a result.

In each of those instances, if you overcame the difficulty that was presented to you, did your life not take a new and more positive direction? Did you emerge from your struggle forever changed, as in more resolute, stronger, happier, more content and better equipped for the next challenge?

If so, what do you think now of your life's greatest struggles? Are they something to disparage or celebrate? Should we despise them or be grateful for them?

My separation and divorce was devastating and extremely painful and I was an emotional wreck for a year. But, I never lost hope that things would get better. After a while, I stopped hoping and decided to make them better.

I became introspective and began to reexamine my life. I actively pursued even more change than what was foisted on me. I struck out in new directions and became enthusiastic about seeking new experiences. I started writing and produced a podcast. I took solo hiking trips in the US and abroad. I feel different, better, more energized and excited for the future. Struggle got the ball rolling. I stepped out of the way.

I learned. I grew. I became a stronger person than I was before. I accepted the gifts of struggle. Now, I will tell you, I am much better off.

I have had many such struggles in my life, just like you. Many wonderful things have always come to me following a great struggle. They are too numerous to mention. Would any of them have taken place without the struggle?

Think of all the truly great individuals you know, the famous ones you admire, the notables you would most like to emulate. How did they become so great? Were they born to greatness, did they stumble upon greatness or did they struggle through to greatness?

Imagine a life without struggle? How would we learn? How would we grow? How would we become strong? It only takes a moments reflection to realize, struggle is a precious gift.

I know why we fear and dread struggle so. Struggle is hard. Struggle is unpredictable. Struggle is painful and cruel. Isn't it strange, though, because we often look back on the aspects of struggles with some sense of satisfaction and fondness after we emerge from them triumphant? There is a reason for that. They were worth it.

The next time you are presented with a great struggle, resolve to overcome it and dwell on these possibilities instead of the dread.

- This struggle could be a prelude to greatness.
- This struggle could be a signal for eminent growth.
- This struggle could lead me off in exciting new directions.
- This struggle could reveal to me some of life's best kept secrets.
- This struggle could allow me to discover my true passion and purpose.
- This struggle could bring me unanticipated opportunities for joy and happiness.

Opposite of what most of us were taught, perhaps we can begin to view life's struggles less negatively. Instead, we could endeavor to embrace our struggles for the precious gifts they bring just as long as we remain open to receive them.

# Powerful Words...

STRUGGLE and BENEFITS are Powerful Words.

The BENEFITS and rewards of success are well know and understood. Less well understood and underappreciated are the benefits of STRUGGLE. Struggle is how we learn, grow, excel, and innovate. It is solely responsible for every intuitive leap in human history. No one is born successful. No one is born with intuition. It has taken the majority of my life for me to understand and accept this reality.

We struggle giving others an opportunity to help us find our way when we are lost, or don't know what to do, because they have learned through their experience. We struggle so we can help others who are struggling find their way, because we have learned through our experience. That is, if we choose to share our experience.

If I were never to have another struggle for the rest of my life, I would think the universe had abandoned me, perceiving I was no longer worth the effort. Not being one to pray for self-enrichment, for this I would have to get down on my knees and pray, "Lord don't you love me anymore? Please, give me some struggles."

I would spare anyone I can the steep leaning curve I have been on for most of my life by simply stating, struggle is a precious gift. For me, this realization has been another step toward enlightenment.

*"The harder the struggle, the more glorious the triumph. Self-realization demands very great struggle."*
*~ Swami Sivananda*

# World of words from within...

What are some of the struggles you have faced which have help to shape you in positive ways?

_____
_____
_____


What Powerful Words or stories come to mind when you hear the word struggle?

_____
_____
_____

Have you seen tangible benefits and rewards from struggle? What are some of those stories? Is there on story in particular form you past about a lost struggle which moves you on an emotional level?

_____

_____

_____

If so, some of these stories are powerful and as such contain Powerful Words. Set them down here or on paper and begin to share them as soon as you can, in any way you can so the value of what you learned can be preserved.

_____

_____

_____

_____

_____

_____

_____

_____

# WAVES

## Look out, here comes another one...

Just when you think things couldn't get any worse, things gets worse. Why is that? Why does it sometimes seem bad stuff happens in waves, or in threes, or without letting up? The answer is, this is the way our universe operates and it is larger than us. But, the opposite is also true. Good comes in waves too. It just seems that more bad follows bad more often.

There is an old Icelandic proverb, *Sjaldan er ein báran stök*. Which translates as, *"there seldom is a single wave."* The meaning is, good or bad events are often followed by more of the same. We have old sayings like this because they are more often true than not. They are truisms, lessons learned from living.

In baseball we say that hitters are in a "slump" when they can't seem to get a hit. In golf, a normally great player who hits bad shots one after another has a case of the "shanks." Alternatively, a basketball player who sinks shot after shot is "on a roll" or we speak of "winning streaks." In each instance, no one realistically expects the player to stay in either of those disparate situations indefinitely.

But, in business or in life, sometimes it seems as though things can get tough and stay that way for a very, very long time. It is human nature to better remember the tough times and how long they seemed to last as we forget just how great the good times were when we thought they would never end.

We gawk at highly successful individuals and it seems everything is going their way. It seems they can do no wrong and everything they touch becomes gold. We are seduced into thinking this is always how it has been for them. We tell ourselves they are the lucky ones and we will never have such luck. Really?

What we didn't see was all of the effort that preceded their success, the years of struggle, sacrifice and failure. Every successful individual has laid a solid foundation for success and placed themselves in a position to garner win after win. Even so, those who are successful still have losses but the odds are definitely in their favor due to their continuous steadfast efforts.

When we suffer, like it or not, it is usually because of choices we have made. When it seems the bad just keeps on coming, could it be because we have laid a very different foundation? One that isn't predicated on success, but rather a foundation which has set us up for failure because of our choices. A foundation not conducive to victory?

If that is the case and you feel you are riding negative waves one after the other, there are several things you can do to tip the odds back in your favor. The first take home message here is no matter how tough circumstances seem to get, or how long they seem to last, all bad streaks will eventually come to an end. Especially, if we begin to intervene on our current circumstances in meaningful and positive ways.

The second take home message is you can construct a new foundation at any time, one that is more conducive to success. I just don't believe there is only so much success to go around that only a lucky few can have.

Take a hard look at where you are and what it will take to catch new waves for a more positive outcome. Ask yourself, are you making quality decisions? Do you have all of the knowledge and tools you need? Do you need to redirect, reinvent, or reignite yourself for eventual success?

Lastly, never ever give up. History is replete with individuals who have given up and thrown in the towel just one moment before all of their dreams and aspirations would have been fully realized.

Remember, just when things seem as though they can't get any worse and you feel as though you can't go on any longer, at that moment, you are the closest you have been to the wave which will turn it all around and make the big difference.

# Powerful Words...

SACRIFICE, FOUNDATION, VICTORY and REIGNITE are Powerful Words.

Seek a sturdy FOUNDATION on which to build your life. This will mean different things for different people. Your core values are the best place to start. In all matters, do not SACRIFICE your values for the sake of an advantage, money, expediency, or a fleeting thrill.

If your cup is overflowing, do freely sacrifice some of your time, money, experience, or service for those in need. It is your responsibility to make sure your cup is full to overflowing.

If you feel you have missed your life's calling. If you feel you are always snatching defeat from the jaws of VICTORY. If you feel you are burned out with nothing left to give, don't settle for your current circumstances. Change them. You can turn it around. You can find your life's calling. You can REIGNITE with passion and purpose. It begins the moment of your choosing and not a moment sooner.

# World of words from within...

Throughout your life, have there been times when good or bad, success or failure seem to come at you in waves? How did you handle those times? What effect did they have on you going forward? What would shift the outcome for you? What are your stories?

_____

_____

_____

Is your foundation sturdy, moral, high-minded, principled, and honest? Does victory come from how well you serve or how well you cheat? Do you sacrifice for all, and save none for yourself? Do you sit, stuck, long burned out, failing to reignite? Why?

Write down your thoughts.

_____

_____

_____

In thinking about the answers to these questions, were any of your emotions stirring? To what events in your life were they connected? Are there stories you could write down and share? Have you identified some Powerful Words, words which resonate with you on an emotional level?

_____

_____

_____

# DESPERATION

## Sand Castles

*Ebb tides that run*
*Tarry little,*
*Carry little,*
*From the shores of yesterday.*
*But flood tides that break*
*Tarry more,*
*Carry more,*
*Of the sands that are today.*
*Sand castles meant to last*
*Are soon faint memories of the past.*
*Let us build them quick today*
*Before another yesterday.*

I wrote this poem one night in 1988 when I was drunk. I wrote it out of desperation. I was hurting in ways which would be hard to describe even now. My life was out of control and I saw it and time slipping through my fingers. Thinking with an addicted brain at the time, I didn't know what to do. There seemed to be no end to my misery in sight. I had no hope. I was scared.

The night I wrote this poem I was thinking about my childhood spending time on summer vacation with my family in Myrtle Beach, South Carolina. It was the first family vacation I can clearly remember. My dad built a castle in the sand for me and showed me how to make one. It seemed like magic.

From a hole he had dug in the sand he would gather and squeeze liquid sand through his fist as layer upon layer would build to form the walls of a castle. It was glorious fun. I wanted it to last forever, the time with my father and the sand castle.

The next day it would be all gone, the time with my father and the castle. I was sad but my dad and I would build another one and we had the fun all over again.

Somewhere along the line in my life I had stopped building sand castles. The joys and wonders life had to offer were lost to me as I drifted in a sea of alcohol. But then, I was afforded an opportunity to change.

The opportunity was really there all along but I couldn't see it. Also, I had to become willing to change. Once I became willing to make needed changes and seized the opportunity, I experienced a new freedom, a new happiness, a new reality.

Time began to slow as mindfulness replaced self-seeking behavior. Life began to unfold and became enjoyable once more. My priorities changed. I let go of the less important things in favor of what was truly important.

Ready to hope and daring to dream, I became an engaged human being once more. Or, maybe for the first time in my life. For me, it was an amazing transformation and it took my breath away.

## Powerful Words...

DESPERATION, OPPORTUNITY, CHANGE and MINDFULNESS are Powerful Words.

So many times in my life I let DESPERATION force needed CHANGE. It's a shame, really. Change out of desperation is always at the end of the path of maximum resistance, hasty, messy, and with fewer options. Wouldn't it be better to choose the path of least resistance through proper planning and at one's leisure where choices are plentiful and to make better choices in the first place? Oh, well. I always seem to have learned my lessons the hard way. I claim progress not perfection.

MINDFULNESS gives all of us the OPPORTUNITY to choose better for ourselves. This forces us to consider all of our options in accordance with our core values. Then, we are free to choose better for ourselves, free from damaging emotions which if left unchecked will hold sway over us. Mindfulness allows us to enjoy being.

# Your world of words within...

Have you acted out of desperation? Most everyone has. What changed as a result? Write down what happened. There are powerful emotions associated with desperate acts represented by Powerful Words. See which words resonate with you on an emotional level. Those are the keys for unlocking those emotions so you can get them out to heal or get them out to share.

What Powerful Words come to mind when thinking about times you may have felt desperate?

_____  _____  _____

Do you practice mindfulness? What can you share with someone about being mindful and how has it changed you? Has the practice of mindfulness given you new insights about yourself and the world?

_____

_____

_____

Do you see opportunities for change, for growth, for improvement? Or, do you feel stifled? Can you identify why? What emotions do the words opportunity, change and desperation engender? Are they strong? If so, they are Powerful Words to you and they should to be explored.

What **BIG** changes have you made in your life and what changes do you have planned? List them here.

_____

_____

_____

_____

_____

_____

_____

_____

_____

# How to Win the
# Battles Within

We may look calm cool and collected on the outside, but decision battles rage on the inside of everyone. You can't often tell by looking. Sometimes small, sometimes large, only the worst internal battles we fight are the ones that show.

These battles may be over mundane things. Should I buy the blue one or the red one or the green one or none of them?

There are decision battles which will have long term consequences. Should I marry him, or her, or am I making a huge mistake?

Internal life-threatening wars may be waged. Am I going to drink or use drugs again today or will today finally be different?

The impetus and arbiter for most of these battles, of course, is fear. Fear of an unknown outcome, fear of making a mistake, fear of being wounded further somehow.

We were more fearless in our youth. We were eager to try the new, the different, the riskier and edgier things. What we lacked in knowledge, resource, and expertise we made up for in overconfidence. But, everything seemed possible.

As we aged and reached our prime, fear began to show up and preside over most of the battles and wars within. We became afraid of losing what we had worked for and accumulated. We traded ignorant fearlessness for educated over cautiousness. Too much began to look impossible to us.

All of my hardest fought internal battles have occurred as an adult. When I became dissatisfied with working for Radio Shack, I was afraid to quit my job and go back to school and I was afraid to stay on as a store manager.

When I was a drunk, I became afraid to quit drinking fearing I would die without alcohol and I was afraid to continue drinking fearing I would die because of alcohol.

When I became burned out as a family physician I became afraid to quit the work I truly loved and afraid to continue on feeling emotionally spent and exhausted and fearing I wasn't making any difference.

When my last marriage came to an unforeseen and abrupt end, I became afraid of losing the person I loved more than anything in the world and afraid of the prospect of moving on down unfamiliar paths alone.

In all of those wars that raged within me, I resisted making decisions as long as I could because of fear. But, eventually, life will force your hand and make you decide. Sometimes I chose well. Sometimes I chose poorly, and that's okay.

With each choice, I learned something about myself. I will tell you I chose best for myself when I asked for, and received, help.

There are hundreds of thousands of quotes, sayings, proverbs, articles and books about how to handle fear. I am sorry to say I have no magic words, wand, fairy dust or elixir for eliminating fear. If there was just one thing out there to eliminate fear which worked for everyone then there would be just one thing out there. That is the honest truth.

What I can tell you is you are not alone in your struggles with the internal battles and wars you face. Somewhere, someone else out there is also battling or has already fought fear under similar circumstances. They are fighting fear and indecision just like you, every day. They could use your help and perhaps you could use theirs.

There is one piece of advice I can give you which will help you to win the wars within. Ask for help. Ask for advice from a loved one, a friend, a professional, someone you trust, someone who is positive in their thinking. In doing so, you have won your first skirmish and are on your way to managing fear and eventual victory. Keep moving, fight, ask for help, decide, learn, and grow.

Remember, we are never so alone as when we feel we are all alone. You are not alone. That is also the honest truth.

*"The battles that count aren't the ones for gold medals. The struggles within yourself - the invisible battles inside all of us - that's where it's at."*
~ Jesse Owens

# Powerful Words...

BATTLES and AFRAID are Powerful Words.

You have seen struggle, I know. Everyone has. You have fought the BATTLES within and some out on the battlefield in war or LIFE. Everyone does. Some fights you have won, some you have lost and some are ongoing.

The trick to winning battles is to keep fighting. Don't let fear stop you dead before you're dead. It is okay to be AFRAID. Who isn't? We are all in this together. Win, lose or draw, there is always something to be gained form every battle. The only time you flat out lose is from failure to fight or if you should quit.

more precious to me, especially my own. There is not a spare minute to be wasted anymore.

As I think about life in general, I believe there that are two ways lives are lost. Of course, the ultimate way is by way of death. But the other way a life is lost, perhaps a more tragic way, is a life wasted.

To live a life according to someone else's terms is wholly repugnant to me. Although, I spent a great deal of my life doing just that. I can also identify with people who labor on burned out doing work they detest, never discovering their true life's purpose, never knowing the joy of pursuing it with passion. It is a great tragedy and a monumental waste of human potential.

This is one of the things that I find so appalling about addiction, the loss of living human potential by the individual involved. No one can be the best they can be if actively addicted. Too much time, energy and resource is wasted on the addiction. People stop constructively developing when actively addicted. In a way, it is a de-evolutionary, deconstructive process until an endpoint is reached - either self-destruction and death, or meaningful sobriety.

So many careers have been upended and lost by way of addiction. It is no less so for the practice of medicine. Addiction rates are even higher in the medical profession than in the general population.

I sit on the NC Physician's Health Program (NCPHP) Compliance Committee. I have also served as chairman of the committee. It is a group composed of individuals from the NC Physicians Health Program staff, the NC Hospital Association, Physician Assistants, physicians in recovery, the general public and members from the board of Veterinary Medicine.

This committee oversees the actions of the NCPHP when dealing with troubled physicians, PA's and veterinarians. I can tell you first hand that this body does great work in helping physicians turn their lives around while protecting the interest of the public at the same time.

They deal with physicians in a way that is compassionate, even-handed and fair. But some participants continue to struggle in spite of our best efforts and in spite of themselves. Regrettably, a few never make it back into good standing with their respective governing boards and their medical careers are self-ended.

There is so much in this world to experience and our time here is finite. I spent somewhere between six and eight years of my life in an alcoholic haze. I stopped growing. Too many times I sat on the sidelines and watched life pass by me. I didn't put myself out there to experience anything new.

I spent every spare moment either feeling guilty and remorseful for breaking my own rules for abstinence or planning when I could drink next, what I was going to drink and how much I was going to drink. It was my madness, my insanity. I will never be able to get those years back.

Still, I do not wish to forget the past nor do I wish to shut the door on it. Thinking about those years now, I see them as a pathway to where I am in the present. Yes, I would have liked to have avoided all the pain that my addiction caused me but that was not the pathway I chose for myself at that time. I chose the path with the **most** resistance.

I might be unable to change the past but I can be thankful for what happened because it has led me to where I am now and it is my past that makes me more aware of my present. My non-addicted brain has fostered a new self-awareness. I have a renewed interest in living and experiencing life as never before.

That's not to say that my life is perfect and that I don't experience setbacks. Of course I do. Everyone does. That's living life on life's terms. The difference is I can now feel, learn, adapt, set new courses, enjoy new experiences, and envision new possibilities. It is part of the new freedom and the new happiness that sobriety brings.

No one wants to see a life wasted. If you know someone who is still suffering, still struggling with a failing business, a toxic or abusive relationship, job burnout or an addiction then by all means reach out to them. Say something, do something that will let them know you have noticed they are having difficulty and that you care.

Let them know that their life, like all life, is precious.

## Powerful Words...

MENTOR, LIVING, EXPERIENCE and SELF-AWARENESS are Powerful Words.

Everyone should have a MENTOR in their life, to fill the role of a wise and trusted counselor or teacher who will offer support when needed. Whether just starting out or should you want to take your craft to the next level, the knowledge and EXPERIENCE passed along from a mentor is invaluable. It is a wise investment of your time. Hopefully, you will be a wise investment of your mentor's time.

SELF-AWARENESS means knowing who you are and where you fit into the world. It means knowing your strengths and weaknesses and how your actions affect you and the lives of those around you. This demands a critical and honest appraisal of yourself and of your talents and abilities. I believe in LIVING fully alive, self-aware and using your natural talents and abilities with purpose and passion.

# World of words from within...

Do any of these words have any application in your life? Have you seen living human potential wasted? Have you seen your own potential wasted? What words describe how you feel when you consider these words?

_____

_____

_____

Do you feel fully alive, truly living and not just existing? What degree of self-awareness do you possess? Can you see the possibilities life has to offer? Do you have a mentor in your life? Should you?

If you were to choose a mentor, who would it be? Write down some possibilities here.

_____

_____

_____

_____

_____

_____

# SHARE
////////////////////////

Anyone who undergoes a Transformation will want to give of themselves by sharing their success with others. It is part of the Transformation mindset. We succeed in life because of hard work using our natural talents and abilities and because we all stand on the shoulders of others who came before us. People we connected with on an emotional level because we heard their Powerful Words.

Just think of all of the knowledge and expertise that was available to us as we were learning. Think of all of the teachers and mentors that have helped to define and shape us along the way. I can't say that I ever succeeded at anything that I didn't have help from someone else.

This does not mean that you should go forth and tell everyone you know, and a good many you don't know, how successful you have become. There is a difference between sharing your success and a list of your successes (wins).

We share our success by doing exactly what made you successful in the first place. There are many ways to share your success. Here are a few.

1) Seeing to the needs of others by providing added value to your employer, clients, customers, or followers. Especially, value that is unexpected or unanticipated.

2) By giving away some of your work product. If you are going to survive in business today then you had better learn how to give before you ask.

3) By helping others as they struggle to become successful. Helping others helps them and you. Not only is it the right thing to do, it is a win-win.

4) Leverage your success in order to help worthy causes that have captured your interest and when you do, feel good about it. There is nothing wrong with that.

5) Don't ever stop working, producing and sharing, as long as you are able. If you do, you will rust or your brain and body will rot. Besides, there isn't anyone else like you on this planet. The world will lose the gift of you if you were to just quit. As long as you draw breath, strive to contribute by designing, building, planning, doing.

I have met a lot of highly motivated people recently through Dan Miller and his 48Days community at 48Days.net. I have never seen such a large group of individuals that are so engaged in helping others to become what they desire to become, to be the best they can be. They understand that success breeds success, that helping others to achieve is the pathway to personal growth and success.

# Powerful Words...

SHARING, SHARE, CONTRIBUTE are Powerful Words.

Growing up, we are taught to SHARE. SHARING feels good. It can impart tremendous joy and satisfaction. I don't believe sharing is **social** responsibility. I believe it is a **personal** responsibility.

If there is much you wish to share, become successful. Be the best you can be at whatever you do using your own unique natural set of talents and abilities. Make truck loads of money if you are able. The more successful you are able to become, the more you will be able to share. It is easier to share from a cup which is overflowing than from a cup being drained dry.

Sharing will help others to become successful. Seeing your example, you will ignite their passion for purposeful action to be the best they can be. Then they will begin to CONTRIBUTE by helping others. So on it goes...

Not striving to become the best you can be, failing to use your natural talents and abilities to the best of your ability and leaving your true purpose undiscovered or hidden is a waste of human potential. Not sharing your success with others is just plain selfish and ultimately, self-defeating.

# World of words from within...

Have you shared your success with others? What are some of the ways you have found to do so? What Powerful Words come to mind when you think about the times you have shared your success with others? Or, when someone shared their success with you?

_____

_____

_____

What did you share or what was shared with you - time, knowledge, expertise, money, food, clothing, shelter, goods, services? How did sharing make you feel? At the core of your stories are more Powerful Words. You will recognize them as such if they move you on an emotional level. Make some notes.

_____

_____

_____

# Next Steps...

If you have gone through the Core Values Inventory exercise and answered questions at the end of each chapter then you have amassed a list of your own Powerful Words from your own life stories. You should try to use these as often as possible in your interactions with the people you wish to serve. These are the words which connect with you on an emotional level. They represent the real you, the authentic you.

When you use your Powerful Words the emotions they reflect will flow through you and connect with others on an emotional level. They will see, know and **feel** the authentic you. This is when things happen. This is when things change, when people connect.

The Powerful Words I have identified throughout this book are listed in **Appendix B**. Add any of these to your list if they connect with you on an emotional level. As you live your life, new Powerful Words will emerge. Add those to your list as well.

All that remains is to share your Powerful Words with the world. Permission to do so is no longer needed. You have the world at you finger tips through the World Wide Web. Whether by conversation, speaking, blogging, publishing, podcasting, art or music there are limitless avenues available to share your message with the world. Just START.

Let loose your Powerful Words!

# Appendix A

## Listing of Core Values

Ability
Abundance
Acceptance
Accessibility
Accomplishment
Accountability
Accuracy
Achievement
Acknowledgement
Action
Activeness/Activity
Adaptability
Adequacy
Adoration
Adroitness
Advancement
Adventure
Affection
Affluence
Aggressiveness
Agility
Alertness
Aliveness
Altruism
Amazement
Amusement
Anticipation
Appreciation
Approachability
Approval
Artistry/Art
Articulate

Assertiveness
Assurance
Attentiveness
Attractiveness
Availability
Awareness
Awe
Balance
Beauty
Being-ness
Being the Best
Belief
Belongingness
Beneficent
Benevolence
Blissfulness
Boldness
Bravery
Brilliance
Briskness
Buoyancy
Calmness
Camaraderie
Candor
Capability
Care/Caring
Carefulness
Celebrity
Certainty
Challenge
Change
Charity

Charm
Chastity
Cheerfulness
Clarity
Classiness
Cleanliness
Clear-mindedness
Cleverness
Closeness
Cognizance
Coherence
Comfort
Commitment
Community
Compassion
Competence
Complacency
Competition
Composure
Concentration
Confidence
Conformity
Congruency
Connection
Consciousness
Conservation
Consistency
Contemplation
Contentment
Continuity
Contribution
Control
Conviction
Conviviality
Coolness
Cooperation
Copiousness

Cordiality
Correctness
Country
Courage
Courtesy
Craftiness
Creativity
Credibility
Cunning
Curiosity
Daring
Decisiveness
Decorum
Dedication
Depth/Deepness
Deference
Delicacy
Delight
Dependability
Depth
Desire
Determination
Devotion
Devoutness
Dexterity
Dignity
Diligence
Diplomacy
Direction
Directness
Discernment
Discipline
Discovery
Discretion
Diversity
Dominance
Dreaming

Drive
Durability
Duty
Dynamism
Ease
Eagerness
Economy
Ecstasy
Education
Effectiveness
Efficacy
Elation
Elegance
Empathy
Encouragement
Endurance
Energy/Energetic
Engagement
Enjoyment
Enlightenment
Entertainment
Enthusiasm
Equality
Ethics/Ethical
Euphoria
Exactness
Excellence
Excitement
Exhilaration
Expectancy
Expediency
Experience
Expertise
Exploration
Expressiveness
Extravagance
Extroversion

Exuberance
Evolution
Facilitating
Fairness
Faith/Faithful
Fame
Family
Fascination
Fashion
Fearlessness
Ferocity/Fierceness
Fidelity
Financial Freedom
Fineness
Finesse
Firmness
Fitness
Flexibility
Flow
Fluency
Fluidity
Focus
Forgiveness
Formidableness
Fortitude
Frankness
Freedom
Free-Thinking
Freshness
Friendliness
Friendship
Frugality
Fun
Gallantry
Generosity
Gentility
Genuineness

Giving
Goodness
Grace
Graciousness
Gratefulness
Gratitude
Gregariousness
Growth
Guidance
Happiness
Hardiness
Harmony
Health
Heart
Helpfulness
Heroism
Holiness
Honesty
Honor
Hope/Hopefulness
Hospitality
Humanity
Humility
Humor
Hygiene
Imagination
Immovable
Impact
Impartiality
Impeccability
Independence
Individuality
Industry
Influence
Informative
Ingenuity
Inquisitiveness

Insightfulness
Inspiration
Instinctiveness
Integrity
Intelligence
Intellect
Intensity
Intimacy
Intrepidness
Introversion
Intuition
Intuitiveness
Involvement
Joy/Joyfulness
Judiciousness
Justice
Keenness
Kindness
Knowledge
Lasting
Lavishness
Leadership
Learning
Legacy
Liberation
Liberty
Lightness
Liveliness
Logic
Longevity
Love
Loyalty
Majesty
Making a Difference
Malleable
Marriage
Mastery

Maturity
Meekness
Meaningfulness
Mellowness
Mercy
Meticulousness
Mindfulness
Moderation
Modesty
Motivation
Mysteriousness
Nature
Neatness
Neighborly
Nerve
Nimble
Noble
Non-conformity
Nurturing
Obedience
Objective
Open-mindedness
Openness
Opportunity
Optimism
Opulence
Order
Organization
Originality
Outdoors
Outlandishness
Outrageousness
Partnership
Passion
Patience
Peace/Peacefulness
Perspectives

Perfection
Performance
Perkiness
Perseverance
Persistence
Personable
Persuasiveness
Philanthropy
Piety
Planning
Playfulness
Pleasantness
Pleasure
Plenty/Plentiful
Poise
Polish
Politeness
Popularity
Potency
Power
Practicality
Pragmatism
Precision
Preeminence
Preparedness
Presence
Pride
Privacy
Proactive
Proficiency
Professionalism
Prosperity
Prudence
Punctuality
Purity
Purpose
Qualifications

Quietness
Quickness
Rationality
Realism
Readiness
Reason
Reasonableness
Recognition
Recreation
Refinement
Reflection
Reignite
Relaxation
Reliability
Relief
Religion
Reputation
Resilience
Resolution
Resolve
Resourcefulness
Respect
Responsibility
Restfulness
Restraint
Reverence
Richness
Rigor
Sacredness
Sacrifice
Sagacity
Saintliness
Sanguinity
Satisfaction
Science
Security
Self-control

Selfishness
Self-realization
Self-reliance
Self-respect
Self-sufficiency
Sensitivity
Sensuality
Serenity
Service
Sexuality/Sexiness
Sharing
Shrewdness
Significance
Silence
Silliness
Simplicity
Sincerity
Skillfulness
Smartness
Solidarity
Solidity
Solitude
Sophistication
Soundness
Speed
Spirit
Spirituality
Spontaneity
Spunk
Stability
Status
Stealth
Stillness
Strength
Structure
Sturdiness
Substantiality

Success
Sufficiency
Superiority
Support
Supremacy
Surprise
Sympathy
Synergy
Tactfulness
Teaching
Teamwork
Temperance
Thankfulness
Thoroughness
Thoughtfulness
Thrift
Tidiness
Timeliness
Togetherness
Toughness
Tradition
Tranquility
Transcendence
Tribe
Trust
Trustworthiness
Truth
Understanding
Unflappability
Uniqueness
Unity
Usefulness
Utility
Valor
Variety
Victory
Vigor

Virtue
Vision
Vitality
Vivacity
Volunteering
Warm-heartedness
Warmth
Watchfulness
Wealth
Wholesomeness
Willfulness
Willingness
Winning
Wisdom
Wittiness
Wonder
Worthiness
X-?
Youthfulness
Zeal
Zen
Zest
Zing
Add Others Here:

# APPENDIX B

## POWERFUL WORDS I Used In This Book

Abilities
Abuse
Acceptance
Accomplishment
Accountability
Achievement
Action
Adapt
Addiction
Adventure
Adversity
Afraid
Anxiety
Appreciation
Art
Artist
Authority

Balance
Barrier
Battles
Begin
Benefits
Broken
Burnout
Can't
Capable
Chance
Change
Choice
Circumstances
Clarity

Commitment
Compassion
Connect
Connectedness
Consequences
Contribute
Control
Courage
Create
Creativity
Criticism
Curiosity
Cynicism
Dedication
Defeat
Denial
Depression
Despair
Desperation
Destination
Determination
Develop
Difficulty
Diligent
Doubt
Dream/Dreams/Dreaming
Drive
Emotions
Empathy
Engaged
Enlightenment
Entrepreneur

Excellence

Excitement

Expectations

Experience

Expert

Explore

Failure

Faith

Fear

Focus

Forward

Foundation

Freedom

Future

Gamble

Generosity

Give

Goal

Grateful

Gratitude

Grief

Grow

Happiness

Hardiness

Hardship

Health

Honest

Hope

Ideal

Ideas

Imagine

Impossible

Information

Initiative

Innovate

Intentional

Intentions

Introspection

Journey

Joy

Kindness

Knowledge

Leadership

Learn

Learning

Legend

Life

Lifestyle

Limitations

Living

Lose

Loss

Lost

Love

Mastery

Meaning

Mentor

Mindfulness

Mistake

Now

Obstacles

Opportunity

Optimism

Pain

Passion

Path

Pathway

Patience

Peace

Perfection

Perfectionism

Performance

Perseverance

Persistence

Personal truth
Pessimism
Plan
Planning
Play
Possibilities
Potential
Power
Practice
Preferred Future
Preparation
Procrastination
Progress
Purpose
Reality
Recovery
Regret/Regrets
Reignite
Rejection
Resilience
Resistance
Responsibility
Reward/Rewards
Sacrifice
Self-assessment
Self-awareness
Self-doubt
Self-esteem
Self-identity
Self-interest
Selfish
Share/Sharing
Skill
Spiritual
Start
Stop
Story

Strength
Struggle
Stuck
Suffering
Talents
Time
Transformation
Trapped
Triumph
Truth
Uncertain
Understanding
Unfulfilled Dreams
Unknown
Value
Victory
Vulnerable
Wait/Waiting
Weakness
Well-being
Willingness
Wonder
Add Others Here:

# NOTES